PHILOSOPHY

9
—
5

# Guardian of Dialogue

# Guardian of Dialogue

Max Scheler's Phenomenology,
Sociology of Knowledge,
and Philosophy of Love

Michael D. Barber

Lewisburg
Bucknell University Press
London and Toronto: Associated University Presses

Associated University Presses
440 Forsgate Drive
Cranbury, NJ 08512

Associated University Presses
25 Sicilian Avenue
London WC1A 2QH, England

Associated University Presses
P.O. Box 338, Port Credit
Mississauga, Ontario
Canada L5G 4L8

The paper used in this publication meets the requirements
of the American National Standard for Permanence of Paper
for Printed Library Materials Z39.48-1984.

**Library of Congress Cataloging-in-Publication Data**

Barber, Michael D., 1949–
    Guardian of dialogue : Max Scheler's phenomenology, sociology of
knowledge, and philosophy of love / Michael D. Barber.
        p.   cm.
    Includes bibliographical references and index.
    ISBN 0-8387-5228-4 (alk. paper)
    1. Scheler, Max, 1874–1928.   I. Title.
B3329.S484B37   1993
193—dc20                                                    92-52715
                                                               CIP

*For Susie, Tom, and Ollie*

# Contents

# Preface

After Wilhelm Jerusalem first coined the phrase "sociology of knowledge" in 1909, Max Scheler authored the first extended treatment of the subject in his "Probleme einer Soziologie des Wissens." Ironically, most discussions have approached Scheler's thought through his ethics, his metaphysics, his philosophy of the human person, or his theories of affectivity or love. My book is unique in that it begins with Scheler's sociology of knowledge and considers his phenomenology as a response to the predicament of modern Western culture as diagnosed in his "Probleme einer Soziologie des Wissens." Furthermore, consistent with this "social" reading of Scheler and influenced by contemporary analyses of ethics and dialogue—particularly those of Emmanuel Levinas and Jürgen Habermas—this book argues that Scheler, in his phenomenological critique of the modern Western *Weltanschauung*, was intensely interested in upholding the possibility and necessity of dialogue—that is, the pursuit of truth by nations, cultures, and individuals in solidarity. Hence, Scheler battled certain currents in the modern Western *Weltanschauung*, many of them still prevalent, that militated against the possibility of dialogue. In addition to offering this "social" interpretation of Scheler's thought, I show both that Karl Mannheim's critique of Scheler from a sociology of knowledge perspective fails and that improvements in Scheler's account of rationality and ethics enhance the idea of dialogue that was so central to his thought.

The introduction presents the historical and philosophical circumstances of Scheler's work and outlines the argument that his analyses of ideal and real factors and structural analogies paved the way for a *critical* sociology of knowledge. That is to say that Scheler's sociological concepts make possible more than simply a neutral description of the modern Western worldview. With their aid, Scheler can argue that especially economic real factors have skewed the cultural development of the West in favor of science and technology at the expense of its religious and metaphysical development. Asian culture, which has unfolded differently, provides a dialogic counterpoint in the "sublime and great conversations" between cultures for which Scheler hopes.

The first chapter presents in greater detail the modern Western *Weltanschauung* that Scheler criticizes. It takes up the growth of science in the West and the epistemology it spawned, the rise of capitalism and the value theories correlative to it, and the social forms of existence with their correspondent philosophical theories of intersubjectivity. In all these areas, a common thread emerges, namely that the modern Western world strips human experience of its own structure of being and value and other persons of their own distinctiveness. It then imposes its own structures on being, creates its own value scheme, and interprets others on its own terms. In the next three chapters, I illustrate how Scheler responded to the philosophical manifestations of the Western standpoint: its epistemology, value theory, and philosophy of intersubjectivity.

In chapter 2, I briefly summarize Husserl's phenomenology as an effort to dig beneath accepted philosophical prejudices and to proffer a more expansive epistemological framework than that permitted by positivistic epistemology. Similarly, Scheler in his "Erkenntnis und Arbeit" confronted mechanistic accounts of perception, reason and understanding, and the relationship between science and philosophy. In my view, Scheler's epistemology aimed at defending an objective order of being that drive-directed perception attends to only selectively. While causal/mechanistic factors may account for this selectivity, they do not explain the production of the order of being itself.

In a similar way, Scheler applies phenomenology to the domain of ethics in his *Formalism in Ethics and Non-Formal Ethics of Value*, discussed in chapter 3. Scheler criticizes Kant for his acceptance of the empiricist theory of will and his narrow understanding of the a priori. Kant never recognized the a priori value ranking that properly ordered human feelings could apprehend. Various forms of ethical nominalism likewise obscure this objective order of value. Throughout his *Formalism*, Scheler highlights numerous mechanisms that selectively reveal and hide independent, objective values, which, as in the case of his epistemology, do not derive from human creativity. In Scheler's view, relativism, reflecting the modern Western worldview, denies this objective order of value to which we attend selectively and credits diverse and arbitrary cultural practices with the production of value. Scheler's objective order of values, on the contrary, makes possible a critical intercultural dialogue in solidarity through which one culture can place another in question regarding the firmament of values under which they both stand. Indeed the richness of those values and the inevitable selectivity of cultural perspectives mandate just such a cooperative dialogue as a necessary complement to Scheler's objective value ranking. The idea of individuals and cultures generating their own aribtrary value schemes without being bound to others in a common search (unless one chooses or contracts to do so) reflects the *gesellschaftlichen* presuppositions of the modern Western worldview diametrically opposed to the notion of solidarity.

Scheler's theory of intersubjectivity, addressed in chapter 4, spells out the philosophical fundaments for the kind of dialogue his epistemology and value theory require. Via a phenomenological critique of the mechanistic approaches to intersubjectivity in the modern Western philosophical tradition, Scheler argues that we can have authentic fellow feeling that is not simply our own feeling reproduced, that we can love others as they are and lead them to become more fully what they are without remaking them in our image and likeness, and that we can know a Thou directly without resorting to analogical inferences or empathic projections onto the Other. According to mechanistic accounts, however, we remain enclosed within our own perspectives, incapable of being broadened by a dialogue with a distinctive Other, whose intervention in our lives invites change. In his epistemology, ethics, and philosophical account of intersubjectivity, Scheler's phenomenology thus shows itself to be the guardian of dialogue.

Nietzsche's idea of a omnipresent, inescapable, and often subterranean will to power poses serious questions for the possibility of such a dialogue. As I shall argue in chapter 5, World War I tested Scheler's philosophical capacity to avoid succumbing to an unrecognized will to cultural power. Scheler's own often biased war writings lend credence to Karl Mannheim's critique that Scheler's pretense to have articulated via phenomenology the objective character of being, values, and the Other is circumscribed by his own socio-cultural determinants. I will reconstruct a Schelerian response to Mannheim that illustrates the difference a phenomenological basis makes for doing sociology of knowledge. Further, I will show that Scheler's own ultimate hope for discovering objectivity and for achieving dialogic consensus rests in the subjective attitude of surrender *(hingeben)* that reaches its fullest articulation in Scheler's theory of phenomenological reduction. Through authentic implementation of Scheler's version of phenomenological reduction—which, I will contend, pays more attention to the distortional influence of socio-cultural factors than Husserlian reduction—one would, in Scheler's view, give up Nietzsche's will to power. One would also free oneself from the modern Western *Weltanschauung*'s passion for control and open oneself to whatever objectivity might be discoverable in unconstrained dialogue. I conclude this chapter by drawing up four arguments from Schelerian sources against the sociologistic menace to dialogue.

In a final critical chapter, I depict how Scheler's critique of the modern Western worldview diverges from Max Weber's and converges with Jürgen Habermas's. However, I believe that Scheler, unlike Habermas, underestimates the place of rationality in ethical theory. In his consideration of the intuitive, prereflective level, I find Scheler's thought also converging with Emmanuel Levinas's ethics. Nevertheless, Scheler's value ranking would have to assume a subsidiary position to the ethical limits established by the intuitively grasped demand of the Other prior to all rationality. Such a modification of Scheler's theory coincides, I believe, with his own theory of solidarity. By appreciating a more positive role for reason in ethical theory and by avoiding any implication of sacrificing persons to an abstract value scheme, Scheler, in my view, could escape residues of the mechanistic Western framework in his own thought and ensure more fully the dialogue that he ceaselessly sought to protect.

A word about the three distinctive periods in Scheler's writing is in order. Scheler espoused at first a noological method while under Rudolph Eucken's influence (until roughly the middle of the first decade of the twentieth century). Then he adopted a phenomenological method (until roughly the early twenties), and finally a metaphysical method. I share the view that neither consistent continuity nor abrupt breaks characterize these stages. Instead, a kind of intellectually accountable progression links these three phases. I think, for instance, that is permissible to argue that Scheler developed his earlier discussion of philosophical attitude in "Vom Wesen der Philosophie" (1917) into his presentation of phenomenological reduction in the later writings. I realize that Scheler assigned a more active role to humanity in its relationship with God in the later writings, but such a role need not contradict the surrender recommended in phenomenological reduction or Scheler's cautions against humanly manufactured "idolatry" in earlier writings. Scheler's progressions from one approach to another suggest that he creatively expanded earlier views without necessarily contradicting himself.

Gratitude is due Bouvier Verlag, Macmillan Publishing Company, Northwestern University Press, Routledge, Chapman and Hall, and SCM Press LTD for permission to quote their publications.

I would like to thank St. Louis University for a Faculty Mellon Grant in the summer of 1987 to pursue research. I am also indebted to James Bohman, Manfred S. Frings, Robert Gibbs, Robert Harvanek, S.J., John Nota, S.J., Vincent Punzo, Peter H. Spader, Kenneth W. Stikkers, and Michael Tueth, S.J., for their helpful suggestions. The technical assistance of Mauricio Gaborit, S.J., was invaluable. I am most grateful to Professor Mary F. Rodgers for her extremely careful reading of the manuscript and for her thorough and helpful suggestions. Also I appreciate the continued patience and interest of the entire Leo Brown Jesuit Community, particularly Tom Rochford, during the writing of this book. Of course, I could not have done this work without the love and support of those three to whom this book is dedicated.

# Guardian of Dialogue

# Introduction: Scheler's Sociology of Knowledge: Critique of the Modern Western *Weltanschauung*

Prewar Germany under Emperor William II was ripe for a crisis. Gaudy public spectacles, ostentatious architecture, art censorship, bourgeois philistinism, and sentimentalism dominated public culture, while universities nursed military ideals and excluded Jews, democrats, and socialists from their midst. World War I, which broke out in August 1914, presented Germans with a release from boredom, an invitation to heroism, and a cure for decadence by galvanizing the *Volk* around the German "mission," articulated by intellectuals such as Thomas Mann, Friedrich Gundolf, Werner Sombart, and Max Scheler. Germany's disillusioning defeat, coupled with the Russian Revolution, which ignited intense and, at times, violent conflicts among German socialists and spurred conservative reactions, produced a state of despair as low as Germany's war idealism had been high. Intellectual, political, and class fragmentation, rapid and unsettling advances in science and technology, the mechanization of life, parliamentary democracy of the masses whose irrationalism Martin Buber deplored—all these elements created an atmosphere of crisis and impending doom. The rise of expressionist art mirrored the state of things by rebelling against stable forms and common sense and by exhibiting discontent with actuality and apprehension about the future.[1]

Peter Gay comments on some of the assorted solutions for this cultural malaise:

> The complex of feelings and response I have called "the hunger for wholeness" turns out on examination to be a great regression born from a great fear: the fear of modernity. The abstractions that Tönnies and Hofmannsthal and the others manipulated—*Volk, Führer, Organismus, Reich, Entscheidung, Gemeinschaft*—reveal a desperate need for roots and for community, a vehement, often vicious repudiation of reason accompanied by the urge for direct action or for surrender to

a charismatic leader. The hunger for wholeness was awash with hate; the political, and sometimes the private, world of its chief spokesmen was a paranoid world, filled with enemies: the dehumanizing machine, capitalist materialism, godless rationalism, rootless society, cosmopolitan Jews, and that great all-devouring monster, the city.[2]

Youth movements, nostalgic romanticization of medieval Germany, the resurrection of myths hostile to rationalism, and pantheistic love of nature addressed this void. Political responses ranged from the violence of the leftist Spartacists to that of the right-wing nationalists who murdered Walter Rathenau, Weimar minister for foreign affairs. Others resorted to utopian projects, glorified violence (e.g., Ernst Jünger), or simply remained apathetic.[3]

Philosophical factionalism paralleled this cultural disintegration. According to Max Scheler, philosophy in the latter half of the nineteenth century experienced increasing nationalization, a growing pluralism of schools and sects, and antithetical developments. Philosophy evolved in this manner because romantic (Schopenhauer, Nietzsche, Burkhardt), irrational (Bergson), pessimistic (Schopenhauer, E. von. Hartmann), and relativistic (Dilthey, Spengler) philosophical currents rose to challenge the predominant rational philosophical culture that had culminated in Kant's thought. German philosophy polarized in three directions: (1) between strictly scientific philosophy and a more aphoristic, unmethodical philosophical literature; (2) between philosophies oriented to the natural sciences and to the human sciences; and (3) between philosophies influenced by Protestant and by Catholic traditions. Scheler also mentions a host of philosophical competitors: naturalism (Haeckel and Ostwald), idealism (Wundt, Eucken, Lotze), Neo-Kantianism (Riehl, Cohen, Natorp, Cassirer, Lask, Rickert, Nelson), positivism (Mach, Avenarius, Ziehen), pragmatism (Vaihinger), realism (Külpe), *Lebensphilosophie* (Dilthey, Spranger), and phenomenology (Husserl, Reinach). According to Jürgen Habermas, the collapse of Neo-Kantianism in the 1920s resulted in a break with Occidental rationalism and paved the way for the German *Dasein* to seize power over its destiny and to harness technology at the service of its own project (Heidegger).[4]

Scheler interpreted these conditions in Germany as symptomatic of a profound philosophical illness that had been developing since the origins of modernity in the late middle ages. In Scheler's view, the blossoming phenomenological movement offered philosophical resources for criticizing and healing this cultural sickness. As such, Scheler's philosophy pertains to a long history of philosophical cultural criticism that can trace itself back to Socrates and Plato and even pre-Socratics like Heraclitus and Parmenides. Scheler's social writings, particularly *Some Problems of a Sociology of Knowledge,* indicate the philosophical and sociological origins of this malady that phenomenology aims to cure.

*Some Problems of a Sociology of Knowledge* contains two sections, one dealing with cultural sociology and the other dealing with one of its subdivisions, the sociology of knowledge. In the first section, on cultural sociology, Scheler defines ideal factors as self-unfolding spiritual activities such as art, religion, metaphysics, and science. Real factors include kinship, power, and economic relationships and the drives correlative to such relationships. In the second section on the sociology of knowledge, Scheler discusses fundamental axioms and the basic types of knowledge under the rubric of "formal problems" and the social conditioning of those basic types of knowledge in a subdivision entitled "material problems."

When Scheler introduces the section on cultural sociology, he speaks first of all of an ordering law that must account for the interrelation of ideal factors, the interrelation of real factors, and the connections among these interrelations. Second, he embarks upon a long discussion of the ideal factors, including August Comte's three basic types of knowledge—religion, metaphysics, and science—and their connections. Third, at the midpoint of his cultural sociology, Scheler argues that real factors do not determine positively the meaning/contents of human spiritual activities, but rather hinder, release, accelerate, or retard the appearance of these contents much as sluice gates *(Schleusen)* control a stream. Fourth, Scheler discourses at length on the real factors, blood relations, politics, and economy before, in the fifth place, returning to the interrelation between ideal and real factors. Thus, in this section on cultural sociology, repeated discussions of the relationship between ideal and real factors in the first, third, and fifth parts, frame the separate presentations on ideal factors in part 2 and real factors in part 4. The key metaphor of the sluice gate occurs in the very center of the essay.[5]

In the sociology of knowledge section, Scheler's subdivision on formal problems clarifies the meaning of *structural analogies.* This notion fills as important a function in any consideration of concrete material problems in the sociology of knowledge as the relationship between ideal and real factors. Scheler observes:

Not only do the unusual facts of primitive collective world images which Lévy-Bruhl, Graebner, Thurnwald and many other ethnological works have discovered become now fully understandable. Furthermore, deep rooted *structural analogies* maintain between, on the one hand, the structures of the contents of natural science, psychology, metaphysics, and religious knowledge, *and*, on the other hand, the structure and organization of the *society* as well as the power relationships among the social groups of a given political era. To reflect on these structural connections of the images of the world, the soul, and God with the strata of social organization is a particularly stimulating task for the sociology of knowledge. This is especially so with regard to the basic types of knowledge (religious, metaphysical, and positive scientific knowledge) and with reference to all the development levels of society.[6]

Scheler, indeed, does make use of such structural analogies, for example, when he depicts in his war writings the intertwining of natural science, ethics, political theory, and history in England. Similarly, Scheler's view that the unity of a culture inescapably pervades its various domains becomes evident when, in concurrence with Walther Rathenau, he argues that the mountain vacationer, who flees a mechanized society, remains bound to it by his very reaction against it and makes use of it with every postcard he writes.[7]

In a related passage from his essay "Weltanschauungslehre, Soziologie und Weltanschauungssetzung," Scheler shows himself aware of the precariousness of such broad cultural generalizations. He wonders whether it is possible to "reconstruct" a whole ethos, that is, the dominant cultural value preferences that condition and pervade everyday valuations. Is it possible, he asks, to reconstruct a whole world view *(Weltanschauung)* from its pieces? He answers that one can have insight into these interconnections *(man . . . einsehen kann)*. In fact, a discipline born of this insight enables one to understand philosophers and authors better than they understand themselves. Only on the basis of this kind of insight can one ever determine how real factors release or suppress the appearance of ideal factors, such as the art of an era. Although Scheler admits that the structural unities of an objective *Geist* penetrate all cultural domains, he distances himself from Hegel's "ridiculous" theodicy, which calls for acquiescence and gratitude for the organic becoming of history. Scheler, on the contrary, believes that his *Weltanschauung* theory permits a recognition of blind real factors and provides a freedom to construct a better history than has been seen. As shall be seen later, the rejection of such broad insight because it is insufficiently "scientific" can actually spring from a particular *Weltanschauung* that precludes its own self-understanding because it has restricted legitimate insights to those of science alone.[8]

When Scheler turns to material problems in *Some Problems of a Sociology of Knowledge*, one *Weltanschauung* absorbs the bulk of his attention: that of the modern West. Scheler comments briefly on religious and metaphysical founders and protagonists, the social vehicles of transmission, and the connections among religion, metaphysics, and science. But when he comes to the sociology of positive science, he embarks on a discussion that runs to ninety-eight pages in *Die Wissensformen und die Gesellschaft* and takes up over one half of the whole of *Some Problems of a Sociology of Knowledge*.

In this largest segment, Scheler depicts the emergence of modern science from out of the medieval worldview and the meaning correlations between modern science and technology and between technology and economy. Relying on the notion of structural analogies developed in his section on formal problems, Scheler argues that neither production technique nor its correlate—positive scientific thinking—is the causal origin of the other. Rather, they both stem from the drive structure of the society's leaders in close connection with its prevailing ethos, that is, the value preferences governing the culture. Similarly, technology is not the mere application of pure theoretical, contemplative science, but both are structural analogates, resting upon a underlying *will to control (Wille zur Herrschaft)*. These structural analogies disclose the presence of a real factor: the economic communities of work and commerce shaping that drive structure and thereby permitting some value preferences to gain ascendancy while suppressing others.[9]

This modern Western *Weltanschauung*, which economic factors release, consists in a distinctive configuration of ideal factors, particularly knowledge types: the entire field of metaphysics all but disappears. At the close of the medieval period, an age of inventions and discoveries suddenly replaced a theological and biomorphic worldview more than fifteen hundred years old. Similarly, a will to control nature and the soul displaced attitudes of loving surrender. Even as capitalist economy involved a will to limitless acquisition, so also modern science no longer held sway over a given deposit of truth, but rather became a "will to methods." This cultural shift resulted in an ignorance of the limits of the validity of formal-mechanistic physics, an absolutization of it and its objects, and a consequent suppression of all authentic meta-physics, whose methods, goals, and epistemological principles differ completely from those of positive science. Even authoritar-ian religions, hostile to metaphysical free thought, yoked their fortunes to the juggernaut of modern science and attacked meta-physics, which gradually fell into decadence.[10]

Thus, Scheler's exposition of structural analogies in "Formal Problems" enables one to see Western culture in its many dimen-sions as one whole. In that cultural whole, as Scheler explains in the section "Cultural Sociology," real factors act like a sluice gate toward ideal factors. Power and economic relationships, in par-ticular, render modern Western humanity blind to a whole do-main of ideal factors, namely, metaphysics and the values accompanying it.

After Scheler's analyses in his earlier sections have produced fruit in an examination of the material problems of the modern Western *Weltanschauung*, Scheler is positioned to appeal for a dia-logue with the *Weltanschauung* of the East. The inevitable one-sidedness of any cultural development prompts such an exchange with complementary cultures. Scheler foresees an intercultural discussion in which Asians will assimilate Western positive sci-ence and technology. Likewise the West, overly developed techno-logically, can both acquire the psychic techniques of nonresistance against suffering and rediscover metaphysics. Should the West learn from the East, a new cosmopolitan era characterized by a "sublime and great conversation" would replace Western political domination, strategic religious missions, and economic centraliza-tion. In addition, Western domestic politics, oscillating between mindless mass popular movements with their accompanying myths and Fascist/ecclesial authoritarianism, could regain its con-fidence in the kind of reason characteristic of metaphysics. Such reason is truly cosmopolitan, with each individual or culture cap-able of making its own unique, irreplaceable contribution to the "conversation." Metaphysics is, as Scheler observes, an absolute and yet thoroughly individually valid form of knowledge.[11]

Scheler is doing more here than simply presenting a general sociology of knowledge. Scheler's purpose exceeds merely search-ing out structural analogies, interrelating real and ideal factors through the sluice gate metaphor, laying down formal axioms, or providing detailed material descriptions. By utilizing this machin-ery of the sociology of knowledge and simply describing Western development, Scheler brings to light its one-sidedness, particu-larly in comparison with Asia. At the basis of this critique, which issues from sociological description, lies Scheler's conviction that the ideal factors of religion, science, and metaphysics constitute three modes of knowing essentially pertinent to the human spirit. Stunted development in any of these domains indicates the presence of real factors exerting their selective force. Such underdevelopment also suggests how diverse cultures might complement and challenge each other as dialogue partners.

It is somewhat ironic that the sociology of knowledge has been used so frequently to disarm cultural critiques by simply pointing out their specificity to particular social strata and thus relativizing their impact. Max Scheler's *Some Problems of a Sociology of Knowledge*, the first systematic treatment ever devoted to a discipline whose name had been coined fifteen years earlier by Wilhelm Jerusalem, served no such purpose.[12] Rather, Scheler availed himself of descriptions of the social conditioning of knowledge for a project of socio-cultural criticism. For Scheler, socio-cultural limitations of insight, instead of resulting in relativism, impelled cultures toward dialogue as the only hope for mutual criticism, learning, and growth in the recognition of values and truths that exceed any single culture's grasp.

Such cultural critique, particularly of the modern Western standpoint, was not something new for Scheler. Indeed, a careful perusal of the works of all three of his periods would indicate his lifelong attempt to show the strengths and weaknesses of that perspective, whether it is described as the mechanistic worldview or the pleonexic spirit of capitalism. In the *Frühe Schriften*, for instance, Scheler reproaches Western rationalism for ignoring the full spectrum of human experience and valuation in his "Beziehung zwischen den logischen und ethischen Prinzipien" and in "Die transzendentale und die psychologische Methode." He also decries the deleterious effects of capitalism in "Arbeit und Ethik." During the middle period, the same project continues, for example, in the fourth and fifth parts of "Das Ressentiment im Aufbau der Moralen" on humanitarian love and value shifts in modern morality and in his critique of Kant, utilitarianism, and *Gesellschaft* in *Der Formalismus in der Ethik und die materiale Wertethik*. Scheler's attack on England and his later diagnosis of the prewar situation in Europe that produced the war in his *Politisch-pädagogische Schriften* advance the same critical undertaking. The later writings, including his sociology of knowledge, "Die Stellung des Menschen im Kosmos," and several of the essays in the second volume of *Schriften aus dem Nachlass*, attempt to situate the mechanistic worldview in its *Daseinsrelativität*. To show in detail how these writings engage in cultural criticism lies beyond the limits of this introduction; it is the task of this entire book.[13]

Phenomenology, central to Scheler's project of cultural criticism,[14] permits a critical assessment of those Western philosophical presuppositions about being, value, and intersubjectivity that undermine the possibility of intercultural dialogue and make it superfluous. Indeed, even a sociology of knowledge undertaken within the framework of Western culture would be prone to take over unconsciously many of those presuppositions unless it carefully scrutinized its own philosophical presuppositions. Thus, Scheler's tying real factors and ideal factors together through the sluice gate metaphor depends on his phenomenological methodology. But these are promissory notes to be redeemed only after Scheler's view of the modern Western ethos in its many ramifications and his phenomenological critique of it have been developed in detail.

# 1

# The Modern Western *Weltanschauung*

In order to understand the role phenomenology plays for Scheler in criticizing the modern Western *Weltanschauung*, Scheler's own understanding of this *Weltanschauung* must be reconstructed in an abbreviated fashion. In this chapter Scheler's portrayal of three institutional features of the modern Western world—science, capitalism, and social forms—is considered. These institutional features reverberate within philosophy, and Scheler's discussion of common Western theories of epistemology, values, and inter-subjectivity have been selected to illustrate this "reverberation effect." Each of these philosophical theories are targets of Scheler's own phenomenological critique, as the three chapters following this one will explain. In the interest of highlighting this "reverberation effect," epistemology is paired with science, value theory with capitalism, and theory of intersubjectivity with social forms. But one could just as well cross-pair these correlates, since scientific achievements echo within value theory and social forms resonate within epistemology. Similarly, there are horizontal relations, with science, capitalism, and social forms effecting each other, just as epistemology, value theory, and theory of intersubjectivity do. In effect, drawing out these pairings and interrelations merely fleshes out Scheler's sociological notion of structural analogies with reference to modern Western culture.

## Cognition

### Science

As the Middle Ages ended and the Renaissance commenced, a new human ethos and drive structure came upon the scene, engendering unexamined beliefs that the human will could exhaustively direct, dominate, and define nature. The organic, contemplative, apractical worldview of the Middle Ages fell as a sacrificial offering to this new, positive valuation of the domination of nature.[1]

The repercussions of this new ethos and drive structure emphasizing the dominative capacity of will was felt across diverse cultural domains, as Scheler points out.

> This idea of sovereign dominion appeared in theology (Scotus's voluntarism, Protestantism, particularly in Calvinism and Puritanism with their exaltation of the mighty will of God), in the view of humanity in psychology (association psychology), in theories of government and society (Bodinus, Machiavelli, Hobbes), in politics (mercantilism and the development of the thought of the absolute state, the concept of sovereignty, the theory of the balance of power)—all this occurred with the same originality and at the same time as it did in the mechanistic view of nature. Also the formal atomism of objects to be controlled and the destruction of the "objective form" idea sprang up simultaneously with regard to knowledge of nature (hence nominalism) and in views of government and society (atomistic singularism and atomism), in biology (Descartes), and in psychology (association psychology and mosaic theory).[2]

Scheler, in his later works, situated this development within a broader historical panorama. In his *Nachlass* "Manuskripte zu den Metaszienzien," he notes that humanity had advanced from a belief in spiritual and demonic power centers to panvitalistic and organological views prior to Galileo. Galileo, in turn, made the lifeless world his focal point and thereby initiated the mechanistic approach. In this approach, one no longer seeks to order the laws of the lifeless world on those of the living world, as did Plato and Aristotle, but rather seeks to found the laws of the living world on the lifeless, inorganic world. In fact, the process of history has involved a devitalizing and desouling reminiscent of Max Weber's notion of disenchantment. The world was an organism for humanity before it became a mechanism in infinite space. The biomorphic or organismic worldview generally preceded the physicochemical (mechanical) one.[3]

Not only does the mechanistic viewpoint disenchant the organic world, but also a certain devaluation, despiritualization, and desouling of the world must have preceded that viewpoint's emergence. The later Scheler imputes responsibility for this devaluation to Christianity, particularly the thought of John Calvin, who stands as the antithesis to world-loving pantheists such as Bruno or Spinoza. Only a world that is essentially reasonless and valueless, experienced as a "vale of tears," can awaken the strongest impulses to control.[4]

> Here the world independent of human work becomes a mere undefined, chaotic, futile and valueless, senseless and irrational aggregate of givennesses. No limit is preestablished for the possible elaboration and domination of this world.[5]

Scheler agrees with Dilthey that the modern grasp of the world, as it has unfolded since Galileo, first of all drove all qualities and forms and all significances of life out of the world of nature. Homogeneous, punctual realities, such as atoms, from which all qualities have been thought away, replaced the forms of Aristotle and the scholastics. These qualityless entities of physics functioned as direct or indirect stimuli for motor behavior. They announced a Nature whose structural patterns seem to emerge by accident. Here one no longer speaks of an intentional relation to what is real in itself and to what possesses its own real structure, but rather of a causal relationship acting upon motor behavior. Whether one's final thoughts coincide with the real that appears in perception is irrelevant to efforts to subdue whatever lies at the source of one's being stimulated.[6] Scheler describes in *Wesen und Formen der Sympathie* how scientific naturalism dismisses any positing of qualities above and beyond mechanistic interactions:

> But for the naturalistic theory this can only amount to a continual piling-up of illusory contents (colours, sounds, values, etc.) *between* the organism and the world. On this view an organism perceiving only matter and motion would have the closest contact with "things in themselves"; every additional quality would be just a further illusion. The naturalistic theory is utterly oblivious to the fundamental fact that the "real" world is always "richer" than any "given" one. Like naturalistic philosophy generally, it is essentially deflationary in its outlook. It approaches everything on the false assumption that whatever happens to be simplest and least valuable must also have the character of *ontological priority* and causal antecedence. Now it is true enough that such things are easiest to grasp from the point of view of a "human understanding" bent on controlling and dominating the world. This is so because such things are the most tractable, widespread, and easily communicable, as compared with the more complex and valuable factors. But that is no reason for supposing that being and value are arranged to suit the convenience of an intelligence operating in terms of practical ends.[7]

This comment indicates further that the mechanistic worldview does not content itself with showing the fundamental causes as inert, valueless particles. In addition, it attempts to reduce all other contents and values to the movement of such basic elements. This reductionistic tendency springs, as Scheler suggests in *Frühe Schriften*, from the division and specialization of the sciences. The sciences, after denying to philosophy any competence in regard to their methodological questions, have attempted to define themselves. But instead of arriving at a preestablished harmony among the sciences, each science has attempted to extend its dominion over all the other sciences. Such disintegrative competition parallels the economic breakdowns of the supposed preestablished harmony that Adam Smith had predicted in the economic domain. Hence from the time of Descartes on, physics has sought to wrest power from biology, life has lost its character as an *Urphänomenon*, and living essences have been reduced to machines, a sum of useful worktools. Scientists investigate life appearances with the same principles and concepts with which they investigate lifeless nature. They can do this, in Scheler's opinion, only because the inorganic natural sciences deliberately abstract from all vital conditions when they apply their methods to living organisms. Furthermore, the natural sciences try to impose their methods on the human sciences just as the economic historian attempts to interpret all political, scientific, and literary history in economical terms. Finally, those sciences that cannot formulate their conclusions in mathematical laws are denied the honorific title of science.[8]

The result of such reductionism, though, is that all differences and rank ordering of beings are levelled out. "Everything, the stone as well as the human being, becomes progressively equal, each a non-independent member of a universal mechanism." In addition, this "levelling" mechanistic view dissolves all laws of structural *Gestalten*. It pares psychic experiences to physicochemical organic reactions. It deflates the *I* to being a mere nodal point where sensual world elements coagulate. It basically overlooks the distinctive essences of life and spirit with their own unique lawlike processes. It substitutes a lifeless, unmoving, geometric image of movement for actual movement whose basic elements involve tendency, dynamism, and passage and whose "ur-image" is to be found in the experienced movement of our organs within the vital-psychic sphere. This envious, reductive overthrow of "higher" contents and processes reminds one of Nietzsche's penetrating analysis of *ressentiment* in the moral-social-political sphere.[9]

Contemporary philosophy of science, especially in its feminist versions, has raised similar questions about the limitations of the mechanistic framework. Evelyn Fox Keller's *Reflections on Gender and Science*, for instance, documents the struggle between hermetic and mechanical views of science just prior to the founding of the Royal Society in seventeenth-century England. For the hermetic tradition, nature was suffused with spirit and could only be understood by the integrated activity of heart, hand, and mind, whereas the mechanical philosophers divorced matter from spirit as well as hand and mind from heart. These mechanical philosophers followed Francis Bacon who urged scientists to strip nature of "her" protective covering, to penetrate to "her" innermost chambers, and to bind "her" to the service of science and make "her" science's slave. Henry Oldenburg, Secretary of the Royal Society, called for a new "masculine philosophy" that would resist what fellow society member Joseph Glanvill called the "power our affections have over our so easily seducible Understanding." In opposition to these mechanistically inclined contemporaries, Thomas Vaughan urged science to "hear with the understanding of the heart." Similarly, Keller points out, contemporary classical geneticist and cytologist Barbara McClintock recommended that researchers "listen to what the material has to tell you." Like Scheler, Keller traces the origin of the mechanistic viewpoint, along with its attendant masculine/feminine polarization, back to the time of the rise of industrial capitalism. Like Scheler, Keller believes that the mechanistic worldview, in attempting to avoid all previous projections onto nature, involves its own projection of disinterest, autonomy, and alienation.[10]

Although the tenor of these comments may have portrayed the mechanistic worldview as somewhat villainous, Scheler nevertheless affirms its relative worth since "the artificial value-free character of the world is itself for the sake of a value . . . the value of controlling the world." In fact, such control is by no means completely contrary to the purposes of nature since the world itself complies with this effort to control it by behaving like a mechanism and permitting itself to be technically directed. Both the mechanistic worldview, as well as its companion, association psychology, have a well-based right to existence, Scheler argues, as long as they are utilized only for controlling the world and the soul and as long as they do not pretend to present the essence of things. Even the Christian church has assigned to the human race the task of controlling nature in solidarity. As shall be seen later, a key element in Scheler's thought is that diverse attitudes and values are of undeniable worth as long as they restrict themselves to their legitimate domains.[11]

Finally, Scheler hints at the critical function phenomenology might serve regarding this mechanistic scheme. According to him, the same mechanistic worldview that evolves in history also develops out of what phenomenologists call the natural attitude, or the common sense approach to the world. Scheler points out that the physical scientist and the denizen of the natural attitude both select intuitive contents of qualities from the fullness at hand only insofar as those contents serve as signs for things, especially stable things in science or practically important things in the natural attitude. Just as the physical scientist observes colors and tones only as signalling the movement of stable points, so the common-sense person attends to colors and tones in terms of their symbolic significance for practical interrelations. In the natural attitude, one notices cherries or hears wagons passing, and the colors and tones that mediate these perceptual unities are of subsidiary importance to the practical desires to eat or to avoid injury. As Scheler concludes:

> In the natural attitude itself, there is to be found a kind of "crypto-mechanism" that must be broken through in order that we might reach the phenomenal being. This motif reaches deeply into science.[12]

Just as phenomenology enables one to see those things that the pressing practical interests of the natural attitude restrict from sight, might it not open up whatever the modern Western *Weltanschauung* also hides?

### Epistemology

In Scheler's view, these developments in science impact on philosophical theories of knowledge particularly at the level of perception, where the knower and the world meet. Philosophical accounts of perception in turn affect characterizations of those cognitive processes that elaborate perceptual data, such as understanding, reasoning, or thinking. In Scheler's view, Western epistemologies from empiricism to idealism manifest the influence of the mechanistic worldview's rise to prominence at both cognitive levels. In addition, philosophy, perhaps overwhelmed by the meteoric rise of modern science, has forgotten the broader context wherein science must be situated.

Scheler makes the case that a deep error has pervaded the philosophical tradition's approach to perception since the time of Descartes, an error that Kant also never overturned. This error consists in founding the concept of a psychologically given stimulus falsely on the categories of physics, that is, on the basis of a nature independent of all life processes. This error has its roots in a philosophical prejudice: the desire to visualize the whole perceived world of physical objects and their reality as the result of a causal inference, whether consciously or unconsciously drawn. Thus, entities defined by physics are said to produce causally the representations and perceptual images given to consciousness. But what these entities in themselves really are appears as a pure construction of thought, devised to explain certain contents of consciousness, such as sensations. Instead of beginning with phenomena given in perception and advancing toward high level theories in physics, one begins with the entity-constructs of physics that function as the stimulus and, as such, explain causally the psychic phenomena of inner perception. Hence, Helmholtz interprets color appearances as facts of inner perception to be explained causally by the physical definition of these colors. Such a physiology of colors involves merely the application of a physicalistic optics to a special case, namely light rays striking an organic body.[13]

According to this dark, mythological account, as Scheler describes it, the physical stimulus and the centripetal neural processes with neural cortex processes alone define a sensation as a "final state" to be located "in" the brain, "in" the soul, or "in" consciousness. Perception itself is a sum or composition of such simple sensations. The resultant composite image is only an ordered group of perceptual possibilities, falsely posited as existing, since, on the other side of consciousness there are only air waves, ether waves, or some construct of theoretical physics.[14]

Modern psychology has attempted to distill out the simplest sensation from which perceptual complexes are built up. In order to find this simplest building block of perception, one would have to maintain a constant stimulus while varying the drive, memory, and phantasy conditions. One could then determine the simplest stimulus or proportional psychic content constant over these variations. This effort presupposes the "constancy hypothesis," namely, that a pure sensation stands in a constant, strictly proportional relationship to the physical stimulus. This hypothesis, which, as we shall find out, Scheler opposes and tries to disprove, has stubbornly perdured because it was concluded on the basis of the mechanistic view of nature.[15]

Under such an account of perception, phantasy appears only as a pale reproduction or copy of originally stimulus-conditioned and stimulus-proportional perceptions and impressions. This view, of course, resembles Locke's and Hume's notions of phantasy.[16] Scheler summarizes the basic strategy of mechanistic psychology:

> In the face of this repeatedly confirmed state of affairs [which contradicts associationist psychology], the sensualistic psychology and knowledge theory still always want to make us aware that the pure sensation, corresponding to (proportional to) its stimulus, is genetically prior in the case of every psychological development.[17]

Clearly, the previously recognized pattern of reducing experience to its more primitive, quality-barren elements and so opening up an abyss between our representations of reality and its real, nonillusory character comes to the fore once again.[18]

What then are the implications of this mechanistically influenced philosophy of perception for cognitive processes that elaborate and organize perceptions, such as understanding or reason? In an essay from his early writings on Kant and modern culture, Scheler reiterates the point of view that the mechanistic perceptual theory disposed of the ancient-medieval forms and substances that communicated themselves to the senses. Mechanistic theory substituted for these forms and substances vague causal stimuli, to be defined according to the prevailing theory of physics. In effect, no external order of nature was now being conveyed to the perceiver at the level of sensation. Instead it became dubious whether the order perceived corresponded to whatever was outside the perceiver. From here, it was only a short step to assign the responsibility for ordering stimuli and elaborating their connections to human thinking, understanding, and reason. Hence, instead of adopting the task of ancient-medieval philosophy, namely, copying or giving back a presupposed order of objects, modern philosophical science experienced itself as "formative" and "creative," burdened with the responsibility of organizing causal stimuli and thus of making nature rational. As a result, modern epistemology attempted to create a closed system of concepts and laws so that discontinuous and lawless sense perceptions could find their place within a consistent Nature. Thus the very formlessness of nature in which the mechanistic account of *sense perception* resulted opened up the possibility for *thinking* to exercise its creative, constructive role:

> Has not this been the direction of the modern spirit, that one (as the sensualism of our day teaches) would try to dissolve all science into sensation? Would not one have seen thought, concept, and law only as "economic" means for the efficient use of sensation and for its linguistic communication? The 'end of knowledge, its *ultimate goal* was not the sensation, rather the *concept* and the *law.* The sensation was only the springboard for creative reason, positing systems whereby we recognized energies such as electricity, magnetism, and a large series of different rays that our sense organs and sensations never grasp. The present weakening mechanistic view of nature, of which Kant was decisively convinced, was one such thought-construction—clearly only devised for the goal of bringing given sensations into a conceptual and quantitatively definable system. According to this view of nature, the nature-investigating reason works out the pieces of its conceptual construction not to reach an order of thought things "behind" the sense world, but rather only to create from orderless impressions a system of nature corresponding to principles of reason. In Kant's language, this reason works out its constructs for the goal of "possible experience."[19]

This division between orderless sensation and order-imposing thought furnishes the common framework within which diverse opposing modern Western philosophical schools compete. Scheler depicts English philosophy in general as evacuating this world of any structures of its own (e.g., Ockham, Hobbes), emphasizing dependence upon the all-powerful will of God or a form of sovereignty, and establishing order in this world on the basis of conventionalism. Hume follows this pattern by noting that temporal change of perceptions lead us to the contradictory affirmation that one and the same thing continually exists and does not continually exist. Hume rejects the idea of an enduring substance behind fleeting perceptions and, in a passage cited by Scheler, invites his reader simply to abandon doubt and to embrace the tried, the true, and the customary.

> As the sceptical doubt arises naturally from a profound and intense reflection on those subjects, it always increases, the farther we carry our reflections, whether in opposition or conformity to it. Carelessness and in-attention alone can afford us any remedy. For this reason I rely entirely upon them; and take it for granted, whatever may be the reader's opinion at this present moment, that an hour

hence he will be persuaded there is both an external and internal world. . . .[20]

English empiricism generally assumes the human spirit to be basically passive. This empiricism insists that one submit oneself to the sensibly given facts in every consideration and exclude from thought everything that can find no immediate correspondence in sensations. Empiricism, in Scheler's view, is essentially anti-constructive and antitheoretical.[21]

Pragmatism, deriving from this empiricism, however, emphasizes human activity. It points out that if one understands by *facts* that which is simply given without any outside activity, there would be no such thing as definite facts. Facts would be nothing more than a fully undefined, fluctuating, and contentless sum of chaotic impressions without unities or organizations or units. Thoughts could never correspond or conform with such chaos. Rather this chaos provides the work material for elaborative activity. A fact, for pragmatism, is always something that spiritual activity already defines and forms. Pragmatism basically involves not a loving immersion in the facts of a sensibly or otherwise given, but rather the active, controlling formation of a sensible chaos on the path toward knowledge. Scheler concludes that pragmatism, by stripping the world of any intelligibility of its own, is but a variant of nominalism and that Thomas Hobbes is pragmatism's grandfather.[22]

Kant took over uncritically and unconsciously from the English and French sensualists the prejudice that the only things given were sensations in an orderless and chaotic fashion. Hence, Kant concluded that all asensual or hypersensual contents of experience were not originally given, but were rather the achievement of a self-legislative, synthetic understanding and reasoning activity. Such factors as relationship, order, substantiality, efficacy, form, materiality, space, time, values, etc., in this view, can never be authentic and true givens, but are only products and constructs of reason. Scheler concurs with E. Jaentsch's view that fundamentally Kantian philosophy, intent as it is on justifying the Newtonian conception of nature, believes that human thought produces all coherence, all order, and all relations and patterns in the chaos of sensation.[23] Scheler pinpoints his critique of Kant in his *Der Formalismus in der Ethik und die materiale Wertethik:*

If the world is first pulverized into a heap of sensations and the human being into a chaos of drive stimuli (which—by the way incomprehensibly—ought to stand in the service of one's naked self-*preservation*), so, obviously, an active, organizing principle is needed, which can restore the contents of natural experience. Stated briefly: *Hume's nature requires a Kantian understanding* to exist; and the *Hobbesian human being requires a Kantian practical reason* if each of these are to resemble the facts of natural experience. But *without* this fundamentally erroneous presupposition of a Humean nature and a Hobbesian human being, such a hypothesis is unneeded. There is no need for the interpretation of the a priori as the "functional laws" of this organizing activity. The a priori then consists in the factual, *objective structure* to be found in the great experience realms themselves, to which first definite acts and functional relations correspond. It is not necessary that somehow this structure be "imported" or "brought into" these experience realms first through the acts.[24]

As this final sentence indicates, by denying any order to the world in itself and by artificially imposing its own order in its place, the mechanistic viewpoint effectively conceals from itself what might really be there.

According to Scheler, it is no accident that the entire period of organism-oriented thought was epistemologically realistic and that the philosophical idealism first appeared when this period had ended and the formal-mechanistic view of nature emerged. This formal-mechanistic approach dissolves stable objects into the spontaneous and never exhaustively controlled movement of whatever entities physics posits behind appearances. The mechanistic standpoint consequently transforms the being of things into a mere created product of human theoretical understanding. The mathematization of theoretical physics implies necessarily the idealism of the inanimate world because one can no longer attribute reality to an appearing object. This idealism need not result in scepticism, though, since science can achieve intersubjective validity.[25]

Scheler eloquently ties these criticisms of empiricism, pragmatism, Kantianism, and idealism together:

The collective thought process (also the *philosophy* of the bourgeois era from Descartes to Kant) and all its forms of so-called "idealism" and subjectivism were exactly the opposite of such a spiritual type [one involving loving surrender to this world], as it has shown itself to us before. This philosophy looked blindly and sceptically upon God and the world, which it grasped as something to be formed, elaborated, and directed through human beings. Because one can only direct and move the world insofar as it is a type of mechanism, this "fortunate working hypothesis for the technician in humanity," namely to see the world occasionally as if it were a mechanism and nothing more, was quickly converted into a metaphysics. It became the pregiven, *"true"* image of the world. This disastrous error is generally in retreat now. Already this new power of a great surrender, the fearless and anxiety-free giving of oneself over to being, the real itself, the heartfilled embrace with the things—these attitudes inform our most recent literature. Already the new European philosophy is beginning—this is not the place to go into it in detail—in a hidden way to change its direction: from the world-alienation of an outlived, subjective, rationalism grown formalized to a living intuitive and experiential contact with the things themselves.[26]

The final few words of this quotation, obviously referring to Husserl's rallying cry of "to the things themselves," suggest that it is phenomenology that will be part of the cure for this culturewide malady.

Finally, philosophical epistemologies modeled on mechanistic science are liable to exclude the very questions philosophy ought to pursue. Such epistemologies involve an artificial turning away from the following crucial data: the various modes wherein things are relative to the person *(Daseinsrelativität)*, layers of value relativity and value differences, the origins of the objects of scientific investigation (e.g., matter, power, energy, life, speech, and others), and the origin of the scientific knowing act and valuing act. Mechanistic epistemologies require sensibly observable proof and prescind from other forms of intuitive, evident knowing. They focus on unending processes of deduction and inductive probabilities, important for controlling the world through willing. All the while, though, they neglect the essence of things, the broader context to which science and they themselves belong. Since such epistemologies tend to dismiss those things from which they prescind as nonexistent or nonvaluable, they are, in Scheler's opinion, fully incompetent for the problems of metaphysics.[27]

In summary, modern Western epistemologies, by relying on the mechanistic worldview to explain perception, effectively emptied the world of its own order. They thus prepared the way for creative understanding and reason to institute its own order. Such developments unleash limitless possibilities for domination and control by the human will.

## Valuation

### Capitalism

Consistent with his awareness of structural analogies, Scheler correlates science and epistemology with broader cultural patterns, such as capitalism. In a remarkable passage from "Die Idole der Selbsterkenntnis," he links cognition with capitalism.

> The monetary economy has the tendency in just this way to strip all values completely, as the mechanistic worldview did for the intuitable sense-qualities. The "commodity-character" of things rests not in some content property of these things themselves, but only in their exchangeability for the sake of increasing their worth. This commodity aspect becomes something of a *substance* to which all the other qualities, e.g., the aesthetic, first are affixed. This is no mere chance analogy, since these two modes of approaching the world [economic and mechanistic] follow the same law. According to this law, all appearing contents of the world generally (those felt values as well as perceived contents) show the tendency to become mere symbols and means of differentiation for those contents upon which the most elementary, general, and pressing drives of a living essence are directed. In both cases, the artificial forms of the money economy and the mechanistic worldview are only tendencies gradually becoming absolutized. These tendencies already permeate the natural attitude behaviors of humanity and diminish the factual quality-fullness of the world for our consciousness.[28]

Scheler adopts the Weberian line of argument that the Protestant Reformation played the key role in the West's development of capitalism. Scheler refuses to trace modern business asceticism to Aquinas's monastic restraint of the erotic drive, as Sombart did. Rather, Scheler asserts that the ideals of monasticism, closely related to the life of the laity, in fact calmed and regulated the acquisitive drive. These monastic ideals never granted to lay businesspeople any naive feelings of self-justification for their greed, and, of course, never embraced any endless *duty* to work and acquire, as occurred under Protestantism. Catholicism's belief in a natural law, flowing from the divine law and calling for obedience under pain of forfeiting one's salvation, allowed the church to envision the whole life of a culture, including its economics, as its concern. Protestantism, however, did not see obedience to this law as binding for justification and thus undercut the ethical-religious governance of economic life. Protestant dualisms between body and spirit, law and gospel, and world and heaven resulted in a prohibition against any ethical-religious interference with the "this worldly" drive to acquire. John Calvin, in particular, placed his active, regimental, organizing will behind the rising entrepreneurship at Geneva and released the newly awakened moral energies of the eternally elect in the direction of capitalism.[29] Scheler observes:

> Regarding the principal *emancipation of the spirit* of economic life generally *from any inspiration* of a spiritual ethical-religious authority and all priestly direction—here is one of the first preconditions of the rise of the new capitalistic spirit.[30]

Protestant dualism, exemplified in its supernaturalism, in its complete surrender to God's grace and denial of free will, curiously ushered in a supernatural religious *devaluation* of this natural world. Now one no longer contemplated the world in love as a locus of encounter with God, instead one made one's peace with God separately and then turned toward the world as an empty source of resistance awaiting the unlimited energy to work. In a manner comparable to the mechanistic worldview, these religious sources of capitalism developed a view of inner nature as a disorderly bundle of drives and outer nature as a chaos needing to be tamed. Neither inner nor outer nature had worth in themselves, neither was in itself already a reason-and-goal directed whole. In Scheler's own words, "A world which is valuable in itself and which unleashes joy evokes wonder and awe; only a devalued world can develop a limitless energy to work."[31]

Just as thought imposes its order on the world evacuated of its own structure by the mechanistic worldview, so labor bestows value and order on the structureless world resulting from Protestant supernaturalism. Moral value accrues to those properties and actions that an individual has acquired through his power and work. Instead of focusing on value qualities already there, subjective work confers value where none was to be found. Labor becomes the creator of all values and all culture, whether one speaks of the political and economic theories of the English, such as John Locke, Adam Smith, or David Ricardo, who base the right to property on labor, or whether one thinks of Marx's labor theory of value. Deleterious effects result, however, when leisure, education, joy, family, politics, and religion lose their independent value and begin to derive their value from work, such that, for instance, one rests in order to work better. At that point, the striving to work leaves behind the context in which it was embedded in the medieval period: a strong, formal, and essentially stable ordering of the universe—an order that embraced both society and its members and that was not, as in the modern era, brought forth through the power and activity of the human spirit. Thus, for example, according to the medievals, marriage, family, status, and call were ordained divinely, unchangeable forms restraining the impulse to work, which unfortunately has been unshackled by the collapse of this medieval *Weltanschauung*. A new human type has come into being who no longer knows what to do to fill up his time and so he works, and by working excessively he makes himself incapable of praying, reflecting, and enjoying himself. Of course, this new type considers such a life virtuous for engaging in industry.[32]

Scheler describes the capitalism that was born through these historical processes not, in the first place, as an economic system, but rather as a historical drive and value system of Western European humanity. This system comes accompanied by cultural systems of knowledge, science, and art. Scheler argues that the capitalist spirit itself preexists its institutional embodiments. This original "spirit," which leads to capitalist institutions, grows out of supernaturally directed and specifically world-hostile motives. This spirit reproduces itself in the institutional forms of an economy that has long since forgotten its religious origins. This drive and value system involves principally the preeminence of the drive to acquire over all other drives, including the drives for power and domination, for sex and reproduction, and for nourishment.[33]

A clear picture of the representative of the capitalist spirit, the bourgeois type, emerges in Scheler's essay "Der Bourgeois."

The *first* type [non-bourgeois] loves adventure and danger and possesses an unconscious sense of his own worth. This sense overflows into his love for the world and the fullness of its qualities and leads him to refrain from any envious comparison with others. He "cares" not for himself and his own, but takes life lightly, lets live, and becomes serious only in regard to what touches the *person*-sphere of humanity. He is characterized by a *great, ungrounded trust in being and life* which excludes a prior all "critical" and "mistrustful" attitudes. He is bold, joyful in sacrifice, and expansive in all things, and he values people according to their *being, not* according to their useful *achievement* for the general purposes. The *second* type lives at the outset under the natural anxiety pressure of a less valuable vital type whereby he shrinks from danger and adventure. This vital type gives birth to the spirit of concern for oneself, and therewith the search for "security" and "guaranty" in all things according to regularity and calculation. This type must *earn* his own being by himself and his own worth. He must prove himself through his achievement, because at the center of his soul lies a void instead of the fullness of the other type. In place of love for the world and its fullness there is concern with it as something hostile, pliable to quantitative definition, capable of being ordered and formed according to his purposes. Where the first type refuses to envy and lets live, the second makes comparisons and seeks to surpass his competitor. This latter type's search for mastery leads to a system of limitless competition and to the idea of progress. According to this idea, a greater *quantity* beyond that of a similar case (human being or phase of life or history) is *henceforth* counted as a value generally. Where the previous type simply intuits or contemplates or proceeds to lose himself in will acts, the other worries and reckons, thereby forgetting the particular worth of the goals by concentrating on the means. He overlooks the fact and essence of things by fixing his attention on "relations." Where the first trusts his nature and its inner harmony, the latter, mistrustful of his own drive-life, erects a system of *securities* through which he might control and discipline himself.[34]

Just as the mechanistic worldview discovers fundamental elements and reduces all higher types of being to those elements, so capitalism involves, in addition to simply narrowing one's focus to work and acquisition, an effort to subvert higher values, an act of *ressentiment*. For instance, a new moral proletariat dispossesses those gifted with higher natures, which they did not work to obtain, and deprives these gifted ones of honor simply *because* they did not earn their natures. Scheler finds a further inversion of values in that capitalism subjects pleasure to the lower value of utility—the end is placed at the service of the means. In capitalism, an infinitely complex mechanism for the production of pleasurable items comes into being, and the limitless drive to work, which produces such goods, emanates from a diminished capacity to find pleasure and, in turn, further lessens that capacity. As further evidence, Scheler points to a the spirit of limitless pleonexia and uncurbed free competition that interprets all social standing as a component of the struggle between classes centered on their own interest. This spirit of greed and competition dissolves all love for work and measures everything on how much money is earned. This spirit spurs the lower social levels to revolt out of hatred, envy, or *ressentiment* against the upper levels whose power and pleasurable life-styles these lower levels despise. The utilitarian moral theory of capitalist societies, particularly England, gives theoretical expression to this value subversion. The vibrant, vital, heroic values of the war-waging Germans, Scheler writes during the war, such as courage, love for fearlessness and danger, the sense for the noble and heroic, knightliness, fidelity, willingness to sacrifice, honor, and the desire for fame are all assessed in terms of their usefulness by the British. The British determine the values of these qualities by submitting them to the judgment of a nonparticipant spectator or public opinion. After all, centuries earlier, Hume had evaluated the feeling of honor in terms of its usefulness and its ability to win its possessor credit. The ultimate subversion—confining spiritual values to practical or mercantile categories—is manifest clearly in a series of examples drawn from English culture. Scheler's war writings highlight England's willful self-encapsulation against new knowledge contents and its opposition to a loving surrender to the world. This overturning of the spiritual in favor of the practical surfaces also in Adam Smith's belief that dominant interests and labor define *Weltanschauungen* instead of reasons and insights. Francis Bacon shares this heritage by dismissing astronomy as an "idle pursuit."[35]

Scheler, whose reading of Nietzsche sharpened his insight into the paradoxes of moral revaluation and taught him to see moral revolutions often as more of that against which they battled, detected these capitalist tendencies in socialist reactions to capitalism.

The fact itself, though, that the freedom-hostile "cure" of rising state-socialism has become the only possible one which can demand the maximum of popular well-being is itself one of the most evil *consequences* of the *dominance of the capitalist spirit*. The rising predominance of the bourgeois spirit demanding "security" beyond what is suitable for the active business spirit expresses itself in, among other things, the bureaucratization of the businesses. This spirit seeking security is itself the *presupposition* under which socialist politics has its successful results. Everything which socialist politics and social legislation are able to achieve in the widest possible measure is not the changing of the ethos or spirit of capitalism, which finally bears and nourishes the capitalist order. Socialist politics and legislation achieve only a kind of diminishment of the grievances and injuries to the well-being of the masses which *can* and *must* result under the existent reign of this spirit. The duration of the dominance of this "spirit" itself is extended and solidified rather than shortened or done away with through these measures. The *basic motive* of seeking maximal security for one's economic existence animates such legislation. We have recognized earlier how this motive's predominance over the courageous, trusting life attitude constitutes the powerful appeal of the bourgeois spirit. Only the working out of these motives is different here, depending on the class interests involved.[36]

Furthermore, when the state becomes an entrepreneur, it takes on the same motivation as the individual entrepreneur. It places itself as the service of business and limitless economic growth. Instead of ruling over the capitalist spirit, the state is ruled by it, except, of course, that the state protects its capitalistic undertakings with a surplus of authority. Thus, Scheler grants some credence to the radical, social democratic criticism that all social legislation within capitalism is only a powerless and provisional surrogate that merely tightens capitalism's stranglehold.[37]

Just as Scheler tolerates the mechanistic worldview as long as it remains within its legitimate boundary, so he seeks to defend capitalism's valid aspects. He proposes that one can sociologically and psychologically separate entrepreneurial initiative and free responsibility from the motor of egoistic self-interest. There are, he indicates, directors and employees equipped with highly developed entrepreneural qualities who are not motivated by such self-interest. The question for Scheler is not the abolition of business or industry, but the development of a society where human solidarity replaces the spirit of capitalism.[38]

### Value Theory

The protagonists of the mechanistic worldview believe that a value-blind causality exclusively rules the whole field of the empirical real. Hence an essential bond between reality and value is out of the question on physico-biological grounds. When the world is thus evacuated of all objective values, as it is by mechanistic epistemology, then moral values become nothing more than subjective appearances in human consciousness. Independently of that consciousness, these values have no existence. Values would then be only shadow images of one's desiring and feeling. "Good is what is desired, bad is what is avoided." Without a desiring and feeling human consciousness, actuality would be only valuefree being and happening, as Max Weber proposed.

Hence, Weber assigned the study of reality to positive science, which was to avoid all value judgments and to issue only practical and technical directives. Science cannot tell one "Value this," but only "If you act this or that way or if you choose to honor this or that god and take this action, this will be the outcome." Of course, Weber went on, mistakenly, to conclude to the impossibility of objective value judgments for philosophy and metaphysics. For the mechanistic view, history sinks into the being of organic nature, with no possibility of spiritual guidance according to objective values.[39]

Here, as ever, Scheler detects more than a mere emptying of the world of values and a consequent subjectivization of them: an inversion of values via *ressentiment* plays a role in the modern Western value scheme. Scheler, along with Nietzsche and Bergson, recognizes mechanistic biology and utilitarian values as the origin of this value inversion. Descartes set the stage by dividing all being into mechanized bodies and free spirits, leaving no middle ground for the distinctive phenomena of life. As a result, each organism, beginning with the smallest, can be understood to acquire repertoires of mechanistic responses to environmental stimuli to ensure its own self-preservation. Characteristic phenomena of life such as solidarity and risk taking fade from sight, and all sympathy reduces to egoism. Following in this tradition, Darwin's view of the survival of the fittest and Malthus's belief that the table has been set too sparsely for organic life to survive convert all developments of organic nature into merely epiphenomenal results of underlying processes of self-preservation. The evolution of organic nature also depends upon the negative activity of exclusion of the nonadaptable through selection. For the human person of the Darwinian type, the will to work in the interest of self-preservation is the prime mover, driving him to conceive the world as workable, as mechanized. Such a personal type prefers to understand living and unpredictable organisms in terms of their lifeless and therefore "reckonable" elements, which can be manipulated without anxiety about outcomes. Whoever possesses such a value scheme becomes constitutionally sceptical against every kind of boldness and daring, against any kind of strength and the will to conquer, even against a willingness to sacrifice oneself for any extravagant good or love, especially when such a sacrifice promises no rewards. One outfitted with such a value framework is bound to view organic life as Spencer does, that is, as a matter of "adaptation," as a complicated limit case of calculable relationships subject to strict mechanistic principles. How much the Darwinian type resembles the bourgeois type articulated above![40]

Scheler detects indications of the tendency to exalt lower values at the expense of higher ones even in Kant's ethics. The weak person of *ressentiment* cannot stand alone with his ethical judgment especially if it is he alone who feels an objective demand. So the generality of a value stance becomes a replacement for authentic value objectivity. This kind of person, instead of pursuing his own investigation of what he ought to do, asks "What do you think? What do *all* people think? What finally is the general tendency of humanity as a type? What is the predominant trend of progress so that when I see it I might enter into the mainstream?" And so the herds of *ressentiment* people gather together to replace "objective good" with their herd consciousness, seeking to act in accord with Kant's "generally valid law of human willing" or with what is typical of the species.[41]

Related to Kantian universalization, understood as *ressentiment* phenomenon, is modern humanitarian love, to which Scheler devotes the entire fourth section of his "Das Ressentiment im Aufbau der Moralen." Scheler comments:

> From this point [the arrival of the general love for humanity] on, an equalizing power is demanded in whose name the dissolution of the feudal and aristocratic ordering of society takes place. Such equalization requires the abolition of all forms of belonging and personal bondedness and the destruction of indolent monks' orders devoid of any usefulness for the common good. . . . Here quantitative criteria suppress qualitative criteria, and, accordingly, the "general love for humanity" grows more powerfully until the French Revolution. During that Revolution "in the name of humanity," heads roll, national and territorial "blinders" are stripped away, and finally the political and economic-social equality of humanity is instituted. Such changes entail an imposed uniformity of life in morality and usage and a "more humane" and common process of education. In the name of this love, world peace is increasingly demanded and a bitter struggle occurs against all life-forms and value-judgments which grow out of the noble life, even out of the warlike caste.[42]

Although it seems somewhat unfair to accuse Kant of promulgating blind conformism, given his emphasis on rational autonomy, or to hold Rousseau's ideas responsible for the French Terror, Scheler has put his finger on currents in the modern Western *Weltanschauung*. That *Weltanschauung* levels values to a least common denominator, denies and obscures from sight value differences and distinctions, and piously covers its deeds by an appeal to "love." These consequences follow when objective values are abolished and the onus of bestowing value is placed upon the shoulders of each subjectivity, desperately willing to resort to any strategy to guarantee its own preservation. Clear linkages can be drawn to mechanistic epistemology's denuding the world of its structures in order to impose its own categorical systematization. Similarly, metamorphoses in the domain of values parallel capitalism's rejection of divine governance and any inviolable qualitative structures so that labor and the drive to acquire can work their will without any restraining boundaries.

## Intersubjectivity

### Social Forms

It is difficult to demarcate the historical boundaries between the four finds of social unities Scheler delineates: the mass *(Masse)*, the life community *(Gemeinschaft)*, society *(Gesellschaft)*, and the collective person *(Gesamtperson)*. Scheler opposes a strict historical evolution from mass to collective person after the fashion of a Comte. Instead, he believes that all four forms and their corresponding ethos are simultaneously at hand in various mixtures. Nevertheless, certain tendencies may predominate in one era or another.

The mass grouping involves no idea-directed action, rather only a blind collective impulse grown out of a many-sided affective contagion. The *Gemeinschaft,* the second form, is characterized by a natural, naive word and concept realism in which common ideas rule the individuals so forcefully that they risk losing their own spiritual individuality. The positive, handed-down tradition appears here as unquestionably given, as firm and fixed as the laws of nature themselves, instead of being recognized as a mere tradition. Individual perception and experience can no more triumph over the collective treasury of traditional ideas than individual actions of discovery, willing, or following one's individual conscience can. Only what confirms and verifies the common mindset even reaches the observation thresholds of the community members. Only reproduction of handed-down, communally sanctioned beliefs—and not the production or discovery of such beliefs—prevails over details as minute as the construction of tools, jewelry, art, and architecture.[43]

Scheler agrees with Herbert Spencer that historically western European modernity, as opposed to the Middle Ages and other cultures of the present, possesses a predominately societal *(gesellschaftliches)* ethos. For Scheler, the communal *(gemeinschaftliche)*

life orientation of the Middle Ages was dissolved by the nominalistic spiritual tenor that prevails in singularism, individualism,
liberalism, formal democracy, contract theory, conventionalism,
or social atomism. Such forms of unity entail a certain artificiality
since individuals do not live with each other, but rather establish
mutual bonds through deliberate conscious acts. Common criteria of truth and falsehood, beauty and ugliness must be agreed
to if there is to be common knowing. Acting and willing in concert
require acts of promising and, particularly, contractual relationships, which form the basis of all private law.[44]

Several shifts occur in the transition from *Gemeinschaft* to *Gesellschaft*. The *Gemeinschaft* is characterized by an active feeling of an
original co-responsibility of every person for every other person, a
co-responsibility that does not depend on prior promises and
contracts. One experiences the *Gemeinschaft* as an organic and
invisible interweaving of all parts of a moral world in time, space,
and beyond that in the kingdom of God. The Christian community's conception of itself as the *Corpus Christi* exemplifies such a
unity. In *Gesellschaft*, however, this co-responsibility of the *Gemeinschaft* gives way to a onesided self-responsibility that each individual must freely assume. In *Gesellschaft*, persons are responsible,
ultimately, only for themselves. A haphazard coincidence of interests between individuals and classes replaces mutual solidarity.
Scheler attributes this lack of solidarity to the "measureless ava-
rice of anonymous or half-anonymous, unresponsible, democratic
streams of people." Consequently, the mutual trust of the *Gemeinschaft* deteriorates into a groundless and primary mistrust typical
of *Gesellschaft*. In *Gesellschaft*, the majority arrives at common national decisions by imposing its will on an unwilling minority.
Even common cultural units, such as that of European nations,
degenerate into a precariously maintained balance of power.[45]

The rise of a predominantly *gesellschaftlichen* social ordering dissolves *Gemeinschaft* into elementary, valueless, particles. The as-
cendance of *Gesellschaft* parallels mechanistic epistemology's
breaking up substances and forms into atoms and capitalism's
disintegration of the stable medieval order into a myriad of tireless
competitors. In addition, a corresponding levelling of all forms of
human socialization occurs.

> A world of differences! This means: all apparent forms of human
> living together (state, church, marriage, nation) not only develop
> through the activity of human subjects, but they arise from human
> acts and can be dissolved and changed through them. These life

forms rest also finally on either contracts or natural power and authority formations. This is the nominalism and conventionalism of the modern world. This is, at the same time, this world's primordial mechanistic belief in nature and history. There is in this world no realized objective value, form, or idea realm, no objective Logos which all mechanistic processes (natural and social processes, soul and life processes) ought to serve. There is thus no Logos in history or in the society *(Gesellschaft)* of human beings who are the highest and most complete of world-essences. And so after these objective forms and ideas about the world have been subjectivized and left to arbitrary choice, all that remains objectively is the mechanism of the world. The spirit of modern democracy speaks audibly in modern individual natural rights theory, in which the state, marriage, and the family are grounded on free contract (unity or subordination contract). Also the principle of original solidarity is shattered with this theory and in its place the doctrine posited by the exclusive self-responsibility of human beings (Protestantism and its idea of freedom of conscience).[46]

In spite of Scheler's criticisms of *Gesellschaft*, he does conceive a positive role for it, just as Hegel allotted such a role to civil society. In the *gesellschaftlichen* structure, it is possible for the individual to build up a mature self-consciousness of his or her incomparable individuality, beyond simply being an "element" of society. Such a possibility is excluded from the *Gemeinschaft*.[47] Nevertheless, this achievement of *Gesellschaft* needs to be "sublated" and incorporated into relationships of solidarity.

> It is valid at the same time not to deny, as so often happens today, the individualism of those who think "liberally." Rather that individualism needs to be spiritualized and penetrated with a religious-ethical content. Further, under energetic defense against all merely pagan, merely modern, pantheistic conceptions of the state (Fichte, Hegel, and Marx), the popular solidarity, experienced in the [First World] war, should be held fast to as an underpinning for the ethical-religious solidarity of humanity. Such popular solidarity is justifiable only when it is overarched by this deeper solidarity.[48]

### Theories of Intersubjectivity

Philosophical approaches to intersubjectivity, traditionally focused on the so-called "problem of other minds," manifest structural analogies with Western science, capitalism, and societal relations. They also correspond to the epistemological and ethical theories characteristic of modern Western philosophy.

According to Scheler, genetic theories of fellow feeling, such as those of T. Lipps or G. Störring, assert that perception of occasioning circumstances coupled with the symptoms of joy or sorrow in another person immediately evokes the reproduction of a similar joy or sorrow previously experienced in oneself. This view, that the other's experience stirs one to reexperience a similar experience of one's own in order to understand the Other, denies any direct fellow feeling of the Other's experience. Besides, it seems to attribute awkward, convoluted, causal-mechanistic processes to actors conceived as basically isolated and atomized and yet seeking to comprehend each other. As such, these genetic views parallel the kinds of interpersonal exchanges usual in a capitalistic *Gesellschaft*, but they do not account accurately for the nature of intersubjective relations. Scheler further contends that, when a person reveals distressful experiences to another and the Other launches into personal reminiscences about the past in a kind of pseudoemphathy, the person in distress in fact experiences a grave failure of intersubjective understanding.[49]

Scheler criticizes further presuppositions of Lipps's stance that one comes to believe in other minds because one empathically projects oneself into the physical manifestations evinced by the Other. This position presupposes: (1) that is always one's own self that is primarily given to one, and (2) that what is primarily given in the case of others is merely the appearance of the body and its changes and movements. While Scheler's full response to these presuppositions cannot be articulated until later, the first presupposition mirrors the isolation of atomized components of a *Gesellschaft*. The second presupposition involves a mechanistic decomposition of the Other into a body detached from all spiritual characteristics. Similarly, the mechanistic framework dissects expressive phenomena (such as a blush) into a sum of separate elements (a patch of redness on the face, rising temperature, perspiration). The interlocutor gradually combines these elements into a whole in order to conclude that the Other is experiencing shame.[50] Scheler sums up his critique:

> Perhaps this may give us a rather better understanding of the supposedly "self-evident fact" that we can only perceive the bodies of other people. We can begin by treating colors, sounds, shapes, etc., as "sensations," when they are really qualities appearing in conjunction with sensation. Or again, we can treat the perception based upon (though not composed of) such qualitative complexes, as a complex of sensations, though sensations play no part in it. We can also forget that on this (doubly erroneous) view of perception it is *no more possible* to perceive the body than it is to perceive the self. If we assume that

it is feasible to perceive with all these presuppositions, then we do indeed reach the remarkable conclusion that we can perceive the bodies of other people but not their selves.[51]

This empathic projection theory of intersubjective understanding displays the usual mechanistic tendency to pulverize human experience into atomized elements. It then attempts a rather clumsy, artificial reconstitution of what never should have been disintegrated in the first place.

The effort to give a mechanistic, causal explanation of human behavior in fact demolishes what it attempts to investigate. Human behavior can be correctly understood only through the distinctive process of *Verstehen*, or intersubjective understanding. In *Verstehen*, one never experiences the living expressions of the other person as the effects of hidden causal processes within the Other. For Scheler, instead, one experiences the acts of the Other (speech, expressions, actions) as proceeding from a spiritual center, given in intuition, and as directed intentionally toward something. If someone to whom one is turned in the understanding posture (and not a scientifically investigative posture) says "The weather is beautiful today," one does not stop and judge, "X says that the weather is beautiful today" or "X is experiencing the judgment process which relates to the fact of the weather being beautiful." Rather the Other's speech provides the occasion that one likewise directs one's intentionality to the beautiful weather. Actually, it is only when this regular continuity of meaningfulness, characteristic of *Verstehen*, is disturbed that one resorts to causal explanation. If someone, for instance, tells a story that is difficult to believe and then someone else says that this person is somewhat deranged, then one no longer interprets this person's expressions as sense-directed intentions. Rather one discovers only an "empty place" where, before, a spiritual center of acts had been perceived. What is given now is mere expressive movements and other movements behind which one might seek psychic processes as causes. In place of the bonds of meaning, causal connections, such as stimuli and responses, assume prominence. In place of objects previously co-intended, there are mere stimuli; in place of intentions, mere processes; in place of meaning relationships, causal relationships; instead of *Verstehen*, *erklären*; in place of the *person*, a mere piece of nature. The substitution of causal explanation for intersubjective understanding—a typical mechanistic procedure—involves explaining normal process by paradigms appropriate only for abnormal cases.[52]

Both the empathetic projection theory and the failure to attain intersubjective *Verstehen* through causal, mechanistic explanation reflect on a philosophical, theoretical plane the "monadization" of individuals typical of social forms in the modern Western *Gesellschaft*. Moreover, the portrait of such an isolated individual within a *Gesellschaft* coincides with the transformations in cognition and valuation in the West. Monads in a *Gesellschaft* are responsible only for themselves and are not constrained by the needs and demands of others. They are absolutely free to do and to will whatever they want to do. Whatever obligations impinge upon them do so because they have willed such obligations by entering into a contract with another. As in the cases of cognition and valuation, here an older interpersonal order of solidarity and restraints has collapsed, and, in its place, has emerged a nearly omnipotent will to create an intersubjective order of one's own choosing and to submit only to requirements of one's own making.

# 2

# Phenomenology and the Objective Order of Being

While Scheler had much to say on the institutional aspects of Western modernity, namely, science, capitalism, and social forms, he was first and foremost a philosopher and a phenomenologist. Thus, the next three chapters are concerned with Scheler's phenomenological responses to the philosophical manifestations of the Western *Weltanschauung* in the areas of epistemology, value theory, and theory of intersubjectivity. The focus is on his largest and most renowned works corresponding respectively to these three domains: "Erkenntnis und Arbeit" in 1926, *Der Formalismus in der Ethik und die materiale Werthetik* in 1916, and *Zur Phänomenologie und Theorie der Sympathiegefühle and von Liebe und Hass* (later *Wesen und Formen der Sympathie*) in 1913. While Scheler utilizes phenomenology to defend objective structures of being and values, as this chapter and the next show, he also envisions these objective structures as preserving the possibility of intercultural dialogue and as mandating its implementation. This second concern of Scheler's emerges more clearly in the next chapter, and his theory of intersubjectivity, to be presented two chapters from now, aims at shoring up the foundations of this dialogue.

To appreciate the phenomenological character of these works, one must consider briefly Scheler's historical links with Edmund Husserl. Husserl's phenomenology grew, in part, out of a response to the same mechanistic worldview, particularly positivism, which Scheler opposed even before he became acquainted with Husserl's work. As is well known, Scheler met Husserl at Halle in 1901 and formed a spiritual bond that Scheler described twenty-one years later as "uncommonly fruitful" for him in "Die deutsche Philosophie der Gegenwart."[1] Scheler later joined the Munich Circle of philosophers in 1907, three to four years after Husserl himself had addressed that group and won them away from Theodor Lipps and over to phenomenology.[2] After losing his position at the University of Munich in 1910, Scheler spent a few years at Göttingen with Husserl and the Göttingen Circle. Scheler's *Zur Phänomenologie und Theorie der Sympathiegefühle und von Liebe und Hass* and the first part of his *Der Formalismus in der Ethik und die materiale Wertethik* were both published in 1913, the same year in which Husserl's first volume of *Ideen zu einer reinen Phänomenologie und phänomenologischen Philosophie* appeared. Both of Scheler's books reflect his lengthy acquaintance with Husserl. Before launching into Scheler's epistemology, the meaning of Husserlian phenomenology may be summarized briefly in order to better understand its influence on Scheler.

## Edmund Husserl and Empiricism

In the second chapter of *Ideen,* entitled "Naturalistic Misconstructions," Husserl begins by praising the motives of empiricistic naturalism. Empiricism, as a form of epistemological radicalism, has withstood all "idols," particularly, the forces of tradition and superstition and raw or refined prejudices of every kind. It has defended the right of autonomous reason as the only authority in questions of truth. It has directed itself to the things themselves and has inquired regarding these things in their "self-givenness," apart from prejudice. In empiricism's view, for philosophy to speak of "ideas" or "essences," instead of focusing on empirical facts, would be tantamount to dealing in scholastic entities and metaphysical ghosts. Natural science has indeed rescued us from such pale specters, and so, according to empiricism, if one searches after "eidetic" givennesses, one relapses into "ideological eccentricities," "scholastic regressions," or nineteenth-century "speculative constructions a priori."[3]

Husserl believes that natural science, by limiting the questions it asks, has wisely avoided entanglement with various age-old sceptical puzzles and their vexing metaphysical and epistemological dimensions, puzzles such as whether the "external world" exists. Thus science has freely pursued questions leading to a correct, fruitful, and comprehensive knowledge of nature. The resulting productivity of science explains, in part, Husserl's jest at the beginning of his later *Die Krisis der Europäischen Wissenschaften und die transzendentale Phänomenologie* over the irony that the natural sciences should be accused of being in a crisis by a futile and unproductive philosophy.[4]

But when positivism boasts of its scientific and prejudice-free character over against other forms of philosophy, Husserl asks on what side the prejudices actually lie. Empiricism, in Husserl's view, despite its good motives, mistakenly identified a "return to the things themselves" with the demand to ground all knowledge through sense experience. To claim, however, that all judgments demand grounding in sensible experience without first having undertaken a study of judgments according to their basically different types is to engage in a "speculative construction a priori." Such an a priori construction is no better simply because it proceeds within an empiricist context. By thus restricting the domain of knowable facts to those sensibly given in nature, empiricism uncritically dismisses other evident data.[5] Husserl goes on:

> There are many questions regarding the fundamental regions of objects and correlatively the regional types of dator intuitions, the pertinent types of judgments and finally the noetic norms that for the grounding of judgments of such type demand exactly this and no other type of intuition. Answers to these questions cannot be merely postulated or decreed. One needs to grasp these matters insightfully, that means exhibiting them through dator intuitions and establishing them through judgments which truly fit themselves to the intuitive data. It seems that this and no other procedure can actually be prejudice-free or purely factual.[6]

Ironically, empiricism, which began as a reaction against irrationality and prejudice, rests on the unproven premise that only those judgments that are provable through sense experience constitute valid judgments.

One finds Husserl's criticism here reminiscent of the criticisms made of positivistic attempts in this century to distinguish meaningful statements from nonsense on the basis of criteria of verification. One may, following Hume, claim that all statements must be either matters of fact or relations of ideas, or else they are nonsense. Still, one must give an account of the validity of that statement itself, which appears to be neither a matter of fact nor a relation of ideas. Without such an account, that statement would seem to belong among those that seem worthy of being cast into the flames. One seems caught in a similar dilemma when one arbitrarily promulgates that only claims verifiable by the senses are prejudice-free.

Furthermore, paralleling Scheler's criticism of the modern Western *Weltanschauung's* narrowing and levelling tendencies, Husserl too opposes the constrictive role exercised by the claim that only sensibly verifiable statements are permissible. Indeed, Husserl's

widening of the meaning of intuition to include categorial structures beyond simple sensible givens was an early step in this
same direction. Furthermore, for Husserl, fundamental regions of
objects, types of *dator* intuition, types of judgments, noetic
norms—whole domains of knowledge—are from the outset pre-
cluded by the ungrounded and arbitrary decree that only certain
types of judgments are legitimate.[7]

Hence, what is called for, according to Husserl is a new beginning in which one proceeds from strictly established individual
cases to general theses in accord with methods illuminated by
stringent, principled insight. Instead of limiting what can be valid
by theoretical proscriptions, Husserl attempts to reach back to
that which antedates all theoretical standpoints. He seeks to return to the collective realm of what is given intuitively before any
theoretical elaboration of it, to that which one can immediately
see and grasp. Hence, Husserl believes that, in order to avoid
error, one must observe his "principle of all principles." That
principle states that one may justify cognition only on the basis
of originary *dator* intuitions and only if one takes what presents
itself originarily in every *dator* intuition as it gives itself and only
within the limits within which it gives itself. If "positivism"
means a prejudice-free grounding all sciences on that which is
"positive," that is, originally grasped data, then, Husserl claims,
it is he who is the authentic positivist. Husserl affirms that "we
do not allow ourselves to be *stunted* by any authority which would
deny us the right to consider all kinds of intuitions as equally
legitimate sources of knowledge—not even by the authority of
'modern science.'"[8]

Later, in his "Vienna Lecture" of 1935, years after Scheler's
death, Husserl drew out the historical dimensions his own philosophical stance by tracing it to Greek philosophy. The ancients
injected into Western culture a "resolve not to accept unquestion-
ingly any pregiven opinion or tradition so that he [the philoso-
pher] can inquire, in respect to the whole traditionally pregiven
universe, after what is true in itelf, an ideality." That Husserl gave
that lecture in Vienna because Jews could not lecture in Germany
testifies to the failure of this rational culture initiated by the
Greeks. But that culture failed, in Husserl's view, not because of
rationality, but because of the refusal to be sufficiently rational, a
refusal to examine all prejudices.[9]

As part of his methodological new beginning, Husserl substitutes for sensible experience the more general notion of "intuition" and thereby refuses to identify knowledge in general with

knowledge based on sensible empirical data only. Intuition, in Husserl's philosophy, functions critically, opening the knower to a broader range of what can count as experience or data. Intuition involves an "immediate seeing" that is irreducible to sense experience, but that can include it. This seeing generally consists in an original *dator* consciousness of any kind whatsoever that constitutes the last justification-ground of all reasonable claims. If one is going to convince someone of a claim, the things themselves must be seen as they present themselves before assent can be given. It is possible that conflicts may arise over what is the correct "seeing," but this no more eliminates the validity of "seeing" than a conflict between forces eliminates the notion of force. This possible conflict of "seeings" suggests to Husserl that there are some intuitions wherein the seeing is, according to its essence, "incomplete." Such intuitions can be confirmed or disconfirmed depending on whether the progress of experience demands the surrender of once firmly held convictions.[10]

Scheler concurs with Husserl's notion of ultimate justification based on an intuitive, immediate grasping of the coincidence between objects referred to and the intentional facts referring to those objects. Such evidence is not isolated from the sum of one's knowledge, and it does not consist in a "feeling of evidence," since the feeling itself presupposes the having of evidence. Further, while there are "evidence-deceptions," such *"Täuschungen"* undergo an *"Ent-täuschung"* in the light of a further evidence. Finally, criteria of knowledge are themselves not originary, but only point to the conditions under which evidences present themselves.[11]

Husserl discovers two general types of intuitions, each of which flows from analogous *dator* acts of consciousness: (1) empirical intuitions that yield sense experience of an individual object, and (2) essential intuitions that grasp ideal unities of meaning or "essences." Although positivistically inclined thinkers reject essential intuitions and restrict themselves to empirical intuitions, Husserl criticizes their view that obvious general truisms, usually expressed in axioms, express facts arrived at through sensible experience. Rather, propositions such as that $a + 1 = 1 + a$, that a judgment is not colored, or that of two qualitatively different tones one is lower and the other higher bring to expression eidetic or essential intuitions.

Having reduced all objects to empirical objects, positivists dismiss "essences" as nothing more than "Platonic hypostatizations" without taking into account Husserl's description of essences as ideal unities of meaning that function as the subject of a sentence. To speak of tone qualities, or the number 2, or the figure of a circle is to discuss ideal objects. In fact, positivists operate with such "essences" in their thinking and are constantly making essential judgments even though they dismiss them from their epistemological standpoint. Thus, for instance, the very claim that only empirical intuitions are valid types of intuitions presupposes unadmitted beliefs about what the essence of knowledge is.[12]

Just as Husserl detects the positivist's unacknowledged reliance upon essential knowledge, so he almost delights in listing the paradoxical, *essentially contingent* properties of the material thing given in perception. A certain inadequacy pertains to the perception of any thing as an essential necessity. It is *necessary* that one *always* perceive a thing one-sidedly, *never* completely, *always* through a series of spatio-temporal perspectives, *always* with a kernel of what is actually presented surrounded by a horizon of what is cogiven but not actually present and of what is more or less vaguely indefinite. A certain incompletion into infinity belongs to the ineliminable essence of the correlation: thing-thing perception. Would positivism ever notice such essential properties, implicitly contained within the material sensible given upon which positivism places such a priority, since its prejudices forbid the possibility of essences?[13]

In fact, Husserl, throughout *Ideen,* untiringly brings to light possibilities that a more reductive, constrained, limit-drawing perspective would never even see. Because of Husserl's notion of horizon, every experience refers beyond itself to further possible experiences, which, again, open up new possible experiences, and so on into infinity. Also, the phenomenological reduction, whereby one brings to focus the domain of consciousness overlooked because of our *common sensible* (or natural attitude) preoccupation with the objects of experience, opens up the intentional conscious activity through which those objects are given. These acts, their contents, and their dynamic unfolding remain hidden to a static sense-data account of experience. Furthermore, just as a noematic object can be approached through a variety and multiplicity of possible noetic acts and stances in dynamic interrelationship, so also, at a higher level, a judgment, such as "S is P," can be considered a noematic kernel, available to possible successive acts of belief, doubt, or rejection. This noematic kernel, in turn, takes on the possible modifications of being held certainly, possibly, or probably, or of being completely rejected. This phenomenological attitude, which differs from mere lived immersion in the natural attitude, makes it clear for the first time that there is such a thing as the "natural attitude," or *"common sense"* way of being toward the world. In fact, the reduction, by freeing one from such unreflective immersion, illuminates many possible ways of turning toward the world, for instance, lived immersion in activity, phenomenological neutralization, or the scientific attitude of various sciences. This field, unearthed by phenomenology, includes whole regions and categories of would-be objects with their essential features (e.g., the material thing for the natural sciences, the psychophysical being for the *Geisteswissenschaften*), which prescribe differing, noninterchangeable methods of investigations. Husserl argues further that there are different kinds of eidetic science, and he resists erroneous prejudices to the effect that the exact mathematical sciences are the only model for eidetic sciences. He also opposes the view that there are no inexact, morphological essences and that transcendental phenomenology cannot also yield eidetic results different in kind from those of mathematics or geometry.[14]

This constant tendency of Husserl's phenomenology to disclose neglected or suppressed possibilities and to release novel ways of looking at things from narrow prejudices compares with the task of the geometer who utilizes phantasy much more than perception when it comes to his models and figures. As Husserl describes it:

> . . . in phantasy he [the geometer] possesses an incomparable freedom in the arbitrary tranformation of imagined figures, in the running through of continually modified possible patterns, and so in the creation of innumerable new structures. This freedom opens up to him for the first time access to the breadth of essential possibilities with their infinite horizons of essence-knowledges.[15]

For Husserl, phenomenology similarly thrives on fiction and imagination for envisioning of new possibilities:

> So one can actually say—if he loves paradoxical speech and if he understands well the multiple meanings involved—in strictest truth that "fiction" makes up the life-element of phenomenology, as of all eidetic science, that fiction is the source from which knowledge of "eternal truths" draws its nourishment.[16]

In addition to countering positivist tendencies to confine experience to sense data and to circumscribe the domain of legitimate knowledge, the phenomenology of Husserl's *Ideen* includes a critique of the mechanistic theory of knowledge, a critique anticipating Husserl's later *Die Krisis der Europäischen Wissenschaften und die transzendentale Phänomenologie*. According to Husserl's *Ideen*, science, particularly physics, seeks greater predictability regarding nature by following the rational motives suggested by *common sense* experience and by articulating a theoretical definition of the sensibly experienced thing. At this point, a distinction appears between the sensible thing and the thing of the "physical intellectio," the latter containing ontological references to invisible atoms, ions, and electrons, which provide causal explanations of natural experience. Gradually the thing of physical *intellectio* comes to explain causally not only the appearances of things but also the conscious acts through which those appearances are given. Causality now bridges the gap between physical being and consciousness. Consciousness itself and such contents as values and secondary qualities are reduced to being derivatives of the entities established by physics, a science that itself has been developed by consciousness. Here Husserl attempts to reverse the centuries-old mechanistic view of knowledge that rests on a forgetfulness of consciousness's own constructive activity in science. This very coming to self-awareness of consciousness serves to relativize physics by showing it to be one activity of human consciousness among many. In Marxist terms, consciousness recovers from its own self-alienation by recognizing its subservience to the thing of physics that is its own product. This condensed critique of the mechanistic account of knowledge coheres with the phenomenological struggle against univocal, reductive modes of considering human consciousness in order to make room for the rich variety of its possible deployments.[17]

At present, strong opposition exists toward Husserlian "foundationalism," because of its longing for absolute grounds that, it is suspected, give false, ideological security, while brooking no opposition. Furthermore, phenomenology's search for essences, it is feared, will seem to have captured the complexity of reality only to those who have created such essences, and, all the while, such essences will suppress differences. While these dangerous tendencies may pervade the phenomenological enterprise, still this interpretation suggests that Husserl was up to something very different from this. He was engaged with an opponent remarkably similar to the kind of opponent that Husserl himself has become for contemporary philosophers. For Husserl, the effort to get behind theoretical suppositions to the things themselves was part of an effort to escape the stifling limitations imposed by the unjustified prohibition of any knowledge beyond sense experience. Whether the objects considered are sense things or propositions, or whether the noetic stances are simple perceiving or a whole scientific system, Husserl's theory of intentionality resists oversimplified assertions that there is only one way or one attitude with which to approach anything given. The given can unfold kaleidoscopically before whichever of one's multiple eyes are turned toward it. Finally, one might find the inquiry after essence, for example the essence of religion, a critical corrective to the narrow and pretentious tendency to assume that one's own religion or those religions in the immediate environs exemplify *the* epitome of religiosity. What philosophers like Derrida, Foucault, or Lyotard undertake with regard to Husserl resembles Husserl's own project in the face of positivistic empiricism of his day.[18]

## Max Scheler's Phenomenological Critique of the Epistemology of the Modern Western *Weltanschauung*

As has been seen already, Scheler, from his earliest period, was already critical of the epistemology of the modern Western outlook, as well as of many other aspects of it, before he embraced phenomenology. In "Die deutsche Philosophie der Gegenwart," Scheler, recalling his first meeting with Edmund Husserl, commented on their conversation on intuition and perception. Even though Scheler was then still close to Kantian philosophy, he had come to the conviction that the content given to intuition was originally much richer that what was discoverable through sensible contents, their genetic derivatives, and their forms of logical unification. Husserl acknowledged that he, too, in a forthcoming work on logic—what was in fact *Logische Untersuchungen*—had analogously widened the concept of intuition via his notion of "categorial intuitions." Such intuitions involve a grasp of logical categories such as being and nonbeing, unity, plurality, totality, number, ground, and consequence. In Scheler's view, Husserl's expansion of "intuition" to include the apprehension of structural relationships beyond merely sensible givens served as the most immediate starting point for the rise of phenomenology. If one can grasp structural features in themselves (Husserl) or within the sensible givens themselves (Scheler), it need not be the case that the world presents chaotic sensations whose only order must result from the synthetic activity of human understanding projecting itself onto the world. If the world appears to intuition as already possessed of its own structure, a fundamental pillar of the mechanistic worldview falls. Phenomenology thus afforded Scheler the means for a critique that had been developing since his earliest period.[19]

Scheler undertook his most mature and complete criticism of mechanistic epistemology in his essay "Erkenntnis und Arbeit, Eine Studie über Wert und Grenzen des pragmatischen Motives in der Erkenntnis der Welt." This essay makes use of diverse phenomenological procedures, although it also incorporates elements of the metaphysics that come to full bloom in Scheler's later works. Scheler published "Erkenntnis und Arbeit" as a companion piece to his "Probleme einer Soziologie des Wissens" in his first edition of *Die Wissensformen und die Gesellschaft* in 1926. Scheler thought that both these works together opened the door to strict, methodical, metaphysical thinking. He stated that the chief goal of *Die Wissensformen und die Gesellschaft* was to pave the way for this kind of thinking as opposed to all mysticism, obscurantism of every kind, and even positivism. He viewed these works both as an introduction to his forthcoming metaphysics and as a defense against the two principal enemies of metaphysics: sociologists who reject metaphysics as outmoded, epistemological definitions of the limits of possible experience and revealed religions with their church structures and dogmas.[20] In Scheler's opinion, these sociological and epistemological investigations converge and complete each other in the common task of criticizing a culture that has rejected metaphysics. As he points out:

> The simultaneous taking up of a sociology of knowledge essay and an extended epistemological and ontological work in one and the same volume can, at first glance, cause one to wonder. But this conjunction has its deeper ground in the principle conviction that guides me, namely that epistemological investigations without an exploration at the same time of the societal-historical development of the prominent type of human knowing and theory of knowledge are doomed to emptiness and unfruitfulness. Likewise any developmental theory and sociology of human knowing—as in an extended manner they were sought first by Condorcet and Comte—must remain directionless, untenable, and unfounded if clearly conscious epistemological essential convictions do not guide the undertaking.[21]

The structure of "Erkenntnis und Arbeit" provides important clues about the connections between epistemology, sociology, and metaphysics. The text consists of seven sections. After the first part introduces the problem of the connection between knowledge and labor, the second section presents the essential nature of knowing and the types of knowing. Scheler then embarks upon a discussion of pragmatism, its principle claims, errors, and insights in part 3. In the fourth part, Scheler praises methodic pragmatism for correctly understanding the mechanistic world view as only an instrumental theory, one of many possible stances toward the world, valuable for technical control so long as it refrains from any pretension to ontological absolutes. A fifth section treats the topic of perception and makes up well over a third of the entire text, the longest section by far of the seven. This section addresses the connection between sensation and perception and perception and phantasy. It basically shows how the mechanistic reduction of perception to sensation artificially distorts the true nature of perception by abstracting isolated and nonexistent "sensations" from the perceptual whole. Up until this point, Scheler's discussion has been primarily epistemological with phenomenology functioning in the critique and relativization of the mechanistic worldview and in accounting for the true character of perception. Notice also that there has been a move from a presentation of what knowing, in general, is to the relativization of the mechanistic worldview as one mode of approaching reality, and then to a highly specific discussion of perception and its relation to sensation. At this point, in his sixth section, Scheler begins an expansion out from detailed discussions of perception to the metaphysical presuppositions of perception, in particular, the nature of reality preceding perception. While this section moves beyond perception to its metaphysical context, the final section, the concluding reflection on the sociology of knowledge, goes beyond this whole discussion of the theories of perception to their sociological context, that is, to the rise of bourgeois culture, which underpins the mechanistic account of perception. Of course, one could easily discuss the mechanistic theory of perception in isolation from metaphysics or from its sociological context, as is usually the case, but Scheler chose to do otherwise.

The movement from general discussions of knowledge and modes of attending to the world to detailed discussions of perception and sensation and back out to metaphysics and sociology shows that Scheler tries to situate discussions of perception in their broader context. He had done the same in his discussion of perception by showing that the mechanistic reduction to sensation has involved an artificial prescinding from the fuller context of perception. It is precisely these richer contexts that the mechanistic worldview, by its simplifying and reductive tendencies, has obscured from sight.

Sociology of knowledge and epistemology are related, with the sociology of knowledge revealing the broad setting to which theories of perception and epistemology pertain without their often recognizing it. Similarly, as shall be seen later, when one adopts a certain epistemological framework, such as phenomenology or mechanism, one's context for sociology of knowledge—that is, how one envisions sociological factors affecting knowledge (e.g., sluice gate or materialist determinism)—will vary correspondingly.[22]

Finally, in "Erkenntnis und Arbeit," Scheler addresses the three problems posed above by mechanistic epistemologies:[23] the problem of perception in part 5, the problem of understanding and reason in parts 1 through 3, and the philosophical context of science in parts 4, 6, and 7. To fill out these general structural comments, Scheler's epistemological critique of the modern Western *Weltanschauung*, as presented in "Erkenntnis und Arbeit," must be traced in more detail.

After listing a variety of possible approaches to the essence of knowledge, ranging from H. Cohen's to M. Schlick's, Scheler spells out the most general concept of knowledge *(Wissens)* possible: knowledge is a relationship of being. It is the relationship of participation *(Teilnahme)* of one being in the nature *(Sosein)* of another being without the known being undergoing any kind of change. This relationship entails no spatial, temporal, or causal relationship. The *Sosein* of the known being is as well *extra mente, in re,* as *in mente,* that is, as an intentional object of the knower. Only the *Sosein* of the known being becomes an *ens intentionale,* in distinction from the known being's *Dasein,* its reality, which remains continually and necessarily outside of any knowing relationship.[24]

Scheler utilizes the *Dasein/Sosein* distinction against reigning epistemological viewpoints. Critical realism, for instance, holds that there is a real world there, but that one's images need not correspond to it. Idealism advances the theory that one knows the essence of things, but their "reality" involves nothing beyond those mental contents. Scheler argues that critical realism rightly sees the being-there *(Dasein)* of the thing as beyond one's knowledge, but overlooks that one can receive the nature of the thing *(Sosein)* as the object of an intentional act and not merely as an image. Unlike critical realism, which places *Dasein* and *Sosein* outside of people, idealism places them both within one's mind.

Scheler concurs with idealism's recognition that *Sosein* can be *in mente,* while he opposes the transfer of *Dasein* to the mind. Thus, Scheler's eidetic depiction of knowledge makes possible his criticism of the one-sidedness of critical realism and idealism.[25]

This description of knowledge also directly confronts mechanistic epistemology's view of the constructive power of understanding since it holds that knowers can partake in the structure of the object, its *Sosein,* and thus they do not create this structure from their own resources. In fact, in the relationship of participation, knowers truly transcend themselves and overleap the limits of their own being and nature in order to partake of what is other. Scheler notes that he sees no other name for such a tendency to self-transcendence than "love" or "surrender" to what is other. Such an act of knowing consists primordially in an ecstatic knowing whereof one becomes self-conscious only subsequently, through a reflexive act.[26]

Rejecting any idea of knowledge for knowledge's sake, Scheler proceeds to describe the three preeminent goals that knowing serves and the distinct types of knowledge corresponding to these goals: (1) knowledge of the deity in redemptive knowledge *(Erlösungswissen),* (2) the becoming and development of the person in self-formative knowledge *(Bildungswissen),* and (3) scientific knowledge for purposes of dominating nature *(Herrschaftswissen* or *Leistungswissen).* Scheler had noted in an earlier essay, "Über die positivistische Geschichtsphilosophie des Wissens (Dreistadiengesetz)," that the positivist doctrine of the three stages of knowledge, represented by thinkers such as Comte, Mill, Spencer, Mach, and Avenarius, misreads these three types of knowledge as sequential phases of history. Rather, for Scheler they are *"essentielle,"* enduring spiritual attitudes, and "knowledge forms" given with the essence of the human spirit itself.[27] Scheler, however, is not content to describe these types of knowing as if they stood on the same plane with each other. Such a "value-free" ranking would cede too much to the leveling tendencies of the modern Western *Weltanschauung.* Hence, Scheler arranges these knowledge forms in terms of the goals they serve, with domination knowledge at the service of self-formative knowledge, which in turn submits to redemptive knowledge.[28]

Scheler, thus, articulates through an implicit form of phenomenological eidetic variation these essences of knowledge and of knowledge types, which form the basis of his critique of pragmatism. Pragmatism basically fails to see that the principle of technical control is only *one* principle whereby one selects possible aspects of objects for knowing. Instead, pragmatism tries to construe all knowing of objects and the idea of knowledge generally as practical in character. Whatever the principle of selection of possible aspects of objects for knowledge may be, truth involves accordance with the things, and knowledge always entails participation in whatever object is chosen for investigation. Knowledge produces practical results because true participation has occurred first; but one cannot reduce knowledge to cognition with practical results nor equate "truth" with the success of action. Pragmatism's one-sidedness becomes further manifest in its overlooking of the uniqueness and the goals of self-formative knowledge and redemptive knowledge. For instance, philosophy, perennially preoccupied with the wonder-evolving essential structures of the world, excludes technical principles of selection in its approach to knowledge and so differs significantly from science. Science ignores questions of essence in favor of gaining predictability and control over the objects and thereby demystifies this world. Although pragmatism occasionally takes account of these differences, nevertheless it misconstrues the rank ordering between knowledge types since it disregards the fact that all attempts at the domination of self and nature are for the sake of the free self-unfolding of the spirit and never vice versa. Scheler cautions that humanity can, after great achievements in positive scientific and technical endeavors, still remain an empty spiritual essence and can even sink into barbarity. Pragmatism, by following the model of science, lacks sufficient critical distance from the mechanistic worldview.[29]

Of course, pragmatism might attempt to blunt Scheler's critique by insisting that there are no essences. Scheler would respond that there exists a realm of thoughts, significations, and propositions that outline constant forms of being—that is, the ideas and basic phenomena that provide the underlying structure for everything observable in the world. Such essential claims are accessible to an a priori knowledge that can neither be supported nor undermined through any possible observation or induction. These essential claims, however, cannot alter the observable world in any way. For the pragmatists, any proposition that would contribute in no way to any alteration of the sensible world is meaningless. Scheler disagrees, though, since such propositions would only be unprovable or lacking in meaning if all of our intuitions were identical with sense intuitions and if there were no other kind of intuition or originary phenomena. The pragmatic principle itself covertly relies on an essential definition of knowledge and meaning that collapses the plurality of intuitions into one type. Thus, Scheler concludes, pragmatism discards all a priori knowledge with a single authoritative pronouncement and without careful proof, thereby handling a priori essences over to arbitrary decision and to the mere expedience of definition and convention.[30]

There are, for Scheler, objective ideal significations that correspond to the *Sosein* of objects, whether *in mente* or *extra mente*, and pragmatism rightly accounts for the *selection* of subjectively thought significances from out of this objective realm. Such selection takes place under the influences of drives and interests of the knowing subject, as can be illustrated by the linguistic terms one employs relative to beings with their own objective structure or *Sosein*. Thus, for instance, one would never refer to a loved friend as a mammal, but, in spite of this interest-directed abstention from that term, one's friend remains structurally a mammal. Or, for instance, those living in nature and following their inclinations possess well-differentiated vocabularies for house pets and hunting animals, but such pets never lose their objective animal structure. Pragmatic concerns determine which aspects of a given object are selected out according to either the spoken terms employed or unspoken attentional foci. Whether the selectivity is linguistically determined or not, it does not do away with an object/ideal meaning realm based on the essential *Sosein* of an object. Pragmatism explains the selection, but it cannot account for the origin of the objective meaning realm nor for the subjective meaning sphere, which, together with the perceptual sphere, is differentiated and developed through a many-sided conditioning process. Practical interests condition perception; they do not produce what is perceived. Similarly, induction grasps accidental patterns, but never manufactures the *Sosein*-constants underlying such patterns and making them possible. Once again, contrary to mechanistic epistemology, Scheler can uphold the objective structure of nature, while permitting the selective viewpoints characteristic of a scientific or pragmatic approach to nature. A more detailed discussion of perception is required before these connections between cognition *(Erkenntnis)* and practical action *(Arbeit)* can be completely clarified.[31]

Having criticized pragmatism and other forms of knowing by reiterating the rights of the objective structure of the world knowable to human understanding, Scheler shifts to a discussion of pragmatism's positive contribution. By turning from the old correspondence theory of truth, which attempted to grasp the ontological structure of the world, and by instead interpreting scientific ideas as *hypotheses,* which may or may not work and so prove themselves true or false, pragmatism has effectively deontologized science and the mechanistic viewpoint. It has converted them into instrumental theories for coming to grips with the world. Pragmatism has, thus, rightly discerned the pragmatic motives underlying positive science. Scheler praises pragmatism for having seen that

> Science leads "nature" insofar as possible back to a prototype of a formal *"mechanism"*—not because nature *in itself* would be *only* a mechanism. Rather, nature in itself, only *insofar* as it is a mechanism or is extensively analogous to one, is *also practically controllable and directable by a life-essence intent on controlling it.*[32]

The mechanistic world view neglects the hypothetical nature of its own constructs. It overlooks how the formal-mechanistic structural image apprehends the thing relative to the mechanistic framework and how it defines nature through signs whereby one can control nature, just as the architect prepares a blueprint before building. But such architectural plans for nature yield no more knowledge of the real fact of nature and its *Sosein* than an address book will teach something about the essence and character of its owner.[33]

Several thinkers have falsely elevated this mechanistic standpoint to the only possible rational view, a trap into which even Bergson fell insofar as he considered *all* thought to be mechanistic and so in need of the supplement of intuition. Even Kant was convinced of the validity of the formal-mechanistic worldview for empirical reality, the explanation of life, and empirical psychology; but he, at least, saw its limits insofar as he contested its metaphysical validity through the "in-itself." The positivists of Scheler's day, particularly Duhem, Avenarius, and Mach agreed on the validity of mechanism. Their principal error rested on the false generalization of the correct insights won in the cognitional practice of exact natural scientists, particularly physicists, to the essence of cognition in general. Mechanists fail to distinguish clearly different kinds of cognition and to derive them from the highest concept of knowing, namely participation of one being in the nature of another.[34]

Fortunately a new breed of methodical pragmatists had appeared on the scene: Maxwell, Boltzmann, Lord Kelvin, and perhaps Einstein in his early period. This group, in Scheler's view, has correctly understood that, for every content of natural events, there is an unlimited number of different "mechanistic models" through which the events can be equally well explained, just as, for any given single technical goal, an unlimited number of machines are thinkable. There are no absolutely final building blocks of nature in this perspective. These theoreticians have realized that the mechanical model does not copy reality outside of our consciousness. Instead, such a model is only a pure thought construction that does not hold for the reality of nature and its real *Sosein*. Rather, models correlate expectations and predictions about nature and the future perceptions that will confirm them. These methodical pragmatists have recognized that the formal mechanistic laws of nature have no ontic significance and that they are valid relative to biological and practical concerns.[35]

To develop this notion of relativity further, Scheler appeals to an evident general epistemological principle that a knower, $X$, to whom an object $A$ is ontologically relative, knows that object $A$ in a cognitionally relative manner as a result. The $X$ itself cannot be explained completely through the same ontological and knowledge principles as the object $A$. However, some different kind of cognition of $X$ must be possible if the ontological relativity of $A$ to $X$ is to be cognizable. As a result, Scheler concludes that the mechanistic view, which exists for the sake of making nature controllable for some living being, is ontologically relative to life processes, and so life processes themselves can never be mechanistically explained. Such processes could be so explained if the mechanistic perspective were relative only to spiritual being, as Descartes thought, since he completely overlooked the existence of life as a independent layer of functions between spirit and mechanism. For Descartes, though, no mechanistic theory could exhaustively account for the soul to which that theory itself was relative. According to Scheler, the scientific constructions developed for a living being's own spontaneous control over nature cannot be applied to that living being itself. Life processes stand forth as free and spontaneous movement when compared with mechanistically explained nature, however much autonomous biological laws may govern such processes.[36]

Through methodological pragmatism and its instrumentalization of former ontological convictions, the mechanistic viewpoint has become self-aware of the conditions under which it approaches nature almost in imitation of phenomenology's recovery of the intentional acts through which an object is given. For Scheler, this awareness immediately suggests alternative possible approaches. One can approach nature as the object of a philosophy of nature through a pure, apractical natural cognition, distinct from the mechanistic view. Further one can look upon nature as offering communications *(Kunde)* from individualities in nature, from electrons to physical macroobjects to stars, even though their impact upon us is barely detectable and may not be conceptualizable or explainable. In addition, one can turn to nature with an attitude of sympathetic understanding, thereby interpreting it as the expression of an life unity ceaselessly creating new images. Finally, nature can be given through a metaphysics of nature that seeks to know the attributes that can be ascribed to the ground of all things.[37]

For Scheler, this limitation of the mechanistic worldview introduced by methodological pragmatism, has "opened our spiritual eyes" to other possible accesses to nature.

> A false, *absolute and metaphysical interpretation* of the cognitional value of the formal-mechanistic view of nature has prevailed since its first appearance in modern times. After the abandonment of this metaphysics of the mechanistic view (which in the first place was the great service of Kant), there has still been a considerable underestimation of its cognitional *relativity*. Its metaphysical absolutization has brought it about that the other four designated grounding types of our knowledge of nature for long periods of history generally have not been noticed and even less seriously valued. It is this false interpretation of the formal-mechanistic view of nature that has completely *blocked* from time to time all ways and paths to philosophy of nature, the communication of nature, the understanding of nature and finally the metaphysics of nature.[38]

Scheler gives several reasons why the mechanistic viewpoint could maintain its dominance over alternatives. Other postures toward nature appear apractical, or, as in the case of teleological investigations, seem to involve mere anthropomorphic projections. Furthermore, if one obtains concepts about nature only through induction and only contingently, in relation to humanity's sensation or brain organization, as the mechanistic framework claims, any search for an intuitively given essence-ontology would be out of the question. After all, the formal-mechanistic laws, taken not as statistical laws but as real laws of dynamic necessity, would actualize such natural ontological structures or basic phenomena merely "by chance." In addition, in Scheler's view, there would be no room for autonomous vital laws, since one would overlook the ontological relativity of the formal-mechanistic view to the life-essence and its spontaneous self-movement.

Instead of recognizing the life relativity of space, time, and movement, one would believe in such "unthings" (Leibniz) as absolute, infinite space, absolute, infinite time (already in physics), and absolute movement.[39]

With the relativization of the mechanistic view, the following once suppressed elements blossom forth: qualities, colors, tones, aromas, individuation levels of nature (inorganic, organic, psychological, spiritual), the possibility of human freedom, the objective/ideal structures of nature in their independence from human consciousness, aesthetic values that are not merely subjective projections of our "feeling-full breast" into nature, ethical values, and secondary qualities. While the cognition of all these forgotten aspects may not help humanity to gain control of things, they are ontologically at hand for the pure, philosophical cognition of nature. The ontological and absolute misinterpretation of the formal-mechanistic view of nature has alienated us from nature and hidden all these wonders from our sight![40]

This criticism of the mechanistic worldview manifests the same phenomenological tendencies as Scheler's earlier critique of pragmatists, critical realists, and idealists for one-sidedly prescinding from the fuller essential structure of knowledge. By tracing the development of methodological pragmatism's dethronement of the ontological mechanistic worldview, Scheler breaks that worldview's stranglehold. He unearths the particular intentional attitude under which the world is conceived in that stance toward the world—namely that of a life-essence trying to dominate its environs. As Husserl's discovery of intentionality released a multiplicity of intentional modes of turning toward a given object, so Scheler uncovers a variety of modes of postures toward nature. After one becomes aware of the frame of mind through which the world is given mechanistically—a frame that mechanism itself neither saw nor permitted to be seen—one's "spiritual eyes are opened." Possibilities of knowing, undervalued and so underdeveloped for long periods of history, now "merit consideration." As a result, the object known—the pale affectless world of mechanistic theory—becomes transformed into a technicolor panorama of values and qualities long unnoticed or undiscussed. Utilizing the essence of knowledge and the essential structure of intentionality Scheler is able to display the rich whole within which one-sided viewpoints must abandon their aspirations to empire and assume more humble positions.

At the same time, Scheler has replied to two of the three premises of Western mechanistic epistemologies. Via eidetic analysis, the notion of *Sosein,* and the selective but not productive character of scientific-pragmatic cognition, he has defended the objective structure of the world, which mechanistic views attribute only to the creativity of cognitive processes beyond perception. Second, through an eidetic grasp of knowledge types and through pragmatism's self-reflection (akin to phenomenology's) and its deontologization of the mechanistic worldview, he has successfully demarcated the bounds within which science legitimately functions. All that Scheler still requires is a careful, detailed discussion of perception. In this task, Scheler will once again offset the constrictive propensities of the mechanistic accounts of perception by recovering a forgotten opulence.

Scheler's account of perception presupposes his earlier essential account of knowledge. Perceptual content, for instance, is neither an immaterial copy of the nature *(Sosein)* of something in one's life milieu, such as Aristotle's and the scholastics' *species sensibilis,* nor is it simply a causal outcome proportional to physicochemical stimuli impacting the central nervous system. It is never a mere sensation complex, but involves an uncommon, changing, limited abstraction, performed by psychic acts, grasping a partial content of the intuitive nature of the thing itself.[41]

Scheler argues that metaphysical force centers *(Kraftzentren)* and force fields *(Kraftfelder)* are the common origin of both the milieu-thing and formal-mechanistic stimuli, such as airwaves or ether waves, molecules, atoms or electrons. These formal-mechanistic stimuli have their effect on the system of lifeless and living force factors, that is, drive factors, which lie at the ground of the perceiving organism. Scheler emphasizes that the bodily organism itself is itself one figure among the other figures (e.g., milieu-things) given to us. These formal-mechanistic stimuli do not define the visible milieu-thing, such as the blue ball or the ringing clock, since the stimuli and milieu-thing pertain to different modes of relating to the world: the scientific or natural attitude modes. These formal-mechanistic stimuli are related logically (but not causally) to the functions of sensation, such as the seeing and hearing and finally, in its totality, the perception of the milieu-thing. These stimuli operate only in conjunction with centripetal and centrifugal nerve processes, from the brain to peripheral nerves. Formal-mechanistic stimuli do not define the figure *(Bild)* of the milieu-thing, which is an objective appearance, but rather they define the perceptual content of this objectively appearing figure. Such a content is continually inadequate and partially given in aspects that mutually refer to each other and call each other forth. The figure itself prexists the readout that the psycho-physiologically unified functions of seeing, hearing, sensing, and perceiving complete, with their sharply pronounced intentional character toward the figure-content and toward its unity. The unified figure, though, is not originally broken up into a seen, heard, or touched thing.[42] As Scheler remarks,

> Is it not simpler to assume that the figures have their *Gestalt* and that all perception splits them only into different aspects by the power of a vast series of dissociation forms that correspond to the drive structures of a life-essence? And is it not simpler to assume, that many individuals, when they perceive a thing, also have the same figures as objects of their perception—only in different aspects, different adequation, different layers of relativity to the nature of the thing?[43]

It is crucial to note that a transconscious existence pertains to these figures of milieu-things, that perceptual sense activity does not bring forth these figures any more than did higher-level cognitive functions such as understanding or reason. Rather, perceptual activity only selects out aspects of what is available. Scheler clearly insists that, contrary to the mechanistic view, this world is not devoid of its own structures and dependent on human activity and labor for its order. Rather, human activity behaves selectively toward structures already there. Here we have no Kantian presupposition that unformed, relationless stuff precedes our thought, which alone bestows structure upon it.[44]

Scheler proceeds to develop two theses regarding the connection between perception and sensation: there are no strict stimuli-proportional sensations, and there are no isolated sensations.[45]

Regarding stimuli-proportional sensations, Scheler begins by showing how sensation originally indicated merely a change in an organism's condition, originally based in touch, wherein the object altered the organism's condition. Then the notion was gradually extended to the other senses after analogy of touch, such that small particles were believed to cross the space between the object and the sensory equipment (e.g. eyes) as the object alters the organism. Hence, one arrives at the mechanistic account of all sensation. According to Scheler, this mechanistic view confuses different levels of being/relativity. The milieu-thing belongs to one layer of being/relativity (*Daseinsrelativität*), that of the everyday life milieu, and the idea of lightwaves, or small particles, or ether waves belong to a scientific mode of relating to the world. At that level of objects wherein a clock rings, for instance, there are no airwaves, and where there are airwaves or lightwaves or ether waves there are no such things as ringing clocks or blue balls, only a complicated system of molecules, atoms, and electrons. The mechanistic view ignores these different modes of attending to the world, natural attitude and scientific, which yield different noematic results. Additional problems arise in that the same individual process, formally-mechanistically understood, can issue in different qualitative experiences or, conversely, different organic components of the nervous system when stimulated can deliver the same qualities.[46]

To show that perceptions are not directly proportional to stimuli, Scheler has to face head-on the most powerful supposition regarding the proportionality between stimulus and sensation: the constancy hypothesis. The mechanistic view had considered all perception contents to be built up out of sensations that, if a single sensation could be isolated, could be shown to be in one-to-one correspondence with a physical stimuli. By maintaining a constant stimulus and varying the conditions of drive laden attention, phantasy, and memory contents, physiologists hoped to isolate a sensation corresponding to such a stimulus. Due, however, to the complexity of the factors involved, this hope has diminished. Those few stimuli bound up with relatively elementary organic experiences, even when they are alike, nevertheless hit upon the organism in differing quantitative and qualitative degrees. A vast number of of factors within the organism (e.g., central nervous system factors, the freshness, weariness, or other mode characterizing the organs, drive factors, maturity and exercise factors) determine the kind and number of stimuli that affect elementary experiences. As a result, Scheler suggests that there is an essential *inconstancy* between stimuli and concrete experiences. Scheler found recent discussions of the constancy hypothesis supportive of his view since they indicated that a repeated stimulus does not issue in the same sensation it produced earlier because the *sequence* wherein that stimulus occurs affects the sensation results.[47]

The basic problem with the constancy hypothesis, dependent as it is upon the mechanistic worldview, is that it prescinds from the complexity of factors involved in perception and oversimplifies the process. For Scheler, the only way in which one could experience a pure, constant stimulus would be if one's life drives, organic moods, and physiological anticipations were out of play, but then one would be dead. Such an experience might take place if all that were involved were a pure bodily mechanism and a percipient spirit, as Descartes conceived it.[48]

Scheler rejects the view that giving up the constancy hypothesis will lead to idealism by recapitulating his belief in the objective structure of nature understood in nonmechanistic terms. Hence, contrary to the sterile Cartesian and mechanistic vision of qualityless particles impacting a machine, the qualities themselves are objective appearances transcendent to consciousness. It is no doubt true that at certain spatio-temporal points physical processes win a "stimulus-value" for the living organism. But these processes explain only the *selection* that different organisms exercise with reference to the incomparably richer, objective qualities.[49]

The second thesis Scheler proposes is that there are no isolated sensations. Sensation is only an abstract piece of the collective reaction of an individual organism to its surrounding world. At stake here is the *activity of sensing*, that is, the functions of seeing, hearing, and tasting, all of which, as discussed above, the mechanistic view recasts on the model of touch. Locke introduced distortions by ignoring the function or activity of sens*ing* and spoke instead of *sensations* as psychic things. Qualities can become contents of the function of the sensing because they are psychophysically indifferent ideal contents pertaining to the objective determinations of figures themselves. In perception, the activities of seeing, hearing, and tasting, decompose concrete things into a manifold of perspectives, into subjective modes of appearance and aspects. Nevertheless, these figures remain intact as far as the contents particular to their ontology are concerned.[50]

Scheler expands his case against the isolated sensations that the empiricist-mechanistic tradition claimed to be the fundamental building blocks to be combined into more complex ideas and phantasies. This sensualist opinion has overlooked that what mature, civilized people name "perception" has resulted from a spiritual and historical process of continuous, progressive stripping away and uncovering of social, collective, historical, and traditional influences. These influences impede the attainment of a pure thing-perception defined only by the *Sosein* of the object. Pure perception, thus, functions originally as an ideal, a direction to be striven for, calling for a negative critical purification of tradition and a weeding out of the false images of drive and wish phantasies. Contrary to the empiricist viewpoint, perception is not the beginning of a spiritual development, it is its end and goal. Hence the human person comes nearer to the ideal figure perception than the animal, the adult nearer than the child, the man nearer than the woman [an example of Scheler's own sexism], and the person of advanced intellectual societies nearer than those from traditional societies [and his ethnocentrism]. Scheler even argues that brain physiology indicates that perception corresponds to higher (more developed) localized brain functions, not the lower ones to which phantasy, for example, corresponds. The brain structure indicates exactly the opposite of what empiricism describes as the primitive and more developed capacities.[51]

All of this criticism becomes grist in the mill for Scheler's ongoing dispute with Kant and Hume. In reality, elements fall out of an original whole instead of the whole being constituted through elements. The idea of an isolated sensation is not the starting point, but is actually an ideal, never reachable end point. Kant, following Hume, considered the starting point of knowledge to be just this chaotic mass of disunited elements, which the conscious subject first brings to order. Scheler concurs with E. Jaensch's assessment that this prejudice of Kant's shows his philosophy to be nothing more than an epistemological justification of the old mechanistic doctrine of Newton's generation. Kant's philosophy rested on a doctrine of perception wherein the basic insights of mechanism were transferred unthinkingly to the still unexamined fundaments of consciousness. Furthermore, as has been seen, the chaos of perception opened the door to the constructive power of understanding and reason.[52]

Scheler further amplifies the complexity of the perceptual process by discussing how drives condition perception. Philosophers have overlooked the significance of the drives for the whole cognitive life (perception, representation, memory, phantasy, thought), whether one speaks of affect and feeling or drive-directed attention and motor impulses. If one adopts the stance that physical stimuli impinging directly on the nervous system produce the contents of consciousness, one will probably have no place for drive impulses either. In considering how drives determine the selection of contents, it is important to focus on what is perceived in addition to the how of perceiving. Once one attends to the objective figure, the "what" perceived, it becomes clear that motor drive behavior facilitates the perception of some aspects of the figure at hand and obscures others. Scheler asserts that beyond the impulses of hunger, thirst, or sex, there are ramifications and differentiations in inclinations, needs, and attitudes that affect what is perceived. If one speaks of a "disinterested" perception, it indicates that the many drives involved have attained a kind of equilibrium, not that there are no drives present. Scheler documents how such drives affect perceptual selectivity and separate patterns or aspects from their ground. He even appeals to biological findings to show the primacy of value qualities in perception. For instance, the lizard does not even hear a pistol shot, but flees at the rustling of a bush. "Path" bees perceive the colors and odors of flowers as lures, while "collector" bees interpret them as omens. Bees in general have a rich sense for bright colors, even ultraviolet, which human beings do not see. However, bees remain unmoved by scarlet since "scarlet" waves are never emitted in conjunction with blossoms in the way that ultraviolet ones are. Scheler concludes: an organism has only those sense-qualities as an alphabet of its possible world structure that can be incentives or markers for objects significant for drive-motor behavior. Such selectivity does not, however, eliminate the figure of the objective appearance.[53]

Of course, Scheler achieves many things by this account of perception. He achieves his purpose of undermining the mechanistic account of perception by showing the richness of experience from which a pared-down stimulus-response explanation abstracts. Pure sensation constitutes a never-to-be-arrived-at goal, so thick is the mesh out of which it must be drawn. After Scheler wards off any reduction of perception to sensation, he immediately embellishes the act of perception by showing the role of multiple drives. He continues this expansion of perceptual activity in the next section by treating the components of phantasy inextricably woven into perceptual contents. It is no wonder that he should go on further to discuss the context of reality underlying perceptual activity in the sixth part of the essay.[54] Finally he hints at the sociological underpinnings of the mechanistic theory of perception. Sociology too is part of the broader context within which perceiving goes on. Scheler enriches the act of perception in direct contrast to mechanism's impoverishment of it. While mechanism strips the world of phantasy, of drives, of complex organic interactions, of values, and of qualities, and while it reduces objective structures to the mere products of physicochemical stimuli or imperial human reason, Scheler attempts to reinstate all these things.

Although Scheler certainly exceeds Husserlian phenomenology by postulating *Sosein* and *Dasein*, metaphysical *Kraftfaktoren* behind the figures that appear, and a context of reality encountered as resistance, still Scheler and phenomenology have much in common.[55] Aside from the eidetic method, the effort to disclose intentional frameworks, and the recovery of whole structures for purposes of criticizing partial viewpoints, Scheler's account of perception shows the same respect for the complexity of perception that Husserl did. Husserl's reduction involved an effort to pay attention to what is given to consciousness, without delving into the causal factors affecting or effecting whatever appears. In fact, the reduction provides an apt tool for avoiding entanglement in precisely those questions. Similarly, Scheler rejects the hope of the constancy hypothesis to isolate a pure sensation exactly proportional to its stimulus. One may dismiss the constancy hypothesis, but one can still talk about what phenomena appear.

Furthermore, Scheler's idea that there is a figure given—as essence, a structure with its diverse qualities, which one grasps partially and through different perspectives with different aspects showing themselves—is undoubtedly influenced by phenomenology. As Husserl noted, the material thing has its essence, and essential to that essence is that it will always be seen partially. This account of perception accords with Scheler's sociology of knowledge: essences and spiritual contents have a lawlikeness all their own while drives and other real factors work like a sluice gate, releasing some of those contents and concealing others. Stimuli acting on nerves and senses do not, however, produce those figures just as economic forces do not produce thoughts, however much they both may cause one either to select or ignore what confronts and stands independently. To deny these objective structures would be to capitulate to the modern Western *Weltanschauung*, to reduce the world in its richness to the clashing of inert atoms, that is, to an anarchy awaiting the imposition of reason's order.

The topic of dialogue does not emerge prominently in "Erkenntnis und Arbeit." But Scheler's phenomenological epistemology, by establishing that a structured world stands over against all the selective perspectives through which it is given, makes the "sublime and great conversation" he foresaw in *Some Problems of a Sociology of Knowledge* both possible and necessary. Such a mutually self-critical conversation becomes possible in Scheler's view because partners to the conversation can arbitrate conflicting viewpoints better if an order of being exists independently of their cultural filters than if each culture elaborates that order of being from out of their own creative resources. Furthermore, such a conversation becomes necessary precisely because cultures intent on mining the richness of being and aware of their own partiality are compelled to seek cooperation with other equally selective viewpoints. Scheler elaborates these connections between his phenomenological findings and dialogue much more clearly in his ethical theory.

# 3

# Common Values and Self-Critical Dialogue

Scheler's value theory, presented most thoroughly in his *Formalism in Ethics and Non-Formal Ethics of Values*, attempts to come to grips with the valuational stance of the mechanistic worldview, just as his epistemological theory had struggled with that worldview's epistemology. Following the pattern of his epistemological critique, Scheler situates the mechanistically influenced ethics of Kant and nominalism within a broader context of objective values whose richness the mechanistic scheme appreciates only selectively. Finally, the narrowness of the mechanistic framework, afflicting as it does a whole culture, brings to the surface basic issues raised in Scheler's sociology of knowledge and treated in depth in his *Formalism*: cultural relativism and the possibility of intercultural dialogue.

## Critique of the Mechanistic Valuational Scheme

### Scheler and Kant

To understand Scheler's critique of the valuational framework of the mechanistic worldview, it is particularly instructive to consider carefully his criticism of Immanuel Kant's ethics. While Kant himself undertook a thorough critique of the mechanistic worldview in his own ethical writings, he, in Scheler's view, absorbed too many uncriticized presuppositions from the very worldview he opposed. Of course, phenomenology dedicates itself to bringing to light just those particularly stubborn presuppositions that could have survived even the severity of Kant's critical scrutiny.

Scheler considers the criticism of Kant's ethics the secondary goal of his *Formalism*, after its primary one of providing a foundation for ethics. Scheler describes Kant's ethics in his preface to the first edition of the *Formalism* as the most perfect ethics of the modern era, in spite of Schiller's charge that Kant "cared only for the servants of the house and not the children." Scheler maintains his reverence even in the face of his belief that Kant mistakenly projected into pure human reason eighteenth-century Prussian prejudices. Scheler dismisses facile criticisms of Kant, by pointing out, for instance, that for Kant virtuous action need not have been against inclination. In fact, action corresponding to inclination could simultaneously follow from duty.[1]

Scheler readily agrees with Kant's critical stance toward the empirical. Kant correctly understood the dangers in making the goodness or wickedness of a person, a will act, or an action depend on its relationship to the particular, accidental existence of goods in the world. The moral value of the will would then be contingent on whether it maintained or encouraged the existence of these goods. If this world of goods should undergo any transformation, the very meaning of good and evil would also shift. As a result, ethics would fluctuate continually according to the historical experience of a changing world. All ethics would then necessarily be relative, valid only because of empirical-inductive circumstances. All of this would be nonsensical for Kant as well as for Scheler.[2]

Kant's ethics effectively prevents one from identifying "good" or "evil" with any characteristics, such as a physical or spiritual property of a human being or affiliation with a class or party. Scheler concurs, since such identifications amount to a type of idolatry, confusing a transcendent value with one of its embodiments. Furthermore, Scheler is in accord with Kant that the simple realization of something of value—e.g., an aesthetic or an economic achievement—of itself, is not necessarily good. Similarly, norms and duties should never be subordinated to the achievement of some practical end. On the contrary, all purposes and all hypothetical imperatives must submit themselves first to the moral norm. Either canonizing any factual development or building an ethics on evolutionary tendencies of the world, life, or culture ignores that such "developments" can bear either positive or negative value-predicates. One can always ask whether such developments are good or not. Ethics does not base itself on socially current notions of good and evil, because, even if the good had never been recognized as good, it still would be good. To use Kant's own example, even if there has never been a sincere friend, everyone ought to strive to be one. Thus Scheler would agree wholeheartedly with Kant's refusal to derive ethical standards from empirical cases and with Kant's insistence that ethical standards serve as a critical standard for assessing empirical cases.[3]

In Scheler's opinion, Kant took for granted the empiricist psychology of the will that was tied intimately to the mechanistic description of the world as a network of deterministic causal relationships. According to this empiricist theory of will, purely reflexive movements result in a pleasurable condition that, in turn, causes, by "reinforcement," the more deliberate willing of further similar movements. For instance, Scheler points out that the sucking movements of the suckling on the mother's breast, at first purely reflexive, result in a flow of milk that produces pleasures. At this point, the suckling begins to will his sucking. This willing takes place again only through the reproduction of the movement's image, given in the "kinematic" and organic sensations that the original reflex movements posited and induced in the first place. The content of willing here arises as a representation of something that produces a pleasure stimulating effect or a reaction of such kind. The "will to do" involves simply reproducing the image of the movement that issued in such pleasure before, and the appropriate actions follow.[4]

Kant grasped clearly that if one were to base an ethics upon this theory of will by itself, one would finally translate good and evil in terms of the impact of events upon our sensible feeling states. In such a theory, there would be no good or evil for a purely rational being or for God, since neither possesses senses. Furthermore, "good" and "evil" would eventually come to stand for mere technical values that result in sensibly agreeable states. In Kant's view of this empiricist theory of will, all choices of contents ("bearers" of nonformal values in Scheler's terminology) would be traceable to the causal relations of things on our sensible feeling states. All content-centered ethics (or material ethics) would pertain to inductive-empirical science, since all judgments of value would be based upon the ascertainable effects that things might produce in our natures, with their specific organization. Ethics in this case would forfeit any critical capacity and would always be relative to the empirical-causal factors at hand. Scheler reaffirms Kant's own conclusion that, if one accepts this theory of will, then every material ethics would be necessarily an "ethics of success." Such an ethics would make the value of the person, of willing, and of all behavior dependent on the pleasurable effects that they achieve in the real world.[5]

Embracing this premise of the empiricist account of will, Kant attempted to found ethics on another basis that might preserve

ethics from the deterministic, causal interrelationships so fundamental to a mechanized, controllable universe. To realize this
project, Kant equated "good" and "evil" with the lawfulness or
unlawfulness of the *form* (and not with any *contents*) of the willing.
Good and evil depend on whether the self acts consistently with
its character as rational agency, that is, whether the self can uni-
versalize its accounts without contradiction. If one attempts to
realize any material contents, such as to promote nobility or usefulness, such purposes have nothing to do with morality. Kant
reiterated these concerns in commenting on the paradox of
method in his *Critique of Practical Reason:*

> the concept of "good" and "evil" should not be defined before the
> moral law (for which it would then appear to be a ground of moral
> law), but rather only (as happens here) after the law and through it.[6]

Scheler, decrying the *desordre du coeur* of the present age that
could even consider the totality of emotional life as a process of
causally moved states, rejects the presupposition of the empiricist
theory of will, which Kant assumed without challenge. Scheler
begins his critique of this theory by noting that "willing to do" is
only a special case of the more generic "willing" that precedes it.
Psychological maturation proves the priority of generic willing
since children will all kinds of contents and states of affairs. Children only gradually come to restrict those original will-contents
according to their ability to do things and their successes or failures in doing them. The ability or inability to do something effectively leads one to select from a richer will-content, forcing one
to give up completely some willed contents and to convert other
willings into mere wishes. Thus the ability to do does not create
the contents of willing, it only negatively eliminates some of
them.[7]

Generic willing itself, however, presupposes values, as Scheler
illustrates by reverting to the situation wherein one picks out
practical objects in the first place. Such objects are not primarily
things of perception, but rather value-things or "goods." Every
willing of something presupposes that the willer feels the value
of this willed thing, a value that exists independently of the willing of it. It is not as if the willing produced the value in the
first place. Rather, from the subjective side, one encounters these
goods and selects them out on the basis of how one ranks values
within one's own spiritual moral tenor. Only after such goods
have been chosen as part of a value complex to be realized does

one meet with the resistance of objects, which, in turn, leads to the adoption of a will-to-do to bring about that complex. In conclusion, Kant fails to see that the value structure of one's moral tenor already limits whatever can be a resistant object or whatever will-to-do can ensue. It is not, as Kant supposes, that the will-to-do flows immediately from the object stimulating sensible feeling-states.[8]

This willing of a value-complex (and the resulting state of affairs) issues in a "willing-to-do" that is not simply a means to the end of the value-complex. The content of a willing-to-do is realized, in its turn, through a kinematic intention, a nonreflective physical readiness to implement a "willing-to-do." This kinematic intention can be realized through quite different organs, which creatively and nonmechanistically substitute for each other (e.g., one can turn off a lightswitch with an elbow when one's hands are occupied, or one can learn to write with one's feet when the hands are injured). As one attempts to carry out this indeterminate kinematic intention with reference to the object to be acted on or changed, kinematic sensations occur, indicating distances, the position of the body relative to its objects, and altering spatial relations to the organs themselves. In the course of carrying out such a kinematic intention or even in the kinematic impulses that precede objective motion, one encounters further "resistance," which can occur if the organs are inhibited (i.e., an arm is tied up with rope) or if the practical object refuses to comply (the weight is too heavy to be moved). Indeed, one often becomes aware of kinematic impulses only after they have encountered such resistances. Kant's notion that objects stimulating sensible feeling-states define the matter of willing can only seem plausible because one finds new purposes and new willings-to-do generated when one experiences this resistance of practical objects. But, as is evident, a great deal of higher-level valuing and willing activity precedes this response to resistances and defines this domain wherein stubborn objects provoke the adoption of a new purpose or a new willing-to-do.[9]

Scheler thus opposes Kant's opinion, shaped by Kant's uncritical acceptance of the empiricist theory of will, that objects define all willing matter through the pleasurable effects they produce. Contrary to Kant, the pleasurable condition to which the object gives rise does not immediately determine one's willing-to-do and its content. Rather, that willing-to-do and its content result from the resistance that the primary practical object presents to one's already formed willing into existence of a definite value-complex.

This willing in turn follows on the already existent immanent moral tenor.[10] In Scheler's view, Kant's espousal of the empiricist theory of will eventuates in a passive conception of humanity since Kant overlooked

> that the content as will-intention as well as the resistant object are already *a priori* limited through the shape of the moral tenor regarding material values. Also he erred about the nature and kind of this "experience" since he *transposed it first into the sensible feeling-states* that the object stimulates in us, particularly in the reaction that the already successful doing posits in our sensible feeling-states. Therewith he fails to see the *level of experience* that he is here treating. The human being is not the passive essence that he presupposes and that must wait upon things for their influences and the sensible feeling states in which they result in order to give his willing a content. Such a content would be defined according to what promotes the greatest *pleasure* or least displeasure. Instead, *these sensible states are founded upon* and follow *the experienced resistances* (and direct themselves according to their type and magnitude) which willing "meets". . . . It is not first the success of factual doing, but rather the resistance experienced already in pure willing that defines the intention of the willing-to-do.[11]

Values (borne by objects and ranked in one's moral tenor) precede willing in general, which precedes the appearance of the resistant practical object, which precedes the willing-to-do, which precedes kinematic intentions, which precede kinematic sensations. Once again,Scheler heads off the mechanistic worldview's penchant for a simple one-way determinism from physical objects to human valuational activity. He simply unveils the rich context that such a simplification overlooks and suppresses. He concludes his third chapter on "The Ethics of Success":

> Kant never observed this fundamental fact for ethics: that a whole primary value *difference* between human beings depends on which objects *can* exercise efficacy on their behavior—and therefore *can* release sensible feelings in them—a difference that depends on what kind of pleasure they are even *capable* of experiencing.[12]

Scheler repudiates Kant's rejection of all material ethics in favor of a formal ethics because Kant ceded too much to the empiricist theory that all willing is subject to the pushes and pulls of mechanistic causal relationships. Before Scheler presents his own material ethics, which he hopes will be as critical and nonrelativistic as Kant's formal ethics, he undertakes a criticism of Kant's understanding of the a priori. As a typical phenomenologist rigorously striving not to absorb prejudices unreflectively, Scheler scrutinizes presuppositions regarding Kant's notion of the a priori. He argues that Kant unconsciously assimilated this notion from the very mechanistic world of which he showed himself masterfully critical in other ways.

To maintain the critical, nonrelativistic nature of ethics, Scheler turned to Husserl's method of essential intuition (*Wesenschau*). Scheler reviews the essential features of essences themselves, ideal unities of meaning, which are neither individual nor universal but which embrace both universal and particulars. The essence "red," for example, is given in the universal concept as well as in perceivable nuances. Furthermore, essential interconnections seem to persist fully independently from what can be observed, described, or grasped through inductive experience and thus from everything pertinent to causal explanations. It would seem, for instance, that no conceivable inductive experience could contradict the proposition that human consciousness is temporal. Indeed, the unfolding of inductive experience itself seems to presuppose just such temporal consciousness as the condition of its possibility. Such essences, are, thus, given a priori, that is before all empirical experience, even independently of the propositions that bring these essential interrelations to expression. But such essences remain fulfilled in the entire sphere of extraphenomenological experience governed by the natural attitude. They underlie the formal laws or structures of human experiencing. Such a priori contents can only be illustrated, not proved or deduced. Procedures like phenomenological "bracketing" only enable one to see these essences. Such essences are grounded in the facts and facts alone and not in any constructions of an arbitrary "understanding." These essences are intuitive contents and not projections or constructs of thought.[13]

In the light of this phenomenological eidetic method, Scheler first faults Kant for assuming that the a priori is equivalent to the formal. All propositions that are a priori valid for special object areas beyond those of pure logic (e.g., that human consciousness is essentially temporal, that physical objects occupy spatial position) make up the realm of the a priori material.[14]

Second, Kant wrongly identifies the a priori with thought and the material with the sensible. Such a view belongs to a long philosophical tradition, including mechanistic views that strip the sensible world of all structures (e.g., relations, forms, Gestalts, values) and attribute their presence to human thought. Husserl, as has been seen, criticized this view as early as his *Logical Investigations*. One arrives at such a conclusion by behaving quite unphenomenologically, relying immediately on handed down prejudices about how things are without consulting the given.

Interpreting the ethical-affective realm in this light, Kant incorrectly held that every willing determined by some matter, instead of by the formal law of reason, cannot be a priori determined. In such a case, the contingent repercussion of some content upon earlier sensible feeling-states causally produces a later act of willing, egoistically intent on recovering that pleasure. In reply, Scheler elucidates the irrelevance of sensible feeling-states to willing by citing strong, energetic, or passionate examples of willing, those of the daring men of action or of great heroes. Such people become so lost in the values they seek to realize that they pay no heed to the reactions of their deeds on their own states, least of all their sensible states. They neither notice their wounds or fatigue, nor expect sensible rewards. In fact, they lack the awareness not only that the deed is directed toward their own ego, but also that it proceeds from that ego. They often claim that what happens because of their deed is the work of God, as cases such as Cromwell, Calvin, or Napoleon suggest. Regarding such people, one might echo Nietzsche's defense of noble morality against the pettiness of the calculating utilitarian, by asking "What had they to do with sensible pleasures?"[15]

More importantly in Scheler's view, however, Kant's spurning of the sensible for the sake of the rational blinds him to the a priori content of emotional aspects such as feeling, preferring, loving, hating, and willing—that is, emotional acts possess their own structures and laws, which are not borrowed from thinking and which ethics can bring to light apart from logic. This a priori *ordre du coeur*, in Pascal's terms, can yield moral knowledge, and it affords the only possible access to the world of values. Kant's neglect of any a priori outside of rationality, amounts to nothing more than an ungrounded, prejudicial narrowing *(Verengungen)* and limiting *(Beshränkung)* of the a priori. Kant thus upholds to the long-standing, false dualism between reason and sense that forces one to overlook the uniqueness of the emotional sphere and misinterpret it as unruly. Once again, phenomenology rescues a sphere of experience denied its own order in the name of the imperious reason, just as it did by criticizing mechanistic epistemologies.[16]

While Kant's mistaken understanding of human emotional life in Hobbesian terms may have prompted his development of practical reason, in Scheler's opinion, it betrays more. Kant's stance here seems to flow from his own individual tendencies, from a certain hostility *(Feindseligkeit)* or mistrust *(Misstrauen)* of the given as such, from anxiety or fear before what he experienced as chaotic forces inside of himself. According to Scheler, Kant shows himself influenced by that hatred of the world that permeates so strongly the thought patterns of the modern humanity, as detailed in Max Weber's study of capitalism and Calvinism. Such despising of the world results in a limitless need for action in order to organize and dominate that world. Here Scheler contends that Kant's ethics unconsciously reflects the very mechanistic worldview that Kant sought to overcome. Scheler's phenomenological critique of Kant's handling of emotional life must be seen as part and parcel of his broader socio-cultural critique.[17]

Scheler further denies Kant's transcendental interpretation of the a priori. Kant construes the links between acts and objects in a one-sided fashion such that the a priori laws of objects must conform themselves to the laws of acts. Scheler, of course, rejects the idea of an understanding that prescribes its laws to nature, laws that are not embedded in natural occurrences themselves. Similarly, he repudiates the idea of a practical reason that must impress its form on a bundle of drives. For Kant, the thing-in-itself represents that aspect of the object that remains hidden insofar as the object does not conform to the a priori functional laws of the understanding. For Scheler, on the contrary, any hidden value and being-contents can be disclosed in all kinds of experiences in the natural attitude and science, in real things, goods, and acts.[18]

For Scheler, Kant's subjectivistic interpretation of the a priori also misses the mark. Stressing the typical phenomenological paradigm of subject and object in mutual interaction, Scheler defends an a priori structure of the realm of values, prior to any ought, prior to any universalization, available to insight even in cases in which such values bind a single individual. The ego, though, is neither the starting point for grasping essence-unities nor the creator of them. While the ego can bear values, it is not their presupposition, not an essence founding all other essences. Paradoxically, even though Kant selects the rational ego as a starting point for his ethics, he diminishes the individual's importance by concluding that whatever is valid for individuals, whatever value might bind them alone, is only subjective.[19]

Finally, Scheler refuses to equate the a priori with the "innate" or the a posteriori with the "acquired." The causal-genetic terms "innate" and "acquired" concern how one comes to recognize the a priori, given as a content of intuition. In Kant's view, since the a priori is a form of spiritual activity (e.g., a judgment form over and above specific judgment contents), one must engage in spiritual activity by oneself in order to recover this form. Hence, for Kant, the a priori must be self-acquired. Scheler agrees with this Kantian emphasis on autonomous insight grasping the good. Scheler believes, however, that Kant overlooks the role of tradition, heredity, authority (provided one has an autonomous insight into its goodness), and education—in all their cultural diversity. Within such processes, the others of one's social group lead one to insight into the a priori, conceived as intuitive contents. Because Scheler conceives the a priori as intuitive content to which one can be led by one's social group instead of a form of activity to be acquired only through self-reflection, Scheler can better accommodate a relativism of insight than Kant. Scheler had already pointed out, in the preface to the third edition of the *Formalism*, that he was more relativistic than Kant. This notion of a priori contents accessible to varied cultural perspectives requires the intercultural dialogue so prominent in Scheler's sociology of knowledge.[20]

Scheler goes on to present his own theory of values. He distinguishes the variable bearers of the values from the invariable structure of the values themselves. This invariable structure, given to the intuitive evidence of preferring, cannot be grasped through induction or deduction. Nevertheless, Scheler attempts to provide confirmation for his value ranking by describing some of the excellent qualities belonging to higher values. The higher values are more enduring. People enjoy they higher values beyond a specific spatio-temporal extension and a large number of partakers can share them at once (e.g., religious values compared to physical goods). Higher values base themselves less upon other values (e.g., the use value of tools is subordinated to the pleasures that make up the higher value of the agreeable). They yield deeper satisfaction and depend less on particular physiological capacities if they are to be experienced (e.g., agreeable values can only be experienced by a sensibly feeling being, spiritual values require no physiological capacities). Scheler's ranking in the *Formalism* situates the values of agreeable/disagreeable at the lowest level; then vital values such as the noble or vulgar; then spiritual values such as the beautiful and the ugly (aesthetic values), right and wrong (moral values), and true and false (cognitional values);

and finally, at the highest rank, the religious values of the holy and unholy. "Good," in an absolute sense, consists in a value that appears "on the act," that is, in the very process of the act, when that act brings about some manifestation of the highest value available. In a relative sense, "good" is a value that appears on an act directed to a higher value over a lower value. In either case, that which is *the* bearer of the values "good" and "evil" is the choosing person, whose individual acts and moral tenor secondarily bear the value good or evil also. Scheler chides Kant for considering only acts of willing to be the bearers of good and evil and for overlooking the many other bearers, including acts of forgiving, commanding, obeying, and promising.[21]

While Scheler successfully criticizes Kant's notion of the a priori, he overlooks Kant's contribution to the question of human rationality. Scheler never entertains the possibility that Kant's notion of practical reason could be rescued from his faulty handling of the a priori. He manifests his lack of appreciation for the distinctive character of practical reason, which Kant carefully developed, when he immediately and without hesitation applies Husserl's eidetic method, originally intended for the structures of the given, to the practical domain. To be sure, Kant's spurning of the sensible for the sake of the rational, perhaps because of a mechanistic hostility to affectivity as Scheler suggests, leads Scheler to base his ethics on the order of feeling. This strategy, however, need not preclude a separate rational justification for ethical norms parallel to Scheler's feeling-based ethics. It will be argued further in the final critical chapter of this book that Scheler's confrontation with Kant and the mechanistic tendencies in his thought skewed his understanding of human rationality. As a result, Scheler failed to attain that phenomenological presuppositionlessness regarding the modern Western worldview for which he strove.

### Ethical Nominalism

Although the first part of Scheler's ethics, covering chapters 1 to 3, concentrates on Kant, the second part places Kant within the more expansive trend of ethical nominalism, which is intimately related to the mechanistic worldview.

According to ethical nominalism, represented by figures such as Hobbes and Nietzsche, ideas of "good" or "noble" are human discoveries, which trace their origin to speech itself. Such evaluative words, lacking any intentional function, serve only as expressions of feelings, affects, interests, and acts of desire. This nominalist theory shares much with Platonism since both deny this world its independent values and disclaim moral facts in particular. Both nominalism and Platonism also shove the entire domain of the moral into the sphere of an unintuitable area of thought. In effect, ethical nominalism denies any particular moral experience since moral discourse is nothing more than a set of expressive reactions of factually occurring processes of feeling and striving. Furthermore, value pronouncements do not mediate any kind of moral cognition, rather they bring to expression only wishes and commands in hidden manners. Thus, there could be no shared knowledge of moral facts demanding acknowledgement, but only concealed solicitations that the Other act a certain way. Moral evaluations can never provide direction for action or willing, and they are only in the final analysis symbolic expressions for already existing power relations between competing wills.[22]

Ethical nominalism, which, in a manner reminiscent of mechanistic epistemology, evacuates the world of moral values and reinterprets them as mere human projections for the sake of covert self-interest, appears in many guises. Emotivist ethics, for instance, asserts that ethical propositions express feelings without any preceding deliberation in much the same way that "Ouch" expresses pain rather than reports it. According to this viewpoint, one does not desire something because of the insight that that something is good, rather one calls that "good" which one desires. Similarly, utilitarianism thinks the judgments as to whether a behavior is "good" or "evil" can be traced to whether that behavior is useful or harmful and so deserving of social praise or blame. In Scheler's view, utilitarianism equates the usefulness or harmfulness that underlies social praise and disapproval with the origin of values themselves. Cultural relativism derives moral "interpretations" from the strivings, interests, and needs of a group. In all these cases, one denies any independent ethical value-phenomena. In the judgments passed on willing or acting, one does not find any value already there demanding conformity. Rather, moral values are only given through the judgments—if those judgments do not in fact produce the values in the first place. Scheler, after a long discussion of Kant's notion of duty, attributes these nominalistic tendencies, characteristic of Hobbes and Nietzsche, to Kant. In so doing, though, Scheler overlooks the objective value accruing to rational agency in Kantian ethics.[23]

One says that one does not find before him something like a value in the objects themselves, for example, in the processes of the will, or in the whole play of modes of behavior that have more value. These on the contrary are only value-free complexes of simple elements of the spiritual life (different in number and nature), which psychology is accustomed to define. First through a judgment which proceeds according to a norm or an ideal, do they come to have value—and only as such can they have value.[24]

In response to Nietzsche's brand of nominalism, Scheler responds that even to mummify one's self-interest by appeal to moral values involves an implicit recognition of the independence of those values and the respect they command (which one is seeking to arrogate for one's private purposes). "Hypocrisy expresses a certain reverence for virtue."[25]

Scheler's attack on forms of ethical nominalism, though, goes much deeper by returning to the facts of moral living. Ethical nominalists mistakenly suppose that psychic processes contain no value in themselves and that all value attributed to these process must be imported or conferred through a judgment in accord with some "measure," "idea," or "purpose." But how do these nominalists arrive at the specific psychological supposition of valuefree psychic processes in the first place? First of all, one does not confer values on a value–indifferent given. On the contrary, in order that a valuefree object might be found, one must withdraw more or less artificially from the original given by explicitly refraining from completing certain acts of feeling, loving, hating, and willing. All primary behavior toward the world generally— the outer world, one's inner world, other people, and oneself— does not consist in representing and perceiving. Rather it is primarily an emotional and value perceiving behavior. Scheler suggests that these emotions and "value-ceptions," so operative in experiencing life, tend to assume secondary importance when one interrupts that experiencing and turns to it reflectively, thereby depriving it of its liveliness. In fact, by suspending the experiential, lived emotional acts in order to study them, the psychologist finds only feeling, but no values, since values appear only at the prereflective level of vital, experiential engagement.[26]

One could only conceive of the psychical as valuefree because one lacks a priori phenomenological investigation of one's prereflective engagement with the world. A causally oriented psychology would abstract from the fullness of psychic life accessible to such a phenomenological investigation. Such a phenomenological inquiry would disclose that there are feeling-states (Gefühlen), such as moods, and intentional functions of feeling (*Fühlen*), such as preferences and acts of loving and hating. In the course of these intentional feelings, the world of objects in their value aspects opens up, often without any representational mediation being necessary. If one assigns the entire feeling sphere to psychology from the outset, then one would never see what the world and its value-content reveals *in* feeling, *in* preferring, *in* loving, and *in* hating. All one would see would be what takes place in personal inner perception, that is, the acts of feeling, preferring, loving and hating. If Scheler is correct here, mechanistic preconceptions about a valueless world feed upon the self-forgetfulness that belongs intrinsically to the adoption of a reflective stance.[27]

In fact, the nominalist viewpoint is so pervasive that one does not even recognize these other sources of ethical insight—on which Scheler builds his own rank ordering of values and ethical theory. For Scheler, the act of preferring founds the feeling of values in the sense that the act of preferring grasps whatever value is higher. We determine this rank ordering of values via an intuitive "preference-evidence" that no logical deduction can replace. The properties accompanying higher values, such as long-lastingness or shareability, confirm what this preference-evidence discloses. These properties, however, do not "prove" the ranking of values, which can only be given in the act of preferring. When one loves a person, for example, one experiences an absolute value without drawing any logical "conclusion" to this effect. Because of this felt absoluteness, one has a sense that to give up this value or to deny it for the sake of some other value would result in guilt and involve a retreat from the height of value existence just encountered. In one's depths, Scheler explains, one secretly recognizes the status of an experienced value and its relativity, however much one may be able to hide this through judgment, comparison, or induction. Scheler, defending Pascal's "Le coeur à ses raisons," argues that there is an emotional type of experience whose objects, values, and rank ordering remain fully inaccessible to understanding. The understanding is as blind to these values as are the ear and hearing to colors. In fact, theoretical ethics must consult these emotional sources as it formulates moral knowledge in judgments. It is no wonder that in the preface to the second edition of the *Formalism*, Scheler refers to his own ethical system as an emotive intuitivism and finds a kindred spirit in G. E. Moore.[28]

The ranking of values given in such intuition does not rest

upon observation and induction. Rather it lies in the essence of these values and the essence of preferring and feeling. If some zoologist or historian, for instance, would relate that there is a species of animals preferring the unpleasant to the pleasant, one would disbelieve him or her and try to show that those animals actually found things we might consider unpleasant to be pleasant. Or, perhaps, one might explore whether some perversion is at work here. The essential value relationship that the pleasant is always preferable to the unpleasant functions as an a priori guide determining what can count even as a legitimate observation or induction.[29]

While Scheler's a priori ranking of values facilitates a Kantian-like critique of any empirical value ranking, Scheler has restored autonomy and independence to values in a way that Kant could not. Contrary to the suppositions of a nominalist ethics, values are not merely human concoctions in the face of a value-barren world. Just as one experiences a mutuality between knower and the known object, cogiven in any act of knowing as essentially independent of that act of knowing, so values exist even if they are not experienced. One can, for instance, distinguish between a value in itself and for oneself, and so on. Nominalist ethics, by reducing all values to creations under personal control, prevents values from making their demands upon one and upsetting one's structured modes of experiencing. Nominalist ethics thus stands as a bulwark of the mechanistic worldview whose premise is control at all costs.[30]

Scheler's focus on the prerational intuitive levels of experience, out of which theoretical ethics emerges, and the exigency of values prior to any creative activity afford valuable resources for contemporary dialogic ethics, as the final chapter will show. The limits of this emotive intuitivism later will also be taken up.

The mechanistic concentration on control affects its methodology in ethics. For Kant, knowledge of the a priori is achieved through self-reflective efforts since the a priori is rather the content of an intuition, which, as Scheler points out in discussing the search for truth, may require a certain amount of activity at first. But such activity paves the way for an insight, that is, a sudden flashing forth to be characterized more as a receiving than an achieving, making, or forming. The prelogical comprehension of values through preferring, prior to judging and at times in spite of strong feelings making the opposite way, highlights the independence of value comprehension from conation. One grasps values that are not realizable through any striving, such as the sublimity of a starry sky or the morally valuable personality of a human being. In the very appreciation of such values, one knows that they do not derive from striving, indeed sometimes one resists their call. Scheler argues that previous ethics has overlooked the powerful appeal of personal models *(Vorbilder)* for will formation because it has attributed moral value only to that which people will, choose, do, command, proscribe, or teach. One does not will, create, or choose one's own moral models, who, on the contrary, first wrest attention and invite imitation.[31]

The very structure of the values disclosed by the less control-oriented methodology of phenomenological intuition also runs counter to the mechanistic longing for mastery. One can manage whether one has certain feelings or not the more the level of sensible feeling-states is approached. Thus pleasures can be stimulated and pains narcotized. Life-feelings, however, above sense-feelings, are considerably less changeable by practical means. Only within narrow ranges, can one alter feelings of sickness or health, vigor or weariness. Even less successfully can purely psychic feelings be manipulated. Those feelings that spring from the depths of one's person and that are least reactive in character, such as bliss or despair, elude any control of the will. Such feelings are experienced as pure "grace." Even though these kinds of feelings overflow into all behavior and willing, one cannot set out to achieve them. Scheler criticizes Jeremy Bentham and his followers, who failed to see that the value and the moral significance of feelings of happiness as sources of moral willing stand in inverse proportion to their reachability through willing and acting. Social reformers, too, can influence practically only the lowest of joys through reforms of socio-economic systems. Those joys and suffering pertaining to the deeper layers of the person necessarily evade such socio-political action. Finally, for Scheler, Nietzsche dramatically exemplifies this *pragmatic prejudice* that envisions moral value as a task for willing and acting and thereby loses sight of the graced character of all human greatness.[32]

These distinctive feeling layers of the human personality permit one to make sense of several phenomena in Western culture, according to Scheler. Eudaemonism's emphasis on achieving pleasure, for instance, often deteriorates into a hedonism preoccupied with the peripheral levels of the person. This deterioration occurs because the eudaemonist discovers that the feelings of bliss and despair—the metaphysical and religious feelings par excellence—stubbornly withstand technical manipulation. As such, prevalent hedonism signals the inner despair and decadence of an age.

Neither drugs nor an ascetic deadening of sensible feeling can substitute for a lack of positive bliss at the core of the person. On the other hand, positive feelings from the deepest layer of the person overflow in every good orientation of the will, even though those who believe that an act of will is the essential condition of all moral value will miss this fact.[33] Similarly, release from suffering and evil is not bliss, as Buddha thought, but rather only the outcome of bliss. History illustrates these coexisting levels of the personality since bliss can survive miserable external living conditions, while despair can be found among the prosperous.[34]

Even as higher values do not yield themselves to human efforts to dominate, the self-conscious and willful attempt to achieve virtue founders. One can see a neighbor in need and take the opportunity to do a good deed, but for the heteronomous motive, in Kant's view, of "appearing good." Hence, Scheler insists that the value good appears "on the back" of a will act as one realizes a higher value without taking any thought for oneself. The very self-consciousness of the pursuit of value detracts from one's surrender to the value itself, as Scheler's earlier references to heroes' complete immersion in their value-projects suggests. Similarly, the truly humble person feels anxiety about the "image" of herself as good and shows her true goodness in this very anxiety. The best people are those who do not know that they are the best, those who, in St. Paul's sense, do not even dare to pass judgment on themselves. Such submission to value without self-reference ought to characterize values such as "salvation" or "self perfection." The realization of these values demands, as a necessary condition, that they not be intended through willing. Indeed, persons might intentionally sacrifice their salvation out of love for another person and in this very act discover their sublime value. Finally Scheler extends this need to forfeit control to nations, which can achieve the character of a national culture not by self-consciously trying to "think German" or "create art as a French person." Nations achieve their culture by allowing themselves to be led by the values of the things occupying their attention. The self-conscious effort to achieve a national culture dissolves in one's hands. In addition, cultural achievement happens behind the back of the artists who entrust themselves selflessly to the task at hand. Moreover, the state would achieve more culturally if it would grant autonomy to cultural realms instead of undertaking responsibility for cultural development itself. These psychological observations all indicate how submission to the highest values runs counter to all mechanistic proclivities to control.[35]

Scheler resists these mechanistic tendencies in other ways throughout the course of the *Formalism*. One never can never definitively decide, for instance, the ultimate direction of his moral tenor. Also, no educator can ever govern or guide that tenor in another without limits. Scheler repeatedly emphasizes the unknowability and unpredictability of personal being. Character traits can express themselves in varied, irregular ways, and the Other always transcends all one's evaluations. In addition, one can know God only insofar as God freely vouchsafes a revelation. Moreover, Scheler distinguishes a *verstehende* psychology seeking intersubjective understanding from an *erklärende*, causal-explanatory one. According to such a *verstehende* psychology, intervening experiences in one's stock of experience prevent that past experience from ever recurring exactly as it did before. One can never offer a foolproof prediction of human behavior, given this temporal flow of experience. Such unpredictability defies modern humanity's hunger to control both outer nature and inner soul. Finally, Scheler attempts to deflate associationist psychology's belief that the notion of similarity is produced in a person when one perception causally effects an association with a previous one. For Scheler, some intuition of similarity is required if one is to pick out the previously perceived object as similar to the present one in the first place.[36]

In the end, Scheler's criticism of nominalist ethics on the basis of the a priori value ranking, which is not of one's own making, only serve to deepen the criticism of Kant at the outset of the *Formalism*. Following the pattern of mechanistic epistemologies, both Kant and ethical nominalism disenchant this world of its own ethical values and offer their own substitutes. Kant's imperativist ethics, which begins with thought of duty as the most original moral phenomenon and from that point wins its ideas of good and bad and virtue and vice, assigns moral value only to that which can be ordered or forbidden. Acts of faith and love, which cannot be commanded, are of no moral value.[37] Scheler concludes that Kant falls prey to the pragmatistic prejudice:

> These propositions are throughout only to be understood through the pragmatistic attitude to accept moral values only insofar as one can intervene in the moral world and change it through command. Pragmatism in the narrow sense is not the only viewpoint to fall prey to this prejudice. Kant shares it.[38]

The situation with Kant, though, is more complex than Scheler portrays it. While Kant—for several reasons that cannot be addressed here—focuses his ethics on moral commands and prohibitions, these commands and prohibitions often curb practical interventions in the world. The categorial imperative demands that a person be passive before the moral worth of other rational agents, whose dignity he may not transgress. In fact, positing an a priori ranking of values with their accompanying metaphysical implications is one way—but not the only one—to set limits for arbitrariness and instrumental-mechanistic purposes, as the final chapter will argue.

## Relativism, Values, and Dialogue

In Scheler's analysis, the diverse perspectives of Kant and ethical nominalism display common symptoms of a single malady afflicting the modern Western *Weltanschauung*. This cultural whole, as has been seen, has perpetrated distortions in the understanding of the human will, the a priori, human affectivity, moral cognition, the nature of values, and human value-activity. The fact that culture holds diverse and intelligent thinkers such as Kant and Nietzsche in its thrall without them even alluding to its covert power suggests once again the question of cultural relativism, a question clearly posed in Scheler's sociology of knowledge and faced head-on in his *Formalism*.[39]

Having asserted his belief in an independent structure of being and a priori ranking of values, Scheler throughout his *Formalism* runs through a series of factors, some of which restrict insight into these independent orders and some of which facilitate insight. To comprehend the role culture plays, one should ponder how these other factors function as impeding or releasing insight. First of all, among restrictive factors, human sensibility suppresses and selects according to the significance of psychic experiences for a body and the immanent goal directions of its activity, but it does not produce or create sense contents.[40] Basic human attitudinal stances toward life, such as hypochondria or optimism, occlude value-qualities. Thus a person might come to believe mistakenly that he is ill even when no physiological problems exist, or she might see a difficult event in a rosy light because she happens to be filled with joy at the time. The culpable egoist, for instance, fails to appreciate the fullness of values in things, people, and actions since he confines his attention to values only insofar as they are important to him. Furthermore, the person slavishly obedient to an authority remains blinded to any values other than those ordered.[41]

Kantian ethics can also shroud the richness of values. Scheler points out that mere universalizability does not exhaust the realm of moral goodness. A distinctive willing, acting, or way of being can be required of a single individual and thus cannot be generalized. Further, self-limitation to universal norms can lead one to bypass key values in need of implementation. Values can call forth moral tasks and actions that are necessary for the present moment and that, if not undertaken *now*, will be lost forever. The full evidence of the good-in-itself can be given only through a careful listening for the wholly unique "demand of the hour" (*Forderung der Stunde*). Scheler repeatedly stresses, however, that this demand can never contradict binding universal norms. Finally Scheler applauds Hegel's criticism that Kant's locating the ethical Ur-phenomenon in the ought of duty, in what ought to be done or not be done, induces Kant to overlook the broader presence of values in a manifold of *already* existent bearers.[42]

Culture, too, checks the possibility of intuitions. Scheler accuses those theories (e.g., Darwinism, Malthus) that derive all organic development from the so-called "struggle for existence" of transferring concepts drawn from human relationships in Western civilization to the domain of life. These cultural prejudices have prevented theorists from seeing that, in the realm of life, solidarity is prior to egoism and species preservation prior to self-preservation. In fact, struggle, which occurs only when living beings stop seeking to transcend their milieu, abide within it, and compete for goods within its strictures, signals the stagnation of life. Furthermore, modern human beings, bent on controlling nature, have blinded themselves for anything amechanistic in the psyche and in nature. One has already seen how the pragmatic prejudice, rampant in Western culture, has blocked insight into the importance of personal models for will formation, into the graced character of human greatness, into values that cannot be commanded or forbidden, and into the nonachievable nature of bliss.[43]

In all these cases in which insight is shackled, Scheler upholds the dual-sided, subject-object character of experience so typical of phenomenology, as he did regarding Western epistemologies. Hence, for example, the realm of values retains its independence and riches from which limited human subjects select.

The proposition that it is characteristic of values that their givenness occurs with relation to a "feeling of something" does not claim that values only exist insofar as they are felt or can be felt. It is a phenomenological fact that, in the feeling of a value itself, it is given as different from its being felt—and this in every individual case of a feeling function. Thus the disappearance of the feeling does not do away with the being of the value. Just as we are conscious of ourselves knowing much in every moment—without having it actually at hand —and that much is knowable of which we are not yet conscious, so also we feel many values as such that we know and that belong to our value-world even as we also know that there are infinitely more that we have not felt or will not feel.[44]

Of course one's body or cultural background, insofar as they function selectively, can, in spite of their suppressive potential, also illuminate hidden values or produce unique insights. Scheler mentions a variety of other factors that can reveal values and yield enriching insights. The flow of experience assists such enrichment. A person can, for example, recollect a landscape, similar to a presently perceived landscape, and she can comprehend that previous landscape in richer measure and in greater depth than she did at the time it was first observed. The opinion that this enhancement constitutes only a subsequent, illusory addition results merely from the sensualist prejudice that memory must always be a poorer, pale shadow of perception. Similarly, as Aristotle pointed out, living morally sharpens one's capacity to root out moral deception and to acknowledge those moral standards of which one falls short. Finally, even punishment can direct criminals' attention to their deepest person-sphere, lead them to ponder their moral character, and thus provide them with an opportunity for an act of repentance, without the act being forced through the punishment.[45]

When one turns to the historico-cultural panorama, even the long process of evolution brings to light qualities long hidden. Scheler denies the mechanistic reduction of colors and sounds to stimuli-induced nerve movements and the mechanistic translation of values into changing bodily conditions and sense feelings. For Scheler, while stimuli condition the *sensing* of qualities or the *feeling* of values, they do not cause the *contents* of those qualities and values. A person comes upon such qualities and values as as independent of himself, however selectively he may apprehend them. Against this background, Scheler interprets evolution:

Only the increasing (in the unfolding of life in an individual and in general) differentiation of the senses in their functions, as hearing, seeing, tasting, bring it about that actual new and richer pictorial quality-spheres appear as well as spheres of feeling also. In addition, always new and richer value quality-spheres *approach* life from out of the encompassing universe. It is not that a poor dead universe of uniform movements hides itself and withdraws before life as life develops itself. Rather life itself cultivates always more and always richer modes of differentiated reaction that allow the fullness of qualities, already existing *in themselves,* to come into sight.[46]

Similarly, humanity's task in evolution consists in realizing the suprabiological values of the holy and spiritual and in unveiling a whole realm of value never seen before. If evolution can lead to the appreciation of values, so can history and tradition, inheritance, tradition, education, and authority—all of which Scheler upholds against Kantian tendencies to emphasize the self-acquired character of the a priori.[47] Here the phenomenological reinterpretation of the a priori as an order of essences available to intuition, coupled with the phenomenological sensitivity to the intentional activity through which objects are given, leads to a greater openness to and valuing of the socio-cultural conditioning of moral insights than Kant seems to allow for. At the same time, Scheler does not slip back into the relativism that Kant, of course, was also interested in fending off.

Phenomenology, too, disencumbers the capacity for original insight. Phenomenology, while digging beneath the naturalist and associationist prejudices, which dissolve the concrete unity of the manifold of consciousness, lays bare consciousness's timeless interwovenness. Phenomenology brings to focus the largely overlooked lived body *(Leib),* that center from which action proceeds, which philosophers such as Mach and Avenarius treat as as if it were a dead object, a bodily thing *(Leibkörper),* an object merely of outer perception. Phenomenology, by reverting to the things themselves anterior to traditional preconceptions, distinguishes and illuminates the qualities of essentially diverse feelings such as sensible pleasures, joy, happiness, and bliss. Kant, however, lumps all of these feelings together as sensible feelings. As a result, the human being independently of Kant's rational moral law could be nothing but an absolute egoist and absolute hedonist, intent on sensible pleasure uniformly in all impulses. Phenomenology liberates one from encrusted traditions so that feeling differentiations never before attended to can emerge. A full enumeration of similar contributions from phenomenology would require a restating of this entire chapter. It is clear, though, that phenomenology allows for novel, noncustomary understandings of the a priori, of methodology in ethics, of human willing, and finally—and most importantly—of a world of being and values that the mechanistic desire for control has kept hidden from sight.[48]

For Scheler, the act of love preeminently brings to light unnoticed value. In love (and its correlate, hate,) the human spirit does something much greater than react to felt or preferred values. Love and hate widen or narrow the realm of values. They do not do this in the sense of creating, making, or destroying values that exist independently of people, but rather in augmenting value comprehension. Love is a pioneer, preceding value-feeling and preferences. One can, for instance, adopt a loving attitude toward the whole of nature, an attitude akin to that of Franciscan spirituality and equally revelatory of hidden values:

> The world of values *opens up* noticeably in every step for the person, the more valuable one is in oneself and the better one behaves. The spirit of the holy person gives thanks ever more perceptively for space, light, air, for the pleasure of the existence of arms, limbs, and breath. Everything is filled with values and disvalues for such a person, but to others such things are value-indifferent. The Franciscan phrase "omnia habemus nil possidentes" expresses the direction toward such a freeing of the feeling of values from the [earlier] named subjective limits.[49]

In addition, only that understanding mediated through love for a person can grasp that person's individual value essence. As Michelangelo depicted it so profoundly and beautifully in his famous sonnet, love is the great plastic sculptor who out of the heap of empirical individual parts, sometimes only in one action or one gesture, can intuit out the lineaments of the Other's value-essence. Scheler does not always conceive love's creative potential from the side of an agent acting on a recipient. In his description of the principle of solidarity, he claims that when one experiences an act of love from the Other, that love includes as essential to its meaning a demand that love be returned. However much a person might deny respect to the Other who respects her, obedience to the Other's command, or trust in the Other's offer of a promise, she must deliberately deny or refuse all these acts of response. She cannot understand the meaning of the Other's act and then behave as if nothing has happened. This capacity of the Other to interrupt her life, to generate unforeseen responses, and to pry open her self-contained existence points to a lively wellspring of fresh value disclosure.[50]

These multiple manners wherein intuitions can be obstructed and nourished suggest that one inevitably approaches selectively and one-sidedly the objective, inexhaustible order of being and values that Scheler defends. But instead of seeing diverse viewpoints as a fecund source for a deeper penetration into that order, as Scheler does, cultural relativism dons new blinders toward objective values.

> Conversely, the origin of *ethical relativism* is such that it holds these values themselves for mere symbols for those evaluations of definite goods and actions (if not mere theories about these things) predominating in its own cultural circle. Such relativism sees the the entirety of history as merely a growing technical adaptation of action to the factually absolutely established values of its generation. It thus arbitrarily construes history of an "advance" toward these values . . . . Such value-relativism remains within the narrowness and blindness of its moral value-horizon, itself morally conditioned through a lack of respect and humility for the moral value realm and its extension and fullness . . . . Such relativism therefore falsely imputes its values to all times or "empathizes" its own experiences into the people of the past. It does all this instead of widening its own narrow limitedness through the experience of the objective value-realm indirectly, that is, through understanding the type of ethos of other times and peoples. If it would understand these other peoples' ethos, it would remove the blinders that it itself possesses in compliance with the value experience-structure of its own time.[51]

Relativists might well step back from diverse limited cultural perspectives, such as those of the Asian or Western worldviews, and highlight their one-sidedness. Relativists may often do so in the name of the value of tolerance, but more often they believe that value diversity proves that there are no objective values. By arriving at this conclusion, they indicate that they have already absorbed by osmosis the mechanistic presuppositions that the world possesses no order of its own except what reason and culture freely constructs. Thus, relativists fail to see that being has its own structure and values their autonomous ranking. They overlook the fact that cultural processes do not create but only selectively delve into these structures of being and values. As such, although relativists may seem to establish a metaviewpoint beyond the limitations of a cultural perspective such as the mechanistic worldview, they are actually only that worldview's newest manifestation. Relativists are as blind as mechanists to an order of being and values that they do not make but that rather makes its demands on them.

The above citation, however, suggests that relativism withdraws not only from the challenge of the order of being and values, but also from the intercultural dialogue to which that order invites one. Scheler illustrates how relativism absents itself from dialogue and absolutizes its own time by an extended analysis of a passage from Wilhelm Wundt's *Ethik*. In that passage, Wundt argues that the variability of conscience has been such that whole peoples and times have considered murder not as a crime but as a deed deserving praise for reasons that moderns would consider objectionable. For Scheler, Wundt's comment, although not intended this way, constitutes an astonishing insult to the honor of historical humanity, with whom the bond of moral solidarity unites everyone. Scheler wonders whether Wundt has in mind the Teutonic moral view that held that murder was permissible. Wundt, however, neglects to mention that the Teutonic code defined murder only as assassination and not as open attacks on another. Thus, the Teutonic stipulation, correctly understood, would not be all that different from the positive law of Wundt's own time. But perhaps Wundt was thinking of the custom of human sacrifice prevalent in diverse cultures. Scheler denies that in those cases there was any intention to deny the being of the person— a trait that belongs essentially to the meaning of murder. Rather in such sacrifices there was an accompanying intention of affirming the being of the person—how else could it have been a sacrifice? In fact, those killed were considered to have been transferred to a higher sphere of being and value—to a heavenly place. Of course, such cultures never permitted or approved human sacrifice to satisfy mere use or pleasure needs or to enhance a priestly caste's power. The subordination of life values to the holy was preserved in such sacrifices, Scheler contends. The intention of hatred and the denial of being of the Other, both essential to murder, would be totally missing in such a context.[52]

Wundt's relativism rests on many philosophical errors that phenomenology shows itself adept at correcting. First of all, Wundt operates with an implicit, prereflective notion of "murder," and hence Scheler commences by defining the essence of murder. Eidetic, essential analysis equips one with concepts sufficiently rich to make the subtle distinctions necessary for assessing another culture and not imposing one's own taken for granted concepts upon it. Contrary to the common supposition that eidetic analysis necessarily disregards differences, in Scheler's hands such analysis rather enables one to become self-critical of one's own cultural presuppositions in order that the distinctiveness of another culture might appear. Second, part of understanding the essence "murder" is grasping the intentions behind an empirical observable action, the meaning that the action has for the actors. Such a *verstehende* method coheres perfectly with a phenomeno-logical concept of intentionality, as Alfred Schutz has shown, and surpasses in excellence any causal-explanatory method, as Scheler has indicated. Such a method is also requisite for accurate understanding of the other culture.[53]

It is most important, however, to notice how Scheler employs these methodologies that enhance empathetic intercultural un-derstanding when confronted with cultures diverse from his own. When relativists find a cultural activity foreign to their own, such as human sacrifice, they, at best, regard that activity as different from their own and look upon it with neutrality. At worst, they might consider it as totally naive and inferior with reference to their own value framework, which has progressed far beyond it. Scheler, on the contrary, because of a deep conviction and respect for the moral solidarity of humanity, anticipates the best from another culture and envisions such anomalies as the starting point for a sympathetic investigation of that other culture. For Scheler, such an investigation calls for purifying one's own naively accepted concepts (such as "murder") and exploring the inten-tionalities behind the observable action of the other. Moral soli-darity would not permit one to dismiss too quickly cultural practices at odds with one's own as first "primitive" steps toward the heights of one's own moral practice. But Scheler's viewpoint demands more than simply not dismissing facilely diverse cul-tures, it compels one not to regard other cultures with neutral dispassion, as if to say "They are different from us and that is that." On the contrary, according to Scheler, each culture stands under the same value firmament that any other does, and each may have insights into values lacking to Others, especially given the pervasive human tendency to narrow one's vision. Far from an objective order of values resulting in arrogant dismissal of other cultures that fall short of others' realizations of these values (the kind of dogmatism relativism always reacts against), these values exact the most sympathetic entrance into the Other's world. They evoke the expectation that the Other can teach about the rich domain of values to which one is often blind and under which all stand.

This move beyond an indifferent relativism is illustrated in Scheler's examination of the ultimate value, the holy. For Scheler, this highest value quality in the rank ordering of values actually guides the construction of all positive representations, ideas, and concepts of God. A theory of religious cognition needs to examine how speech shapes and transmits the unified whole of revelation, how dogmas handed on in traditions and church organizations circumscribe it, and how the sharp definitions and systematic contents of theological science articulate it. Because, however, values are given prior to and independent of images and representations, there can be a unity regarding the core of the idea of God between individuals and groups, however far apart they may be in their conceptual articulation of God. The God of a farmer is not the God of a theologian, and the God of Moses is very different from the God of St. Paul. In spite of this, Scheler affirms that more people grasp God in a common way through love than through a common concept. Anyone who overlooks this fact dissolves the unity of religious valuation, which first forms and establishes the deepest unity of humanity, into a welter of insuperable differences on an intellectual plane. This ignorance of valuational unity transforms God into an object of dispute and intellectual rancor and finally into the source of bitter, violent conflict, as all the religious wars of history have shown. By anticipating that those different from himself can instruct him about the same God they both love, Scheler presents a position antipodal to such religious intolerance and violence. But, paradoxically, the attitude of relativists, who regard those different from themselves with neutrality or indifference, may be closer to that stance that produced the great religious wars than Scheler is.[54]

Scheler's absolute ethics, far from suppressing relativity in ethics, demands it.

> Nevertheless, in the *most radical* "relativity" of moral valuations lies no basis for the supposition of a relativism of the *values* themselves and their rank-ordering. Only this follows, namely that the full and adequate experience of the cosmos of values and their rank ordering and therefore of the presentation of the moral meaning of the world is bound *essentially* to a *cooperation* of different forms of ethos, unfolding according to their own historical laws. The correctly understood *absolute ethics* is the one that forcefully mandates this difference, this emotional value-perspectivism of times and peoples, and this basic openness in the formative stages of an ethos.[55]

For Scheler, it is impossible that the entire fullness of the kingdom of values and their ranking order could be given to any one individual, any one folk, any one nation, or any one moment in history.[56]

Against this background, the mechanistic worldview and its offspring, relativism, would appear to imperil the intersubjective and intercultural dialogue of which Scheler always dreamed. By undermining the objective order of values and ascribing the origin of values to the creativity and will of diverse cultures and individuals, mechanism and relativism have eliminated one of Scheler's central motives for dialogue since there is no longer the hope that the one culture might illuminate another regarding values *under which they both stand together*. While relativists can admit that each culture is one-sided since each has qualities missing to the other, they lack any critical impetus to scrutinize and evaluate their own one-sidedness. For nonrelativists, it is always possible that the Other's one-sidedness springs from a better insight into the order of being and value held in common by both parties.

The nonrelativists' position at times may seem unpalatable because so often objective values or subjective values masquerading as objective values have been employed by nonrelativists to exercise power and conceal that exercise at the same time. Scheler was no stranger to such Nietzschean suspicions. As a result, when Scheler uses examples of how one might apply objective values in a dialogic setting, he often emphasizes how objective values provide an opportunity for *self*-correction rather than for correction of the Other. This emphasis, though, need not rule out the possibility that genuine reciprocal criticism might be called for.

Even if one disagrees, however, with Scheler's a priori ranking of values—and a good Kantian could claim that objective norms of self-consistency can be found implicit within that free, rational will without reverting to any value ranking—Scheler's criticism of relativism does not rest completely on his a priori ranking of values. At the heart of relativism, as Scheler is depicting it, lies a deep-seated predilection not to be challenged. To be sure, relativists do away with the ranking of values that might call them to account. But also, their neutral, purely descriptive attitude toward different cultural value systems keeps them at a safe distance. Their indifference staves off any possible indictment from the other culture. If one detects in the relativists' position, however, an emphasis on how bizarre other cultures may appear or on how these other cultures' intolerance falls short of the tolerance of the relativists' culture, then one knows that their relativism disguises an absolutization of the values of their own culture, as Scheler has perceptively remarked. But these relativists would be even less likely than neutral, indifferent relativists to allow another culture's values to query their own.

In this author's opinion, this predilection of both types of relativist to avoid a challenging exchange reflects the ethos of *Gesellschaft* and its resistance to relationships of solidarity. For either relativist, each culture must establish for itself what is true or valuable since each culture is responsible only for itself. There is no responsibility for a culture to allow itself to engage another culture or to be interrogated by its values, unless for some interest it freely chooses to do so. For the relativist, each culture does as it wills without being beholden to any other. For Scheler, on the contrary, the intercultural struggle for knowledge of being and value in solidarity proceeds on a different basis. In such a struggle, other cultures from the outset have a claim on ours, they demand to be listened to and recognized for what they have learned. Furthermore, one culture can anticipate that its delicate efforts to understand the other culture will be rewarded by the education that the other culture offers. Cultures in solidarity do not pursue private projects as isolated monads immune to questions from without, but rather show themselves as vulnerable and welcoming before other cultures, with an endless readiness to learn from them and grow. Thus, Scheler's important notion of solidarity must be taken, in tandem with his idea of an objective order of being and value, as calling for an intercultural community of dialogue. By exempting themselves from this dialogue, relativists, for all their pretense to survey cultural relativities from a transcendent, noncomittal perspective, show themselves much more a prisoner of the Western *Weltanschauung* and its societal ethos than they recognize.

# 4

# The Fundaments of Dialogue: Scheler's Theory of Intersubjectivity

Max Scheler's philosophical critique confronts the modern Western *Weltanschauung* at its foundation, namely its tendencies to denude the world of its own structure of being and value and to substitute an order imposed by will. Utilizing phenomenology to burrow beneath mechanistic prejudices, Scheler practices advocacy on behalf of being's own structure and the a priori ranking of values. The paradigm of these objective orders spanning diverse cultures, which penetrate them only partially and one-sidedly, encourages an intercultural dialogue more than the mechanistic framework that puts great stock in the power of will to fashion its own order. In this sense, Scheler's phenomenology can be seen as a guardian of dialogue. Scheler's concept of solidarity, when conjoined with his objective orders, also fosters such dialogue more than the atomistic model of intersubjectivity typical of the Western *Gesellschaft*. Quite consistently, the mechanistic worldview, which tends to militate against dialogue, has construed the philosophical character of intersubjectivity itself in mechanistic terms. Hence Scheler's *Wesen und Formen der Sympathie* must be examined now to see how he attempts to rescue the notions of fellow feeling and love and the philosophical explanation of intersubjectivity from the distortions that they have undergone within the mechanistic framework. Perhaps here—in the clarification of the acts and structures fundamental for all dialogue—Scheler's phenomenology will appear to be quintessentially the protector of dialogue.

## Fellow Feeling

The first section of Scheler's *Wesen und Formen der Sympathie* addresses the character of "fellow feeling" (*Mitgefühl*) and develops a complementary metaphysics. First of all, Scheler, relying implicitly on phenomenological method, attempts to ferret out the eidos "fellow feeling" as distinct from other intersubjective feeling processes. Fellow feeling is not a feeling of the *same* feeling that the other feels *(Miteinanderfühlen)*, as occurs, for instance, when two parents stand near the deceased body of their loved child. Nor does it involve one of the several forms of emotional infection and identification, which Scheler describes in detail (as, for instance, the cheer one experiences because one's companions are cheerful, the non-Westerner's identification with a totem, Dionysian frenzy, hypnotism, eros, mob action, or the assimilation of one's identity to that of his parent). Such forms of identification *(Einsfühlung)* effectively suppress the distance between the persons that must be maintained if *Mitgefühl* is to take place.[1]

True fellow feeling involves a distance between oneself and the Other. To be sure, one adopts a feeling-intention toward the joy and the suffering of the *Other* wherein knowledge of the *Other's* feeling occurs. But, in such fellow feeling, the Other's feeling does not transfer to the observer so as to become his or her own feeling. Unlike what occurs in *Miteinanderfühlen*, he does not experience the same sorrow the Other may be feeling, but rather he experiences the Other experiencing the Other's feeling as the Other's and not as his own. Nietzsche, too, misunderstood the distinctiveness of fellow feeling by conflating it with infection. Nietzsche believed that, in fellow feeling or pity, a person feels sorrow with the Other and thus multiplies misery through her fellow-feeling. To the extent, however, that someone identifies with the Other and the Other's suffering becomes his own, he would become so focused on removing what is now his own suffering that he would become incapable of authentic fellow feeling. In identification, he becomes self-preoccupied with contagious feelings that are his own to the detriment of authentically entering into the Other's experience through fellow feeling.[2]

In discussing forms of identification, Scheler combats those who would reduce mother love, which, as love, is even a rung above fellow feeling, to a form of identification. In the view of these reductionists, mother love derives from the drive for self-preservation insofar as a mother tries to subsume her child into herself and under the dominion of her own will to survive. On the contrary, in Scheler's opinion, a phenomenological return to the facts discloses a conflict between maternal instincts that seek to draw the child back into the protective womb and authentic mother love. Genuine mother love battles against such instincts and aims at the child as an independent essence, who gradually develops from organic darkness into the increasing light of consciousness. Both fellow feeling and love stand over against modes of identification wherein the distinctiveness of the Other, whose feelings are distinct and whose independence is irreducible, is obliterated. Just as Scheler opposed those who would reduce all ethics to the pursuit of self-preservation and pleasure seeking without taking into account the unique character of higher-level spiritual activity and values, so here he distinguishes fellow feeling and love from lower level identification in order to separate mother love from mere instinct. This reductionist tendency in the analysis of feeling evidences the presence of the mechanistic worldview.[3]

So-called "genetic" theories of fellow feeling obscure its self-transcending character. According to these theories, the Other reports experience to someone and elicits from her the reflection, "How would it be if this had happened to me?" This question, in turn, leads her to reproduce imaginatively similar experiences in herself through which she finally can come to understand the Other. Such an artificial theoretical construction derives from the psychology of the French Enlightenment and presupposes the egoistic nature of humanity. Fellow feeling becomes a self-focused feeling reaction wherein one's own suffering or joy takes precedence over the suffering or joy of the Other. According to Scheler, however, one *never* focuses on one's own feelings in true fellow feeling. The feeling-state of B with whom A commiserates is wholly in B, and it neither migrates into A as he fellow-feels, nor does it produce a similar condition in A. Thus, for instance, a person can enjoy the Other's joy directly with the Other without necessarily being in a joyful mood himself. To corroborate his account of fellow feeling, Scheler appeals to the situation wherein a friend in need recounts an experience to a person, who, in turn, takes such a recounting as an opportunity to narrate similar personal experiences. Clearly, the friend in need will be disappointed and thus will try to redirect the listening friend's attention away from such personal preoccupations and back to those experiences with which the first friend initiated the conversation.[4] Scheler concludes:

> This genetic theory does not clarify the positive and pure fellow-feeling, which is a true grasping beyond oneself (*Hinübergreifen*) and entrance into the Other person and the Other's individual condition, a true and actual transcendence of one's own self. . . . Whatever in

one's own experience through reproduction shoves itself between fellow-feeling and the state of the Other—such a thing is only a obscuring medium for authentic, pure, positive fellow-feeling.[5]

The main difficulty of this mistaken description of fellow-feeling is that a person's capacity for fellow-feeling would be limited to only those experiences of the Other that he had already experienced and so could reproduce. But this unduly restricted explanation of *Verstehen* ignores that one can immediately feel suffering and joys and values that she has never experienced before: one who has never felt anxiety over death can nevertheless understand it and sympathize with another's feeling of it. Indeed, this type of fellow feeling makes possible such things as the conversion of the Buddha, who, raised in pomp and pleasure, beheld all suffering of the world in a few appearances of sickness and poverty and reoriented his whole life. Scheler mentions also Tolstoy's account of the "Master and Servant," wherein the master, with his closed, narrow, little heart, undergoes his first pure act of fellow feeling for his freezing servant and thereby opens himself to all those aspects of experience that he was unable to see, neglected, or failed to understand.[6] If understanding another meant merely reexperiencing only what one had already experienced, one would be as entrapped within one's own world as when the mechanistic worldview interposed constructs of will and reason between the knower and the objective order of value and being. Furthermore, if these genetic theories of fellow-feeling are followed, change and conversion, the possibility of being enlightened in dialogue with a completely alien culture, would be out of the question.

Those who would counter that one must, at least, have experienced "elements" of such experiences display the mechanistic proclivity to atomize experience. For what are the "elements" of fear or anxiety before death and how can they be synthesized into a single feeling? Just as a person can envision colors he has never seen before without building them out of previously experienced colors, so he can overleap his stock of experience to understand feelings never felt before. Whoever believes otherwise effectively reduces the richness of the world of color and feelings to the limited dimensions of a single person's or culture's past experience. As in the case of Scheler's view of being and value, the larger world always exceeds one's limited capacities to appreciate it and entices one onward to continual discovery.[7]

Scheler resists the mechanistic underpinnings of the genetic account of fellow feeling. Fellow feeling is not the product of causal factors, as if someone's history deposits sediments of feelings with which she eventually fellow-feels, or as if the perceived suffering of another stimulates a proportional state in oneself.

> We see daily in our life that there is a rhythm between closedness and openness, between idiopathic self-enclosure and entrance into the life of other people in fellow-feeling. Fellow-feeling does not run its course only in dependence upon the changes of outer stimuli, but varies widely and independently from such stimuli. In the presence of great suffering and its outer signs, fellow-feeling often will not occur. Then, on the other hand, often without such powerful stimuli, a trifle will open our whole soul for days and weeks to human joy and suffering—as if suddenly in a dark room a light were kindled or window opened. Here the function of fellow-feeling appears clearly as independent over against those conditions in oneself that are stimulated from without.[8]

Scheler, always aware of the intimate bonds between epistemology and metaphysics, affirms that his "epistemology" of fellow feeling correlates with metaphysical principles. On the one hand, Scheler repudiates any egocentric metaphysics wherein one illusorily takes one's own environment for the world itself. Fellow feeling dissipates the illusion of egocentricity, including the natural attitude tendency of each to relativize the Other and the Other's interests to one's own. Also, fellow feeling reveals the equal value of human beings *as* human beings (although some people are morally superior to others). On the other hand, various forms of monistic metaphysics, which envision persons as modes or functions of a superpersonal spirit, mistakenly proceed from an understanding of fellow-feeling as infection or identification. For Scheler, fellow feeling brings to light the distance between persons and their respective and reciprocal awarenesses of difference. Only a metaphysics of substantially diverse concrete act centers called "Persons" would do justice to fellow feeling, as Scheler's depicts it. Such a metaphysics further coincides with one's constant experience that the Other possesses an absolutely intimate Person, which one knows is absolutely inaccessible to all possible co-experiencing in spite of all moments of intimacy. Indeed, it is in fellow feeling that one learns that finite people cannot see into each others' hearts, let alone into one's own heart. In addition, theories of love based on monistic metaphysics go astray. For if one conceives love as treating the Other as if the Other were identical with oneself, then all other-regarding love should collapse into self-love. In fact, love is an understanding going unto the other individuality, different from one's own, *as* other and different. In spite of such differences, in love, one emotionally affirms completely the Other's being who the Other is. Egocentric and monistic metaphysics are two sides of the same coin in contrast to a personalist metaphysics attuned to the otherness of the Other. This otherness, given both in fellow feeling and in genuine love, parallels the independence whereby being and value defy any mechanistic attempts to domesticate them. In brief, monistic and egocentric metaphysics debar the possibility of dialogue between distinctive, reciprocal personal centers.[9]

Scheler's differentiation of fellow feeling from forms of identification and infection, his critique of genetic theories of fellow feeling, and his rejection of egocentric or monistic metaphysics combat underlying mechanistic presuppositions. But rather than stop here, Scheler turns to another manifestation of the mechanistic worldview—its spurning of life. In his preface to the second edition of *Wesen und Formen der Sympathie* (1922), Scheler describes additions he has made to the first edition published in 1913. He has added the discussions on emotional identification, which he discriminates from fellow feeling, and on the metaphysical theories of sympathy, including those sections on metaphysical monism, which he rejects as inadequate to the experience of fellow feeling. In whole new sections on unity with the cosmos and the founding relations between identification, fellow feeling, and love, Scheler's tone alters markedly. Instead of opposing identification and monistic metaphysics, as he had done previously, he now dwells on the *value* of entering into unity with cosmic life forces.

This effort to achieve unity with the cosmos runs counter to life-distancing trends, which preceeded the mechanistic worldview in the seventeenth century and resulted in it. Scheler begins his fifth chapter of the first part, "Die kosmische Einsfühlung in den Gemütsgestalten der Geschichte," by contrasting Indian spirituality with that of the Greeks, the early predecessors of the mechanistic standpoint. The Indians, people of the Asian woods and not the city as in the West, share neither the north-European attitude of seeking mastery and control over nature nor that distant wonder and love for the plastic forms and patterns of nature characteristic of the Greeks. Rather, the Indian lives in nature, in vital identification with it and with its universally intuited All-Life (*All-Leben*). The Indian does not rank animals and plants under humanity either, contrary to the Greeks, who saw humanity as the pinnacle of nature's hierarchy, and Judeo-Christianity, which placed the entire universe at the service of humanity. On the contrary, the Indian looks upon all living creation and the expressions of life hidden in the inorganic as "brother" or "companion" or "friend."[10]

The ancient Greeks were the first to set spirit against life and thereby demote the importance of identification as a method for knowledge of nature. In place of identification, a whole new tier of *spiritual* relationships between human beings and nature, other human beings, and God, came to the fore. This tier became possible only through authentic fellow feeling and spontaneous spiritual love. The Orphic movement and the mystery religions, with their modes of identification, constituted a romantic reaction against these spiritual processes opposed to identification with nature and promoting the city-born "Apollinism" of the Greek thinkers. Judeo-Christianity, with its completely spiritual God, effected a delivering and desouling of all nature and paved the way for a rising dominion over nature. In Christianity, all identification with nature was branded as pagan (at least until St. Francis of Assisi). Christianity urged one to detach oneself from nature and channel that energy into a acosmic love for Jesus Christ. Christianity thereby transformed nature into lifeless objects fit for domination by the spiritual will of humanity, whether in bodily ascesis or technology. Numerous philosophers, from Schelling to Fechner, have reiterated that Christian intuition and thinking and Christianity's theistic formulations have fostered a deadening and mechanizing approach to all subhuman Nature. Only in the sacraments has Christianity preserved traces of a vital identification (e.g., participation in the body and blood of the Lord in the Eucharist) that the Christian mechanization and desouling of nature generally abandoned. As Scheler noted earlier in *Wesen und Formen der Sympathie*, humanity has lost various capacities, while gaining others, in its evolution toward present-day civilization.[11]

Francis of Assisi modified these trends in Christianity by brilliantly synthesizing acosmic personal love with cosmic-vital identification. Without any predecessor in Christendom, Francis bridged the gap between humanity and nature by seeing sun and moon, fire and water, animals and plants as his "brothers" and "sisters" and not as objects for human condescension or mere resources for exploitation. Francis committed "heresy of the heart" in the face of Scholasticism and its doctrines of the strictly isolated informed structures and the aristocratic, hierarchic layering of nature. Furthermore, his attitude toward nature gave birth to a social mission similar to the Buddha's struggle against the ancient Indian caste system: the moderating of status and class oppositions and the bringing of charity to the common people. For Scheler, the origin of Francis's spirituality lay in the erotic overtones of the Provençal cult of spiritual love that shaped his life, his noble gallantry, his delicate reverence for women such as St. Clare, and the self-abandonment and devotion of his vital-spiritual center to the core of creatures. The final root of all identification, according to Scheler, is eros, and Francis brought together eros and agape in such a mutual permeation that he spiritualized life and enlivened the spirit as no one had done before.[12]

Francis's experiences parallel those of adolescence wherein the child discovers for the first time an erotically charged world.

> Already with phase of *puberty*, a change in the image of Nature takes place, which one can describe as the sudden *enlivening* of all natural appearances. These appearances take on a new, intensive expression-character. Nature itself appears to give an answer to the formless, chaotic longing that now begins to stir in the child in its changing modalities. Nature becomes filled with thousands of dynamic powers, which call forth at one time anxiety, which was never known before, at another time delight, which likewise was unknown and appears as "new." In this situation, the doctrine of projective identification says as little as it says for the understanding of prehistorical animism of the primitives. What is involved is not only a new experience of Nature, but also the experience of a *new Nature*. The *dynamic* process side of Nature—all "Becoming," "Growing," "Fashioning," in contrast to the already completed being in space and time—comes forth here.[13]

In addition to the discovery of eros in adolescence, loving sexual activity opens up for civilized humanity a source of metaphysical knowledge and access to cosmic-vital identification. The Franciscan revolution and adolescence, like other value transformations discussed earlier, open one's eyes to a world of values offered to him before; these values may never have been recognized, especially insofar as he has been under the sway of the mechanistic approach to nature.

Scheler envisions this identification with nature, so clearly embodied in Francis, as providing an alternative to the mechanistic conception of nature. Natural science adopts its own legitimate, but limited, stance toward nature, but *Nature*, as if it were a partner seeking dialogue, provides a richer field of expressions for a nonmechanistic understanding.[14]

> We must again learn to see into Nature as did Goethe, Novalis, and Schopenhauer, as if "into the heart of a friend." In addition, we need to limit the "scientific," formal-mechanistic consideration of Nature, important as it is for technology and industry, to the specialized, "artificial" behavior pattern of physicists, chemists, etc. The formation of humanity (and of its heart) must precede every "specialized" approach to Nature as if it were an opponent to be controlled. Thus we must pedagogically reawaken cosmic-vital identification in the first place and revive it anew from out of its stupor among Western humanity with its capitalistic societal spirit (Gesellschaftsgeistes).[15]

Because of its one-sided evolution, Scheler remarks, the West needs to abandon the conception that civilized, masculine, European humanity provides the "monarchical" capstone of a world development for which other cultures have served only as discardable stepping stones along the way. Scheler argues that there are two modes of escaping such forms of restricted vision:

> On vital grounds only identification and on spiritual grounds only the art of understanding (Verstehens) of other forms of worldview and their structures promise slowly the adjustment (Ausgleichung) of specific narrownesses and particularities. These narrownesses encompass us all, as blinders shield the horse's eyes.[16]

The mechanistic worldview reduced fellow feeling to identification with the Other or to a projection of self-reproduced feelings into the Other and suppressed any attitude toward nature other than the scientific-technical one. It effectively obliterated the very otherness that could place it in question and liberate it. Scheler's effort to preserve the distinctiveness of the Other in fellow feeling and the autonomy of Nature, with which one can identify without needing to dominate, run parallel to his attempt to preserve objective values and an objectively structured world that confront every selective cultural pattern with their inexhaustible wealth. It is not surprising that this mechanistic worldview would dismiss all cosmic-vital identification (Einsfühlung) as only a projective reading of specific human feelings into (Einfuhlung) the animal, the plant, and the inorganic—a mere "anthropomorphism."[17] By such an interpretation, the mechanistic view maintains its hegemony, deflects its opponents' charges, and rebuffs dialogue. What is even more interesting is how this mechanistic worldview seems to have made Christian spirituality (other than that of Francis of Assisi) an accomplice to its own purposes. The mechanistic perspective manifests itself not only in a reduction that reduces spiritual activity to causal forces, but also in a spiritualism detached from its vital roots. Nietzsche, of course, most perspicuously detected these subtle linkages between aloof spirituality and the passion to control.

To conclude his discussion of fellow feeling, Scheler lays out the "founding laws" of sympathy. To be able to feel another's feeling state vicariously (Nachfühlen)—at a distance—one must at some time have identified (Einsfühlung) with the subject type who has that feeling. One does not have to have already experienced every feeling-state of the Other in order to understand what the Other is experiencing, though. Einsfühlen thus founds Nachfühlen. But vicarious feeling (Nachfühlen), in turn, founds fellow feeling (Mitgefühl). Vicarious feeling is a feeling of the Other's feeling, more than a mere knowing about it or a judgment that the Other has that feeling. In vicarious feeling, one grasps the quality of the Other's feeling without it migrating into oneself. Fellow feeling, though, involves the added component of actual participation in the Other's feeling as presented in vicarious feeling. Fellow feeling nevertheless presupposes that one feels the Other's feeling as the Other's own and not one's own. For Scheler, the distinction between vicarious feeling and fellow feeling becomes clear when the cruel person takes account of the victim's suffering, feeling it by vicarious feeling, and then goes on to take pleasure in it— something inconceivable for true fellow feeling. Fellow feeling, for all its participation in the Other's feeling, still enables one to recognize the independence of the Other person with whom one fellow-feels. As such, one recognizes the equality of the Other and overcomes residual forms of autoeroticism and egocentrism. Fellow feeling thus prepares the way for spontaneous benevolence (Menschenliebe), or love for the Other because the Other is a human being. Finally, as benevolence establishes a similar real equality between vital egos through fellow feeling and as it penetrates the deeper psychic levels, it disposes one to love a person. In such personal love, directed at the individual person-center, one has gone beyond general benevolence that grasps each person only as an exemplar of the human type.[18]

For Scheler, these founding relations are important because one must develop the lower-valued, more general capacities in order to cultivate the higher-valued and less frequently occurring powers of the spirit. If this identification of humanity with the whole of nature is lacking, humanity gradually finds itself cut off from its great, eternal Mother, Nature, in a way that does not correspond to the human essence. As a result, humanity exploits and destroys nature, reckons use- and achievement-values as superior to the values of life, and ignores the importance of life values for cultural-spiritual values.[19]

This value distortion shows up most clearly in sexual practices. With the devaluation of life values and of identification with Nature, sexuality loses its expressive meaning and becomes a mere means subordinated to goals of pleasure, procreation, quantitative reproduction of the race, eugenic planning, power, interest, or gain. In other words, sexuality becomes *zweckrational* instead of communicative or dialogical. Scheler believes that mechanistic metaphysics, although no longer prominent in physics, psychology, or sociology, has become part and parcel of the "the relative natural attitude" of the commonsense person in the West. Hence, this commonsense person believes in general that sexual instinct takes precedence over sexual love, self-maintenance over improvement, and the individual over the community. In brief, the values of life have been deposed in favor of utility because this mechanistic metaphysics now rules in the theory and practice of the West's common life, in nearly all morals and institutions, as well as in the collective spirit of Western sexual living and the sphere of the erotic.[20]

## Love

Scheler's treatment of love in *Wesen und Formen der Sympathie* advances his criticism of modern Western understandings of intersubjectivity. He begins by distinguishing love from fellow feeling and benevolence. Love involves none of the distance and "condescension" that characterize benevolent well-wishing. Furthermore, love differs from fellow feeling, which is value-blind, in that love refers to value. In fellow feeling, for instance, one can rejoice with A's pleasure over B's misfortune, whereas, in love, one would find oneself not only fellow-feeling A's pleasure, but also evaluating it as improper, as not in accord with A's own finest possibilities. In addition, love is not a feeling, but rather an *act* and a *movement*, a spontaneous rather than reactive condition. Love plays a founding role with regard to fellow feeling in that fellow feeling varies according to love; hence, one fellow-feels more intensely the more one loves. Further, some general kind of love (e.g., for a whole nation, race, or church to which the person belongs) underlies a person's willingness to fellow-feel with someone he does not love, as when someone expresses sympathy to someone whom he does not personally and individually love. One can fellow-feel with someone she does not love in this sense, but it is impossible to love someone and not fellow-feel with them.[21]

Love's endurance despite changing feeling-states proves that one cannot reduce it to a complex of feelings and strivings. The pain and suffering that a loved person causes does not alter one's love for that person. In the many changes of joy and suffering, which take place day-by-day between people, love and hate relations perdure unaltered. Further, love and hatred differ from acts of preference and rejection whereby one cognizes values. Love and hatred instead refer to objects, not values, insofar as these objects possess value. One does not love values, but that which possesses value. Love plays a founding role regarding preference insofar as love's intentional movement allows a higher value of an object to flash forth so that one can then prefer that value. Love and hate are actually wholly original and immediate modes of emotional behavior toward a value-content such that they do not even include value apprehension (as do preference and rejection). Their primitive character can be seen in the facts that one cannot give reasons for love, that whatever reasons one does give fall short of justifying love, and that other objects with the same value-objects do not elicit love. Rather, reasons follow on love instead of leading it. In fact, one's choice of evaluative standards depends on whether the values are borne by a loved or hated object. In the end, though, one does not love or hate the object because it possesses attributes meriting a high evaluation. Hence, once neither judges a love letter by its grammatical precision, nor traces one's love for the Other to the Other's grammatical accuracy. This originary, nongrounded character of love calls to mind the age-old charge that love is blind. Scheler, on the contrary, asserts that simply because love sees with different eyes than the eyes of reason, one cannot conclude that it does not see as well as reason. Love and hate have their own evidence that is not to be measured by the evidence of reason. Finally, love and hate do not consist in striving, for the disquiet of striving is missing in love and hate. Love does not try to realize some project with regard to the object of love, as if the Other were a field for mechanistic domination.[22]

Love is above all creative. As a movement, love does not gaze with affirmation upon extent values, nor do values embodied in the object prior to love's onset draw out love. In both of these cases, love would be determined mechanically by an empirical fact outside of itself. Rather, love entails an intention toward higher values than those already given. It anticipates positive qualities not yet given. Love discerns an ideal value structure, which belongs to the "true" and "actual" person. Such a value structure lies implicitly within the person loved such that the lover does not import one's own values into the Other. Love posits no goals that the Other must achieve. Instead, its movement brings the higher value to appearance, as if it streamed forth from the loved person without any seeming exertion from the lover. Authentic love opens the lover's spiritual eyes to always higher values in the loved person. Love enables one to see, rather than making one blind. In fact, it is the "cold Other," who accuses the lover of overestimating or idealizing the person loved, who in fact does not see the particular individual values in the person loved because this "cold Other's" sight has not been sharpened by love. This "cold Other" is, in fact, the blind one. The lover sees more objectively because of a unique, individual insight into the loved Other, as opposed to the Kantian insistence that the objective is equivalent to what is generally and universally valid.[23]

For Scheler, love, in spite of its movement beyond the empirically given, persists in its respect for the otherness of the loved Other. The lover engages in no project to make the Other better (*Bessermachen*) by adopting a pedagogic attitude toward him. Love accepts the Other as the Other is, and no conviction that "you ought to be such and such" conditions love. Jesus, for example, lays no binding imperative upon Mary Magdalene as a prerequisite of his love for her. In love, "You should be such and such" is replaced by "Become what you are" ("Werde der du bist")—its movement toward higher value is based on what is already there. Lovers do not project any of their own values, nor do they invest the Other with imaginary values that the Other lacks.[24] As Scheler puts it:

> That would be an illusion. Naturally there are such illusions. But surely they are not conditioned by love for the object. Rather, they are brought about through the opposite, through the inability to become free from one's inclinations on behalf of one's *own* ideas, feelings, and interests.[25]

Such false "love" fails to escape the orbit of the self. Feuerbach seems to have taken a similarly false notion of love for God and converted it into the essence of religion: human beings live in the illusion that they love another, while factually they love only themselves, a mirror image, which they have created. For Max Scheler, on the contrary, there is a real God and a real Other there, however much one's own egotism might abstract from their fullness or inhibit them from irrupting into one's life in a moment of dialogue. Just as Scheler battled the theories that fellow feeling involves only the projection of reproduced feeling into the Other or that all talk of identification with Nature is only anthropomorphic eisegesis, so also he labored to preserve the possibility of a love wherein lovers can escape themselves. Lovers genuinely love Others as they are and even lead them to higher values—all without subjugating the Others to themselves. False love and false theories of love reflect the pervasive Western mechanistic tendency to denude this world of its objective traits and values and replace them with merely subjective meanings and values that a personal will to power imposes.

Scheler dissents from the belief in a love for "the Good" that might translate as "Love people insofar as they are good" or "Hate the evil insofar as they are evil." Love does not depend on exterior qualities, nor is there some Platonic form bestowing goodness on objects and eliciting love for these objects. Rather, love itself is the original bearer of good. In the exercise of love, the good shines forth in the lover. This dynamism of love reappears in Scheler's doctrine of solidarity. The laws of intersubjective understanding teach that, in its essence, love evokes a loving response. Thus, if evil people fail to make a loving response, this failure indicates a lack of original love in their lives. In solidarity with evil people, one recognizes that one is responsible for them and must extend creative love to them in order to evoke a loving response. Instead of opting for "love for the Good," solidarity demands that one love even evil persons, because their failure is one's own and because love can create goodness where none was to be found before.[26]

Of course, there are parallels with the solidarity requisite for intercultural dialogue. Just as a person should not love people only if they are good, so he should not limit his conversation to those who are like him. Just as the evil person's evil is one's own, so the truth that another culture bears is a part of one's own culture insofar as that other culture has penetrated into the objective being and values accessible to all. Just as one places hope in the evil person's capacity to change, so one hopes for growth from an interchange. Finally to let one's love be repulsed by the other's evil or to let the other's difference dissuade one from dialogue is to succumb to passivity and to forfeit creative opportunities.

Virtually the entire second half of Scheler's discourse on love finds him embattled with the "naturalistic theory of love." Philosophical currents within this theory include some of the reductionistic interpretations of fellow feeling he had opposed: positivism (first of all Feuerbach), correlative philosophies of history, and Freudianism. In Feuerbach's historical purview, the sex drive is restrained and splits apart into partial drives producing maternal love, the love of children for parents, and finally love for one's kind and fatherland. Freud, in a similar vein, begins with childhood suckling and the stimulation of the "erogenous zones of infancy." Through secondary drive impulses, one seeks to repeat such sensations, and these sensations become the final "building material" for all mature kinds of sympathetic feelings and all kinds of love, including the most sublime and spiritual forms. Freud names the drive impulse to experience such sensations "libido," and he considers it prior to and more basic than the more complicated construction of the sexual drive.[27]

Scheler's critique of the naturalistic theory of love, particularly Freudianism, relies on his phenomenological return to the facts that delineate the essences of life and spirit. But this critique depends above all on his conviction that the naturalistic theory of love is part and parcel of that narrowing of vision and suppression of novelty that the mechanistic worldview in its zeal for control has introduced. As Scheler comments:

> This crux [of the naturalistic theory of love] consists—besides the already disproved view that the act of love can be clarified generally as a "complex" or "developmental product" of simpler spiritual elements—in its complete overlooking of the originariness of "spiritual" and "holy" love, as well as of "love for the individual soul." The error of the naturalistic theory does not lie in that it perceived the facts designated by these words, but only falsely and insufficiently "explained" them. No. It does not even see these facts generally; it is particularly *blind* to them. . . . The naturalistic stance blinds itself to the fact that in the course of vital development principally *new and deeper being and value-levels* appear. In these new levels, whole realms of *objects* and values for developing life can come into view. In the presence of the unfolding of life, these being and value realms first open up their qualitative fullness and begin to disclose themselves. For the naturalistic theory, mere new and illusionary contents emerge *between* the vital essence and the world (colors, tones, values, etc.). A vital essence that would sense only static bodies and their movement

would stand, according to this theory, nearest to the "things in themselves." Every new quality signifies a new illusion. The basic fact, that the "true" world is always "richer" than the given one, is overlooked by the naturalistic theory in principle. This thinking, as that of the naturalistic philosophy in general, is basically "deflationary." It approaches everything with the false founding axiom that whatever is simplest and least valuable takes on the character of an *ontologically prior* and an ontological "origin." This axiom presupposes that being and values should be directed according to the convenience needs of a reason schematized for practical goals. These simple and least valuable things, it is true, are easiest to grasp for a "human reason" considered in terms of directing and dominating the world. These things are facile to grasp because they are most tractable, widespread, and easily communicable, in contrast to those things that are more developed and valuable.[28]

Scheler's other criticisms of the naturalistic concept of love echo his earlier critiques of the mechanistic worldview. Thus, the system of instincts can select out certain objects or bearers of values, but it produces neither the act of love directed to such objects nor the a priori ranking of values. Moreover, Scheler opposes Freud's mechanistic explanations that the sexual drive arises from a striving after a distinctive kind of pleasure (e.g., that found in suckling) and that this origin involves a more or less accidental "fortuitous" coincidence of exterior circumstances. Rather, vital love underpins the development of an ever-present, but, at first, unconscious and vaguely directed sexual love, which only gradually comes to fix on its particular sexual object. Scheler, with his usual eye for the distinctiveness of levels and acts, insists that there are originally diverse qualities of love that are irreducible to each other: brotherly love is not sublimated sexual love. Once again, Scheler's phenomenological procedure requires an eidetic analysis flowing from a return to the facts instead of reliance on the mechanistic presumption that everything must be reduced to its least common denominator.[29]

## The Other I

Scheler's final section, originally only an appendix in the first edition of the *Wesen und Formen der Sympathie*, focuses on the "other I." The subtitle of the section sums up its theme: "Investigation of the Eidetic Nature, Epistemology, and Metaphysics of the Experience and Real Positing of the other I and Life-Essence."[30]

Scheler's first task is to articulate the distinctiveness of the methods and objects of what has been traditionally referred to as the human sciences (*Geisteswissenschaften*) as opposed to the natural sciences (*Naturwissenschaften*). Scheler objects to the intention of experimental psychologists to submit higher functions such as thinking, willing, or religious acts to experimental testing. For Scheler, the collective contents of the noetic acts are neither interiorly perceivable, observable, nor capable of experimental modification or technical control because of their essential character and not because of some superable methodological failings of the present. What is accessible to experimental inquiry lies exclusively within the limits of vital-psychic, goal directed, automatic being and becoming—beneath the realm of free, spiritual, personal acts. While the effects of these spiritual acts within the vital sphere, however, permit empirical scrutiny, the realm of spiritual-noetic being remains transintelligible.[31]

Through the method of *Verstehen*, a listener receives a speaker's free and spontaneous disclosure, to which no spontaneous knowing or cognition by that listener can attain. Persons possess the capacity—not shared by the rest of nature—to be silent, to refrain from communicating in such a way that no automatic, bodily expression even betrays their restraint. Nature, on the other hand, inevitably manifests itself in its bodily, physiological processes and so remains continually open to spontaneous cognition from without.[32]

In *Verstehen*, one can apprehend the acts of the Other in a non-objectifiable manner. One listening to a speaker's free self-revelation participates in that speaker's spiritual being in a manner different from all perception of objects. One does not require a foundation in such perception for this participation. Therefore, the *verstehende* psychology, as cognition of concrete persons and concrete systems of their noemata, differs fundamentally from all psychology that treats psychically real being insofar as it is objectifiable. Experimental psychology can never achieve—even at some more advanced stage of its development—what the *verstehende* psychology accomplishes as the foundation of the human sciences. These extensive methodological refinements, of course, ensure a nonmechanistic access to the Person.[33]

In addressing the question of the general evidence for the Thou, Scheler declines to start with isolated human consciousness asking whether other minds exist. Instead, the world of the

Thou or the world of the community constitute an independent essential sphere of beings, as do as the spheres of the outer world, the inner world, and the sphere of the divine. In the case of each of these irreducible spheres of being, the sphere itself is pregiven as a background before the positing of any possible object in the sphere. These ontological spheres establish general, essential presuppositions for any theory of knowledge. The sphere of the Thou would be a priori present even to a Robinson Crusoe, who would find evidence for this sphere in the experience that he lacks fulfillment insofar as he is cut off from others. The very attempt to prove the existence of the Other must presuppose what it is trying to prove.[34]

Having given this response to the problem, Scheler undertakes a critique of the two other leading candidates for a solution. First, the "analogy" theory argues that one concludes to the existence of the Other by observing another body analogous to one's own, which must embody an "I" analogous to one's own. Second, the "projective empathy" theory states that belief in the existence of the Other is founded on a projection of one's own feeling processes into an the appearance of an alien body. In these mistaken theories, Scheler detects the influence of mechanistic biology after Descartes. Here the soul, separate from its own body, attempts in vain to move through the body of the Other and reach the Other's soul. The most the analogy theory can conclude, if it is not to commit a *quaternio terminarum*, is that one person's soul is united to his or her body, which is like that body over there, which would lead him or her to believe that he or she is over there. In Scheler's view, both of these theories depend on two starting points: (1) only one's own "I" is first and foremost given to one, and (2) what is first and foremost given to one of the Other is the Other's body, through whose changes and movements one comes to believe in its ensouled character. Such presuppositions seem plausible to a mechanistic theory because stimuli reach one's sense organs only if the body of the Other has emitted them and because whatever psychic communication occurs depends on such physical processes.[35]

If theoretical premises end up isolating consciousness and necessitating convoluted processes to bridge the divide between them, phenomenology would insist that one return to the things themselves instead of taking for granted such theoretical premises. "Nothing is more certain that this, that we can think the thoughts of the Other as well as our own and feel her feelings as well as our own." In fact, it is often the case that one can only separate one's own thoughts from others' with great difficulty. When examining one's thoughts, someone can easily wonder whether they are his own or whether he may have filched them from something he read, from a conversation he has forgotten, or from a tradition he follows. Furthermore, in Scheler's view, the facts of child psychology and anthropology indicate that children and non-Western people live so immersed in the experiences of others that an individual can only very slowly lift her own spiritual head from out of this rushing stream. Only gradually does she discover her own essence that, now and then, contains its own feelings, ideas, and strivings. But even then ideas and experiences, whose factual origin is completely hidden, pervade one's consciousness. One's own "I" is not the first thing that is first and foremost given to one.[36]

Scheler further counters the Cartesian dualism underlying the first starting point above by pointing to the fact that a person does not first perceive psychic experiences and subsequently the bodily movements and expressions correlative to these experiences. Instead bodily expressions, including language, enable particular psychic processes to stand out for perception in the first place. One notices and remembers, for instance, expressed feelings of joy or love, while unexpressed feelings swiftly dissipate. Similarly, poets find the right words to express what has never been seen before because often the dominating linguistic schema of the time blocked one's vision. Since body and language can obscure a person's own self-perception as much as perception of the Other, Scheler refuses to privilege self-perception over perception of the Other, as the analogy and empathy theories do.[37]

Moreover, Scheler disapproves of both the soul-body interaction theory and psychophysical parallelism because both theories lock all human beings in in their own psychic prisons. Within such prisons, they await whatever missives the metaphysical causal-nexus magically emits in their direction. A quick recourse to the phenomenological facts dispels any dualism between the spirit and the body.

> Surely it is correct that we believe we can grasp one's joy directly in one's laughter, one's sorrow and pain in one's crying, one's shame in one's blushing, one's praying on one's folded hands, one's love in the tender gaze of one's eyes, one's rage in one's clenched teeth, one's threat in one's clenched fist, the significance of what one means in one's expressed words, etc. Someone may say to me that there is no "perception" here because there "can" be none and there "can" be

none because perception is only a "complex of physical sensations." Someone may also say that surely there can be no such thing as a sensation of the psychic contents of the Other—surely there are no [physical] stimuli here. But I would ask this person to step back from such questionable theories and return to the phenomenological fact.[38]

No doubt, discrepancies crop up between the experiences the Other intends to communicate and the Other's expression of them. In such situations, the interpreter must revert to ratiocination. Even here, however, ratiocination will rely upon simple, immediate perceptions of the Other.[39]

The central point is that a person does not perceive "bodies" or "souls" first, as the framework for considering intersubjectivity handed down from Descartes suggests. Rather, he experiences unified wholes, from which, secondarily, he can choose to focus in the direction of the inner or other perception, upon the Other's body or the Other's thought processes. But it is essentially impossible to take the unity of an expression (a laugh, a threatening or tender look) and split it into a sum of appearances, as if one were simply dismantling the exterior appearance of a body into its components. Thus, one cannot decompose a blush of shame into its elements and assume that a qualitative redness covering a cheek can, when conjoined with other sense elements, amount to a blush. Some might interpret the mere redness of a cheek as symptomatic of overheating, anger, debauchery, or the glow coming from a red lantern. Instead, one recognizes the actual condition of the Other as a whole, first, before one ever isolates a splotch of redness from its context.[40] Through this analytic dissolution of experience into atoms, the familiar visage of the mechanistic account of perception grins at one, an account that indeed underlies the falsely posed problem of other minds:

Perhaps this may give us a rather better understanding of the supposedly "self-evident fact" that we can only perceive the bodies of other people. We can begin by treating colors, sounds, shapes, etc., as "sensations," when they are really qualities appearing in conjunction with sensation. Or again, we can treat the perception based upon (though not composed of) such qualitative complexes, as a complex of sensations, though sensations play no part in it. We can also forget that on this (doubly erroneous) view of perception it is *no more possible* to perceive the body than it is to perceive the self. If we assume that it is feasible to perceive with all these presuppositions, then we do indeed reach the remarkable conclusion that we can perceive the bodies of other people but not their selves.[41]

## Conclusion

Even as Scheler opposed the southwest German school of Kantianism for separating metaphysics from epistemology, so also he insisted that accounts of intersubjectivity, love, and fellow feeling be considered in concert with the epistemology and metaphysics of an era. These philosophical areas are so intertwined that one would not, for example, expect to find an ethical personalism coexisting with a metaphysical monism that denies the substantial existence of the spiritual person. Scheler ties the strands of ethics, epistemology, and theory of intersubjectivity together to illustrate their philosophical connections:

> The old "contract-theory," which historically grew out of the Epicurean school, corresponds exactly to the analogy doctrine and the doctrine of the subjectivity of qualities and forms (with its accompanying conceptual nominalism). Let us reverse the presuppositions of these doctrines by assuming that we can know some content of consciousness, for example, the blue of this pen lying before us, identically in common with another human being. Let us further assume that it is not the case that there are "two" blues that are the similar effects of a quality-less thing on the Other's and on our physical nerves and psyche. If both these assumptions were true, then the reasoning by analogy for "every" content of consciousness of the Other would fall by the wayside.[42]

It is not accidental that the Epicurean value scheme, built on a subjectivizing of all values and secondary sense qualities, should lead to a contract theory wherein isolated individuals, dwelling in their own subjective worlds, could only establish artificial relationships, which would not exist unless they will them into being. Such a view foreshadows rather accurately the modern mechanistic worldview, the target of Scheler's critique in his sociology of knowledge, epistemology, ethics, and, as this chapter shows, in his account of fellow feeling, love, and intersubjectivity. Using phenomenology as his method, Scheler has attempted to uphold an objective order of being and value, which mandates an intercultural dialogue undertaken in solidarity. He complements this metaphysics and ethics with a theory of intersubjectivity claiming that people are not atomistically self-enclosed in their worlds as the Epicurean and mechanistic standpoints avow. Rather, a person can have authentic fellow feeling with another's feeling, which is not simply his own feeling reproduced. One can love others as they are in such a way that they become more fully what they are without remaking them in her image and likeness. Finally, one can know a Thou directly without resorting to analogical inferences or empathic projections. These tenets of Scheler's theory of intersubjectivity provide the fundaments for the type of intercultural dialogue for which Scheler's metaphysics and ethics calls. Scheler's *Wesen und Formen der Sympathie* thus deploys phenomenological method to criticize the mechanistic culture of the West at the high philosophical level of its theories of intersubjectivity and to protect the possibility of dialogue with those who are different.[43]

Immediately after Scheler points out the links between ethics, epistemology, and intersubjectivity in his remarks on Epicureanism, he reiterates the need for investigations into philosophical *Weltanschauungen*. Such studies, while not pronouncing on the truth or falsity of such *Weltanschauungen*, will attend to the necessary interconnections of their systems of ideas. He proceeds to suggest that the contract theory and the argument from analogy both express an underlying alienation from the social whole conceived as somewhat anti-individual. In *Formalism*, Scheler insinuates that the belief in a separate substantial soul for individual persons belongs to the same configuration of ideas as the argument from analogy and the contract theory. Furthermore, the philosophical principles of this single common *Weltanschauung* play a part in shaping, for instance, the doctrine of exclusive responsibility for oneself and not for others, the religious concentration on the individual soul's relationship to God at the expense of religion as a communal way to God, the idea of "perpetual peace" on the basis of contracts between states, the pedagogic emphases on the enlightenment of the individual, and the economic system of free competition.[44]

Philosophical principles, however, do not unfold in a vacuum, as Scheler's sociological concept of structural analogies implies, for philosophy correlates with socio-historical events. Scheler, for instance, observes in "Der Bourgeois" in *Vom Umsturz der Werte*: "The merchant's fear of being cheated has become the very category of intersubjective perception." The contract theory itself, he adds in *Wesen und Formen der Sympathie*, probably first arose when immigrants from outside overran a population, shattering its bonds of blood—the original glue holding the community together. Furthermore, the contract theory reflects a predominantly *Gesellschaft*-type of society in contrast the natural law theory deriving from Aristotle, the Stoa, and the Church. The natural law theory appeals to original instincts that precede any acts of promising or contracting and that prevail especially in a *Gemeinschaft*. Natural law theory itself simply formalized and extended underlying *Lebensgemeinschaft* relationships.[45]

Scheler's mostly critical comments on the theories of fellow feeling, love, and other minds in *Das Wesen und Formen der Sympathie* simply battle against the philosophical expressions of the underlying *Gesellschaft* relations dominating in the West. Scheler, however, works out his positive presentation of the new society, that of a spiritual *Gesamtperson*, in his *Formalism*. Scheler's critique of philosophical errors on intersubjectivity lays the remote groundwork for this vision of the society to come. This new society consists in the participation of independent, individual, spiritual persons in an independent, individual, spiritual *Gesamtperson*. Such a society refashions the old Christian belief that independent believers belonged to the mystical body of Christ. In this new society, everyone will be self-responsible (as one never fully was in the *Lebensgemeinschaft*) and yet coresponsible for all others (as one was not in the *Gesellschaft*). Solidarity entails a form of "one for all and all for one," whether one shares interests with the Other or not. This new social form does not involve a synthesis of *Lebensgemeinschaft* and *Gesellschaft*, but one discovers in it key features of each: independent, individual persons as in the *Gesellschaft*, and solidarity and real communal unity as in the *Gemeinschaft*. Such a new social essence is not to be realized by pitting the forms against each other, but by aiming at a higher form, integrating the best aspects of each. It is clear that within a *Gesamtperson* the authentic dialogue in solidarity between respectful and respected individuals would occur, the very dialogue given philosophical foundations by Scheler's theory of intersubjectivity.[46]

# 5

# The Way beyond Sociologism

The deep-seated, violent clash between the culture and nations of Europe during World War I severely tested any philosophy that aspired to an objective, transcendent order discoverable through intercultural dialogue. How Max Scheler, in his war writings, fell under the sway of an unrecognized will to cultural power, although occasionally he struggled against such bias, is discussed below. Treatment of the war writings serves as a prelude to the critique of Scheler that Karl Mannheim developed, which can seem justified, given Scheler's war writings. Mannheim criticizes Scheler's sociology of knowledge by denying that Scheler's eidetic claims are compatible with the force of socio-cultural determinism, more or less recognized by Scheler himself. Since Scheler never directly responded to Mannheim's charges, an attempt to answer Mannheim's critique is constructed. At the same time, the implications of Scheler's phenomenological starting point for the sociology of knowledge and the possibility of intercultural dialogue is shown. All these efforts necessitates a careful consideration of Scheler's account of the attitude proper to philosophy and his related reinterpretation of the phenomenological reduction. Finally, how Scheler's thought can combat sociologism while making dialogue possible is described.[1]

## Scheler's Writings on World War I

In the *Der Genius des Krieges und der Deutsche Kreig*, written in 1914, Scheler traces the origin of World War I, paradoxically, to the period of peace prior to the War. In that period, the nations of Europe, seething with "yellow and cutting" feelings against Germany, had disguised these feelings under the masks of business interests and international courtesy. For Scheler, the horrifying hatred of Germany bursting forth at the opening of the

War has served as a "thunderstorm of the moral world," "purifying the air" from the venom built up during peacetime.[2]

Scheler's mention of the masks of "business interests" and "propriety" refers principally to England, Germany's chief antagonist during the peaceful era prior to the War. England, the motherland of modern high capitalism, has subordinated spiritual and life values to use values and technology particularly in its limitless industrialism, which has devastated its countryside and its people. Such practices find their theoretical expression in the Darwinian-Spencerian concept of life: all development is an epiphenomenon of individuals struggling for survival in a anarchic setting. Similarly, political "liberalism," from Locke onward, has insisted on the contractual origin of the state and the doctrine of the divinely willed "natural harmony of interests" latent in the midst of the most selfish of pursuits. It has denied any central controlling agency over the elementary unities composing the world, the soul, or the state. England has approached other nations with its use values as its first priority, disregarding their cultural differences for the sake of its profit. Instead it has propounded a mechanistic "balance of power" politics for the preservation of peace (and profits) instead of pursuing bonds of authentic solidarity. The English army is nothing but a mechanized tool of the government for colonial acquisition interests, the mere "trailblazer of the merchant *(der blösse Schrittmacher des Kaufmanns)*." Since the War poses such peril to profits, the English can only consider it irrational and seek its quick resolution through a deftly designed treaty.[3]

Because Germany's cultural traits reflect more a *Gemeinschaft* than a *Gesellschaft*, it devotes itself to the principle of the universalism of life that transcends individualism. Germany embodies this principle in the will to life of the state that persists beyond the timely interests of generations, manifests itself identically in all individuals, transcends private interests and tendencies, and shows its vitality in a willingness to go to war. The state that has ceased to grow and that focuses only on its own "survival" effectively commences to die, succumbs to paralysis, and forfeits its own essence—it is a state in decline. "War, though, that is the state in its most actual growing and becoming itself. It is politics *katexochen* . . . ."[4] Furthermore, the German army is not a tool, but an expression of the ethos of a people that values bravery over pleasure and utility, honor and fame over life, strength over advantage, and the affairs of the state over the individual comfort. Such a militarism of conviction *(Gesinnungsmilitarismus)* differs from a militarism of purpose *(Zweckmilitarismus)* that utilizes its army as instrument to achieve the greedy goals of a nonmilitary class, as in England. The former militarism is more compatible with peace than the latter. The readiness of Germany to sacrifice its most loved and talented youth symbolizes the rich, high life of its people *(Volkes)*; and the contrary tendency, to preserve the most talented, signifies a biological decline.[5]

In what is obviously a piece of war propaganda, Scheler expands Nietzsche's criticisms of utilitarianism, prominent in the first essay of *On the Genealogy of Morals*, into a full-blown attack on English culture. In this assault, Germany represents noble morality and England a more conniving slave morality. Furthermore, Scheler enlists his own a priori ranking of values, articulated in lectures before the outbreak of war, for the German cause by portraying England as focused on the lower use values, while Germany aims at the higher values of life. Scheler's war writings seem to prove Nietzsche's point, namely, that the will to power can press any ethical principles, even those of a material value-ethic, into its service.[6]

In spite of Scheler's efforts at self-legitimation within this obviously propagandistic work, sometimes he still heeds the demand for truth. Scheler recommends humble readiness for submission to God's final verdict on the outcome of the War, coupled with trust in one's own rightness. In addition, Scheler rejects any conscious or unconscious appropriation of God for one's own side since the one God would then dissolve into a plurality of gods. In all German talk of "our old Prussian God," the "our" is not the "our" of the universal "Our Father." One should drop all talk of a German God and avoid concealing one's own self-interest by feigning service to a wholly universal and authentically monotheistic God, as Scheler saw the English doing. Scheler's insistence on obedience before an independent God, who is not the product of wishes and interests, but who can place them in question, reflects his basic critique of ethical nominalism and the mechanistic *Weltanschauung*. Further, he displays certain nonpropagandist openness when, like Nietzsche, he urges a personal reverence and affirmation of one's opponent in war; hatred for the enemy should be out of the question. He even willingly admits the weaknesses of dutiful, simple, punctual, and well-organized Prussianism, which has evoked such aversion throughout Europe against Germany.[7]

In spite of these scattered self-critical comments, Scheler devotes his ingenuity principally to attack England. In addition to castigating the English value scheme, Scheler's tirade attributes to the English a deep, organic untruthfulness that explains why they conceal their misdeeds even from themselves and why no one should trust their self-justifications at face value. Because of their "cant," the English disguise their hatred as "love for the weak," whom England has received a "divine mission" to defend. England teaches other cultures to "free" themselves from cultural eccentricities so that the English can secretly exploit their economic energies. English "freedom of speech" appears magnanimous by allowing one to say what one wishes, but it conceals that mistrust of the Other and that lack of responsibility for the Other so typical of English liberalism and contract theory. Scheler unearths how this "cant" appears analogously in the structural domains of philosophy, literature, religion, history, economics, and sexual activity.[8]

In "Die Ursachen des Deutschenhasses" (1916), Scheler's biased, polemical reconstruction of the English construction of the world destroys the very possibility of dialogue between cultures. Scheler recalls that the Germans found their chancellor's admission that the German invasion had breached Belgian neutrality an act of "noble, free honesty." The Anglo-American world, however, interpreted differently this same action in the familiar judgment, "Not only did the Germans invade Belgium contrary to all right, no, they even have the shameless cynicism to say that they did so and admit it." Scheler then wonders how the Germans would have reacted if England would have invaded Belgium and if Lord Grey, instead of admitting it, would have juridically justified the invasion by utilizing the English legal tradition to deny that any such violation of a people's right had even occurred. Scheler speculates that the Germans would have negatively responded, "See their hypocrisy and cant."[9]

In this partially imagined complex interchange, which Charles Cooley would term an example of the "looking-glass effect," a German philosopher interprets the English interpretation of the Germans' interpretation of the action of their chancellor. Clearly Scheler, relying on his earlier characterization of English cant, believes that the English twisted the chancellor's forthrightness (the German interpretation of his action, of course) into "shameless cynicism." The English behave this way since forthrightness is so foreign and threatening to the English soul.

Moreover, if the English had invaded Belgium, their cant would never have allowed them to admit any wrongdoing. On the contrary, they would have presented themselves as justified, thereby lowering ideals to conform with their reality. In this example, Scheler, following the pattern of Nietzsche, not only imputes the worst motives to the English. But also, via his notion of cant, he discredits their self-justifications as nothing but deceptions unconsciously welling up from the organic untruthfulness endemic to English culture and, thus, deserving no acceptance from outside parties. In this war polemic, Scheler models an interpretive procedure wherein one ought to mistrust the Other's interpretation of oneself and even the Other's self-interpretation. One ought to deconstruct and reinterpret any interpretation by the Other on one's own terms instead of the Other's. If such a procedure were to become normative, though, would one not be back at the point where each person and each culture remains encapsulated within its own viewpoints, which are necessarily imposed on each other? Further, if there is no fellow feeling and love beyond one's projections onto the Other, what possibility would there be of coming to mutual recognition of an objective world or an a priori ranking of values either? Scheler's wielding of the categories of the sociology of knowledge (e.g., structural analogies) and Nietzschean suspicion in his diatribe against England run counter to some of the most basic discoveries of his phenomenological method. In the war writings, the nadir of dialogic possibilities is reached, whose apex appears in Scheler's critique of Wundt in the *Formalism* or in his suggested Asian-European dialogue in the sociology of knowledge. Of course, one ought never to forget that this hermetic self-enclosure of perspectives, which marks Scheler's war polemics,coincides with one of the bloodiest wars the human race has known. If each one, as persons and cultures, is irremediably confined within his own viewpoint, then perhaps violence is inevitable and reason serves only as violence's handmaiden.[10]

## Scheler and Mannheim

Scheler's writings on the War make palpable the challenge that cultural determinism poses for the objective character of being, values, and the Other in Scheler's phenomenological perspective. Karl Mannheim thought that Scheler's eidetic system could not survive this challenge, especially as articulated by the sociology of knowledge, even though Scheler had also incorporated related Nietzschean sociological analyses. Mannheim, in his 1925 essay, "Das Problem einer Soziologie des Wissens," discusses recent interest in the sociology of knowledge and criticizes positivist and neo-Kantian approaches to the sociology of knowledge. These discussions preface the decisive debate he constructs between phenomenology, especially Scheler's, and historicism, which Mannheim himself espouses.[11]

Mannheim's critique of Scheler begins with the question of how Scheler can proceed historically in factual investigations and statically in his doctrine of esences. Mannheim, however, seems to imply mistakenly that essential investigation pertains to some other world, and he fails to grasp the subtle connections between essence and factual experience, which Husserl himself explained. Further, Mannheim opposes Scheler's separation of *Realfaktoren* from *Idealfaktoren*, conceived by Mannheim along the lines of Marx's substructure/superstructure distinction. According to Mannheim, the substructure already involves mental interaction between agents, which, in turn, shapes the spiritual activity to be found in the superstructure. Because, however, Scheler includes among his *Realfaktoren* blood relations, politics, and the economy, it seems unlikely that he would disagree with Mannheim on this point.[12]

Mannheim raises a more germane objection against Scheler's positing of a spiritual domain that contains its own immanent logic of meaning, from which the real, historical factors select. In Mannheim's opinion, Scheler can think that ideal processes unfold according to a dynamic of their own, independent of real factors, only because he considers their unfolding *after they are completed*. This reflection after the fact leads Scheler to the impression that something preexistent, resting fully in itself, has realized itself in the development of an idea. For Mannheim, one needs to consider the becoming of ideas themselves and particularly their functional relationships to concrete occurrences and their existential roots. If one does this, one cannot maintain the presupposition of preexistent world of ideas. Mannheim instead affirms the correctness of the materialistic conception of history, "according to which the being, the reality, creates the idea content *(das Sein, die Realität den Ideengehalt schafft),*" as long as one does not hypostatize being as matter.[13]

Since Scheler seems to dissociate being and truth and to neglect how being *creates* idea-contents, a major inconsistency appears in Scheler's theory:

> All concrete norm-orderings are characterized by Scheler as histori-
> cally and socially determined [*determiniert*], and also the human being

at any time is grasped as standing in history. But all this takes place only insofar as we are not treating the apprehension of those essence-unities whose adequate realization is the mission of humanity. As soon as these are treated, the historical human being becomes suddenly a conqueror of temporality and seems possessed of the superhuman capacity of shaking off all historical bondedness.[14]

From Mannheim's view, Scheler must presuppose that he himself has the superhuman capacity to grasp all those essences that others have not seen fully because of their cultural-historical limitations. If the philospher's intuition of essence can effectively transcend the temporal flux, then why is history necessary at all? Why should there be any cooperation between diverse peoples if Scheler himself already sees what they are mutually struggling to find? Scheler' static conception of eternity with its essences and the foreign standpoint of historicism that he has imported into his phenomenology tear his system apart. Because of his incorporation of the historical, Scheler should have given up the pretense to have grasped essences. That he claims to have discovered temporally transcendent essences for which the rest of humanity is still searching in solidarity smacks of cultural arrogance. His conclusions, no less than those of anyone else, are the products and projections of their existential background.[15]

Mannheim, as a historicist, opts for an in-itself of the historical object whose essence is such that one can grasp it only in its aspects, from different historical spiritual standpoints. One can justify such a "thing in itself" since, whether one speaks of factual being or the essence of a historical epoch, one experiences something given that prohibits arbitrary pronouncements, even though this "in-itself" cannot be comprehended from any one perspective. Thus, the stubbornness (*Massivität*) of facts resists being interpreted away. On the other hand, though, these facts cannot be given independently of some system of meaning, as positivism mistakenly supposed. Positivism also failed to make explicit its own interpretive system, including its own own metaphysics and epistemology—something that Scheler at least admitted, in Mannheim's assessment.[16]

Mannheim issues his final verdict on Scheler's approach to the sociology of knowledge:

If one will see the process [of knowledge] to be radically dynamic, the only solution remaining is to hold that one's own standpoint is relative, but constituting itself in the element of the truth. And to express the difference between Scheler and our solution in contrast, we can say that while we presuppose that God's eye rests on the process (that also the process is not meaningless), Scheler must presuppose that he sees the world with God's own eye.[17]

If Mannheim is right, then Scheler really has not broken through to an objective, independent realm of essences and values. He remains ensconced in his own historical cultural viewpoint as were Germany and England, misinterpreting each other during the War. While Mannheim might seek "objectivity" through an overlapping of perspectives, Scheler's supposed essences exaggerate how much one can escape one's background and self.

A reconstruction of Scheler's response must begin with Mannheim's opposition to a spiritual domain with its own immanent logic of meaning. One cannot deny that Scheler admits such a domain since he describes the task of sociology as determining what in a sociologically conditioned appearance is conditioned by the "autonomous self-unfolding of Geist" and what is conditioned through real factors. Preliminary examples of this "autonomous self-unfolding," however, show links to real factors. Scheler points out how Raphael needed politically and socially powerful patrons so that his genius could come to expression. Similarly, Luther's ideas on faith and the internal spirit could not have spread without the backing of politically interested princes and the rising bourgeois. In these examples, which do not seem out of the ordinary, real factors serve the function of furthering, propagating, or distributing the creative cultural products of individuals. Immediately after these examples, Scheler proceeds to oppose any theory, such as Hegel's, that would claim that the course of cultural history is a purely spiritual and logically meaningful process. So far, Mannheim's reference to "something preexisting, resting fully in itself" and realizing itself in the development of ideas seems to target Hegel's thought more than Scheler's.[18] Scheler explicitly rejects any understanding of ideal factors in terms of the unraveling of a Hegelian absolute spirit. Rather, such factors consist of more than simply the cultural achievements of individuals, which real factors support and spread. Scheler argues that between ideal factors there are essential, and not accidental, interdependencies in their being and becoming, however difficult these essential links may be to discover. As instances, he refers to developments between religion, metaphysics, and science; between Levy-Bruhl's "primitive" mentality and that of civilization; and between organological worldviews and mechanistic ones.[19]

It is appropriate to focus on Scheler's own analysis of the connections among religion, metaphysics, and science since these form the anchor of his sociology of knowledge. These three types of knowledge differentiate themselves from each other in a necessary sequence. Religion, while not being a primitive form of metaphysics or science, nevertheless *always* already fills the spirit of a person or group when metaphysics or science comes on the scene. Similarly, natural philosophy—and presumably metaphysics—precede the science of nature as the "mother-lye the crystal," and the greatest philosophy has always been not merely the "owl of Minerva," but a pioneer of science. In addition, cultures such as Egypt or China failed to develop a methodological, cooperatively organized, specialized positive science because they lacked the basic forerunner of science: free *philosophical* speculation. Scheler, as we have seen, denies Comte's assessment that the three types of knowledge develop progressively, with religion and metaphysics gradually falling by the wayside. Instead, their gradual, historical unfolding has culminated in the disclosure of three essential, lasting, spiritual attitudes and knowledge forms, which the human spirit in equilibrium will, of its essence, possess. According to Scheler, there are three different motives, three different categories of acts of the knowing spirit, three different aims, three different personality types carrying on these enterprises, and three different social groups linked to them. Such essential interconnections depend, of course, on the same possibility of insight into essence that underlies Scheler's essential rank ordering of values, grasped or neglected as they are in various cultures, depending on whatever real factors predominate.[20]

Mannheim contends that Scheler only establishes this unfolding *ex post facto* and then declares the process to be essential to dynamic ideal factors, unfolding independently of real factors. In order to uphold this charge, though, Mannheim must assume that mere empirical events, including real factors, have produced only contingently connected systems of ideas and that Scheler has artificially elevated these ideas into "the structure of an immanent system of meaning resting only on itself." But could not one say, in reply, that, within the historical processes—including the real factors affecting ideation—Scheler could have detected an *essential* pattern of development of three *essential* knowing forms that *essentially* belong to the human spirit? The empirical, historical events, including the web of determining real factors, need not led *only* to contingent historical generalizations, which could have turned out otherwise. They can also provide the occasion for essential (i.e., nonrevisable, incapable of being otherwise) interconnections to emerge and be captured by insight. After all, in Husserl's phenomenology, most essences emerge from empirical, historical data. Mannheim's critique would only undermine the possibility of essences and essential connections if one presupposes from the start that there are (essentially!) no essential interconnections and essences. Scheler's position on ideal factors in opposition to Mannheim's stands or falls on whether an intuition of essence is possible or not.

Because such essential connections between ideal unities can be traced, one can see how real factors eliminate, interrupt, bypass, encourage, or expand them. Furthermore, Scheler utilizes these essential interconnections, not as a means of isolating ideal from real factors, but rather as a means of identifying precisely where real factors engage *(eingreifen)* ideal factors. Having a set of essential interconnections between ideal factors (e.g., between religion, metaphysics, and science) provides the condition of the possibility of recognizing the efficacy of real factors. Hence, Scheler criticizes the Western *Weltanschauung* for its suppression of metaphysics (an ideal factor) and its consequent distortion of the balance of knowledge forms pertaining to the human essence. In both cases, he finds symptoms of the predominance of real economic factors in the West, closing the sluice gate on certain ideal factors.[21]

Mannheim's own idea of a really existent *Ding-an-sich* placing critical controls on diverse perspectives, which never exhaust it, involves an *essential* characterization of knowledge and interpretation. Historicism thrive on just such a typically unacknowledged essential presupposition, which itself seems to transcend history.

Scheler, though, seems willing to posit a larger domain of essences than Mannheim, as Scheler's three essential knowledge forms and his a priori ranking of values suggest. But again these essences and essential value rankings remain a priori and can be filled out and realized or violated in a variety of striking ways, as an example from the domain of value theory can elucidate. The Aztec human sacrifices, for example, understood not as murder but as a valuing of spiritual and religious values over life values, could have been highly instructive for the Spanish *conquistadores*, often intent on sacrificing personal values for use values. Scheler's essential value ranking, as this instance suggests, serves as an interpretive tool for recognizing *how* cultures have realized values in original ways or *how* they have distorted them. Recognizing and appreciating these values and their interrelationships calls for continual cooperation and criticism among the diverse peoples that embody these values. Ethical insight and development do not stop at discovering a priori essential ranking of values, but begin there. Moreover, it is possible for one to lay out a *theoretical* ranking of values and yet need constant reminding, renewing, and illuminating regarding these very values through encounters with their diverse value-bearers. The firmament of values that Scheler lays bare does not raise him above others, exempting him from the cooperative search for ethical insight, but in fact it exacts a more vigilant participation. By erroneously interpreting essences as completely filled with content, such that whoever knows them would require no further ethical insight, Mannheim overlooks the dynamic, heuristic function that essences serve within Scheler's framework.[22]

Mannheim's barren *Ding-an-sich*, lending itself to various interpretations, reflects the typical modern Western tendency to evacuate the world of meaning in order to allow humanity to project its own interpretations and meanings upon it. Mannheim, in turn, could counter that his *Ding-an-sich* does function as a critical control on interpretations. But, if so, one must, at least implicitly, be grasping some essential content whereby one can judge certain interpretations as falling short. Mannheim himself seems to admit, for example, an essence of Hellenism whereby one is able to pronounce faulty descriptions of Hellenism as one-sided. If the *Ding-an-sich* serves as a critical control, it must be other than an empty *Ding-an-sich*.[23]

Finally, Scheler would have to take issue with Mannheim's notion that reality creates the idea-content, that real factors cause ideal factors, instead of determining only which ideal factors are noticed. After all, in Mannheim's view, real factors would equally cause both the correct and incorrect apprehension of the essence of Hellenism since both descriptions of Hellenism consist of idea-contents. Even though both descriptions are alike in being caused by real factors, Mannheim insists that one can distinguish their differences and decide which description approaches the essence of Hellenism grasped as a critical standard. Making such an evaluation presupposes an appeal to an eidetic intuition whereby one distinguishes a correct from an incorrect essence. Simply pointing out that both descriptions spring from differing causal factors seems hardly sufficient to convince anyone that one apprehension is superior to the other.

Scheler, in contrast to Mannheim, places the sociology of knowledge within the context of phenomenology. Phenomenology, beginning with the disciplined implementation of reduction, focuses on the contents given to consciousness, without questioning their causal origin. The phenomenologist then unveils essential structures through eidetic variation on the basis of these contents (for Husserl) or directly through the reduction itself (for Scheler, as shall be seen). While the sciences and natural attitude take for granted these essential features of the world, of the human spirit, and of valuation, phenomenology elucidates them as preceding and founding these other domains of knowledge, including the sociology of knowledge. When one approaches the sociology of knowledge from such a phenomenologically established framework, one will not understand real factors as *causing* the ideal comprehension of these structures of the world, value, or the human spirit that phenomenology has already clarified. Rather, real factors will determine what aspects of those structures any particular culture or person attends to or embodies. Both Mannheim and Scheler would admit that socio-cultural influences affect knowledge, but they differ on whether real factors cause *the ideal factors themselves* or whether they cause *the selection of ideal factors from a constellation which exists independently of those real factors*. Scheler, in effect, is propounding phenomenology as an alternative to a causal, mechanistic foundation for the sociology of knowledge.

This mechanistic approach, by interpreting ideal factors as the causal products of real factors, would relativize any notion of an objective world, any objective scheme of values, and any objective claims about intersubjective *Verstehen*. What one thinks to be objective would depend on the different causal forces to which one has been exposed. All viewpoints would be equally right and wrong insofar as real factors (albeit diverse ones) cause them all equally. But, then, on what basis could one raise questions about the adequacy of this causal/mechanistic scheme itself? In addition, this causal/mechanistic account would all but abolish any prospects of dialogue wherein one could learn from the superior viewpoint of another. Phenomenology, by undergirding a sociology of knowledge critical of mechanistic presuppositions, fittingly acts as the guardian of dialogue.

## The Phenomenological Reduction

Scheler's fullest answer to Mannheim's question of how the philosopher escapes cultural relativism lies in his treatment of phenomenological reduction, which itself presupposes earlier discussions on the attitude proper to philosophy. In his essay "Vom Wesen der Philosophie (1917)," Scheler refers to a fundamental spiritual attitude (*geistigen Grundhaltung*) whereby one can identify the true philosopher, even as the true artist or true religious genius posesses his or her own unique stance toward the world. In his later works, Scheler continues speaking of a human mode of living (*menschliche Lebensart*) that metaphysics presupposes. The Greeks were well aware that, in order to apprehend being correctly, philosophers required a definite propensity pervading their whole personality and lacking to what Husserl would later call the person of the natural attitude.

> This propensity—which we will here investigate more exactly—was for the ancients first of all a moral propensity, but not therefore of a onesided, will-directed nature. It appeared to them as a propensity wherein no positively grasped goal was to be reached or so-called practical "end" was to be actualized. Rather through this propensity, one was supposed to set aside that restriction of spirit that lies essentially in the stance of every natural worldview. This narrowness of spirit inhibits the spirit from coming into possible contact with that realm of particular being that is the being seen by philosophy. Through this propensity, a barrier belonging constitutively to the natural attitude should have been exploded, a veil concealing that being should have been stripped from the eyes of the spirit.[24]

Just as the Greeks held that one must learn in a more or less blindly obedient way to act and will in an objectively good manner before one would ever be able to see the Good as good or to realize it insightfully, so they required a distinct attitude for theorizing also. For Plato, this disposition of philosophy consisted in love for the essential, the purest and highest form of eros. Scheler, too, describes this attitude as a love-defined propensity at the heart of the finite human person to partake in the essence of all possible things.[25]

This idea of a philosophical bearing, which affords some hope of overcoming cultural blindness, was not something that Scheler simply tacked onto his overall philosophy to respond to criticisms such as Mannheim's. Just as Scheler sought to incorporate affective capacities in the perception of objects and values, so he believed that the whole human being must be fully engaged, with the concentrated entirety of its highest spiritual powers, in order to philosophize authentically. Furthermore, Scheler's concerns mirror those of phenomenology in general, which always considers objects in correlation with the acts of consciousness whereby objects appear.[26]

Scheler regards love as the foundational activity pervading this philosophical posture. Love and hate, the most original, comprehensive, and foundational acts among all emotional acts, constitute the common root of practical and theoretical behavior. Through these grounding acts alone, one's theoretical and practical lives find and preserve their ultimate unity. In "Liebe und Erkenntnis," Scheler observes that the Greeks understood cognition as love for a positive being and a positive value, namely a certain fullness of being—an attitude quite different from the Buddhist turning away from positive being. In Scheler's view, and contrary to Plato's, love involves no striving, but rather rests in the being and structure of an object, never demands that the object be otherwise than it is, and grows deeper the more it penetrates an object. Far from distorting one's view, love augments the intuitive fullness and meaningfulness of the world. A person's own worldview widens and deepens, the more widely and deeply he loves. In fact, following Augustine, Scheler even argues that one cannot attribute the growing fullness of an object in the presence of love only to the activity of the knowing, loving subject, since whatever is loved responds to love by giving itself, opening itself, and revealing itself. The authentic phenomenologist turns toward being like a lover toward a friend.[27]

This loving philosophical attitude contrasts with those of the person of the natural attitude and the scientist. When accompanied by the moral acts of humility and self-control, love frees one from the natural egocentric, vitalistic, and anthropomorphizing tendencies marking the natural attitude. Like philosophy, science escapes the natural attitude with its individual, popular, and racial relativities. Philosophers, however, in contrast to scientists, must set aside their willing and surrender (hingeben) to the pure what of their object. Philosophy sets aside precisely those motives and attitudes that stamp the modern Western Weltanschauung and its science, namely, a practical interest in controlling the self and the world. Philosophy brackets such concerns in the hope of bringing to light those essential structures and values that can found a critique of Western modernity and every onesided Weltanschauung.[28]

Before elaborating this attitude requisite for philosophizing in terms of phenomenological reduction, the later Scheler adopts his usual strategy of situating all reflection in its metaphysical context.[29] According to Scheler, a person at first ecstatically immerses herself in the world, like plants or animals, until she suffers a resistance experience of reality, which forces her to bend back (reflect) upon herself. Reflection and consciousness thus take shape from the experience of reality; they are not its ground. Even in daily life, one is generally an extrovert, grasping and observing physical reality first and foremost, and, only when he finds himself disturbed by it or struggling with it or when constraints impede his elaboration and forming of it, does one refocus upon psychic facts. Neither consciousness of one's drives nor consciousness of curbed impulses leads to the experienced resistance. Rather, the ecstatically experienced resistance elicits an act of reflection through which one becomes conscious of the drive impulse itself. Consciousness comes into being as the result of one's suffering the resistance of the world. For Scheler, as for Merleau-Ponty, people are through and through compounded of relations to this world, especially at the level of drives and desires, long before they reflect upon it or refuse it their complicity in phenomenological reduction.[30]

While Scheler lauds Husserl's discovery of the technique of reduction, Husserl's unawareness of our prior, drive-laden engagement with reality prevented him from clarifying the reduction sufficiently. Husserl's "holding back" (Zurückhaltung) of the positing of being implicit in the natural attitude cannot mean simply the withholding of the judgment of being, since any child could then perform the reduction. Moreover, Scheler wonders how the mere withholding of existential judgment would open up that new object world, unseen in the natural attitude, which Husserl so often mentions. For Scheler, judgment takes place at a higher level than one's primordial encounter with reality and its objects. Indeed, people do not even grasp objects as objects or form judgments until reality shocks their ecstatic outreach and leads them to pull back and reflect. The much more difficult task, calling for the rigor Husserl seemed to associate with the reduction, involves setting aside the reality-moment itself by setting out of power the unintentional, prejudgmental functions that yield this moment.[31]

The functions one brackets in phenomenological reduction include willing, all active attending to scientific realities, and the drive directed life-force (and passive attending) that pertains to the natural attitude. For the sake of the pure spiritual action required to grasp essences, one must also set out of play the body and the forms of apprehension defined by the vital ego. One liberates spiritual acts from all service to goals, tasks, and needs of the vital ego. One refrains from the blind impulse to sustain one's culture in its struggle for survival and superiority via the mechanisms of cultural conventions and prejudices. As a result, one centers the ego of one's spiritual person similarly to how one objectifies the body, along with its vital being, and takes control over it. Reduction does not imply the negation of reality, nor the tearing of the person substantially from the body, although it can entail loosing oneself from the functional binding of the person to the body. By restraining willful life-urges, reduction allows being to reveal itself. As such, the technique of reduction brings to fulfillment that loving surrender to being so typical of authentic philosophizing and so foreign to the natural attitude and science. One must read Scheler's later account of reduction in the light of his earlier discussion of the genuine philosophical bearing in "Vom Wesen der Philosophie."[32]

Scheler's extensive attention to the philosophical attitude and the phenomenological reduction reflects his awareness of Nietzsche's challenge. Scheler pays special heed to the will to control, which characterizes any natural attitude, but which the Western *Weltanschauung* and its scientific proclivities particularly reinforce. The will to control stands as the central enemy to that loving surrender that alone can bring to light those essential features that the will to control itself distorts even as it conceals its own distorting. In response to Nietzsche, who acknowledged only life functions, Scheler upholds the functions of spirit, independent of and transcending the functions of life. Only spirit can relinquish the need to control and achieve authenticity. It alone can implement the technique of reduction, rein in life functions, and surrender in love. It would seem that the disciplined passivity of phenomenological reduction would constitute Scheler's final response to Mannheim's charge that the will to cultural power rules out eidetic attainments.

Moreover, Scheler's theory of reduction exhibits a keen awareness of distortions of knowledge entering even at the level of one's precognitive encounter with reality. Because Husserl's interpretation of reduction confined itself to the cognitive level of merely withholding an existential judgment, Scheler revised the practice of reduction in a more rigorous direction. On the one hand, Scheler certainly insisted that phenomenology alone could provide a foundation for the sociology of knowledge without giving away the possibility of validity claims. On the other hand, his treatment of reality and reduction indicate his sensitivity to social determinisms and the potentiality for self-deception and culturewide illusion at the level of the most primitive interface with reality. Scheler's reinterpretation of phenomenological reduction shows that, while phenomenology had much to teach sociology of knowledge, it also had much to learn from it.

## Sociologism and Dialogue

Sociologism holds that, since all knowledge is socially caused, one cannot arrive at truths that transcend the culture wherein they are discovered. Sociologism clearly would jeopardize the possibility of an intercultural dialogue wherein one culture would learn from another's truths. By extending Scheler's own thought, four negative criticisms of a sociologistic stance can be elaborated. However, these criticisms do not depend on Scheler's ontology or his ethics. Hence alternative philosophical positions favoring objective standards of truth and rightness could find these criticisms congenial.

First, the very recognition of socio-cultural one-sidedness presupposes a transcendence of that socio-cultural one-sidedness. After criticizing critical realism in "Idealismus-Realismus," Scheler concurs with P. Linke who argues that the experience of deception regarding a thing does not exclude cognitional insight, but, on the contrary, presupposes an insight into the nature of the thing. According to Scheler, phenomenology shows that, in every discovery of deception, one experiences the "supposed" nature of the thing being "demoted" to the status of a mere image. At the same time, the true nature of the thing *now, after* the "un-deception" *(Ent-täuschung)*, takes that demoted image's place. Scheler sums up this hidden presence of truth in the midst of deception with regard to phenomenological evidence: "Naturally there is such a thing as evidence deception; but only in de-deception *(Ent-täuschung)* is the deception itself apprehensible."[33]

This discussion is relevant to sociologism. Socio-cultural blinders do hinder insight into being or values, but how can one recognize that another's outlook falls short of an insight unless one already has the insight the Other lacks? Mannheim admitted as much when he acknowledged an essence of Hellenism whereby one can criticize one-sided notions of Hellenism. A complete sociologism, though, would cancel any possibility of criticism since, at the most, all that could be claimed would be that one view differed from another, not that one view understood being or value better than another.

Second, sociologism confuses the temporal frameworks of va-
lidity-claims. Scheler's suggests this criticism in "Das Nationale
im Denken Frankreiches":

Those investigators who articulate a thought or write a sentence because they hold it as corresponding to the spirit of their nation or
serviceable for their nation bypass the highest principle of all science:
to will to serve the *truth* and it alone. However, investigators can
legitimately depend upon the spirit of their nation, but only if this
dependence shows up after the fact (for a critic coming on the scene
later). This dependence appears after those investigators, in a pure
sense only, have given an open and free hearing to the facts and
conclusions that investigators of other cultures have found regarding
the problem occupying them. This is the only kind of deep and valuable dependence upon the national spirit that Goethe had in mind.
The national in its spiritual type should move the spirit of the investigators as if from behind—it is not permitted to draw them forward
as a goal or purpose. . . . It is the greatest self-deception when people
believe that they are working in the deepest spirit of their nation by
allowing themselves to be determined by what they think their national spirit requires instead of by being determined by the force of
the things [being considered]. On the contrary, such nationalists are
heading in a direction wherein a nationality destroys its own unre-
peatable type and becomes nothing more than an international cliché.
This is the case today among those nationalists who in every nation
utilize more or less the same [nationalist] phrases and so increase
the amount of conformism in the world. On the other side, only the
strongest holding back from that reflexive national motive guarantees
that the *authentic national* spirit will unveil itself and achieve expression in its full particularity. Truthfully, that nation gains its own depth
when it is willing to lose itself. Such a nation thinks not of itself,
but of the things alone [which it investigates]. A conscious national
philosophy would be a non-thing.[34]

The temporal sequences here are important: in the authentic
search for truth, the things themselves pull one forward. Only
subsequently, "for a critic coming on the scene later," (*für den
nachkommenden Betrachter)* can one unearth the national, sociological roots of a thought.

Scheler has correctly understood the difference between the
truth claimant's future orientation in intending to make and uphold a validity claim and the past orientation of a subsequent,
retrospective investigation of the sociol-historical factors (e.g.,
one's nation) influencing that claim. Alfred Schutz speaks of the
"in-order-to" motives of an action, the purpose in the mind of

the actor, and the because motives, those past occurrences and environmental factors events lying before the just completed action (in the pluperfect tense). The difference between these two temporal orientations shows up when someone submits a claim to another and supports it with evidence, anticipating that it will be dealt with in terms of its own validity or invalidity. The claimant would be utterly shocked to find a respondent exploring background events in the claimant's life that might "explain" the because motives for the claim. Thus, the woman who argues that abortion should be legally permissible would feel dismay if her dialogue partner responded to this claim by tabulating the courses in women's studies this woman took in her past and by stating that these historical data "explain" her claim. Because a respondent can approach the same claim in terms of the in-order-to motive in the mind of the claimant or in terms of the because motive influencing (but not causing) that claimant, sociologism has mistakenly concluded that because motive analyses could undermine the validity of claims. These two approaches simply occur on irreducible planes. The proper distinctions to ward off such sociologistic reductionism and to keep open the possibility of dialogue, though, are already implicit in Scheler's perceptive discussion here.[35]

Third, sociologism resembles pathological indecisiveness. The ubiquity of hidden socio-cultural determinants easily leads to widespread scepticism about the possibility of making any valid claims. The anticipation that social determinants will undermine any validity claim results in a loss of philosophical nerve wherein one no longer even dares to venture a claim. Scheler lays the groundwork for a response to this view in "Die Idole der Selbersterkenntnis." In that work, Scheler describes certain pathological tendencies to concentrate one's attention on oneself or one's body at the expense of the world beyond. Hence, instead of trafficking directly with the world, sick individuals reduce their entire environment to a sum of stimulants for their feelings, especially their sensible bodily feelings. In the sphere of willing, normal willing focuses on a goal to which subactions are subordinate, pursues that goal ecstatically, until resistances are encountered, and then, as a first tendency, assigns the ground of resistance to the outer world. In pathological willing, though, the acts that are means to the end become the focus, and "hesitation" or pathological indecisiveness occurs. Stuttering persons, for instance, reflect so much on what they are now saying and its correctness that they cannot easily articulate a coherent thought. Similarly, mentally ill persons can become so preoccupied with walking to the door, grabbing the door handle, and turning it that they never take the first step.[36] Scheler summarizes:

> There follows then a pathological pressing forward of the question "can I?" before the question of "do I will it?" or "should I?" And from this results pathological indecisiveness.[37]

Those who deny the possibility of valid claims from the start because of the inescapability of sociological conditioning seem to have fallen into this type of pathology. To raise validity claims even in the face of the recognition of sociological determinisms is to focus ecstatically on the goal, the truth to be sought, without heeding the pitfalls. One remains so focused unless resistance is encountered in the form of counterevidence or better arguments pointing in the other direction. To risk making such a claim to truth is to shake off a form of sociological self-consciousness that is as crippling as the self-conscious pursuit of pleasure is for pleasure, or as self-conscious moral activity is for authentical moral action. To venture a claim to truth is to imitate heroic greatness, to lose oneself in the search for truth without any reckoning about one's own safety. The daring truth claimant abides in that future orientation described above, without worrying about whatever because-motives will later be discovered to have been influential. Here there is no need for pathological indecisiveness. The question of "Can I do it?" does not rule out the effort to try. Without such daring, dialogue would cease.[38]

Fourth and finally, sociologistic reductionism is, ultimately, unduly narrowing. It effectively encloses each within his or her own culture and beyond that within his or her own personal history such that all anyone ever knows of truth, value, or the Other depends on what is projected into them—as one's own socio-historical background compels one to do. Sociologism deprives one of the hope of mutual enlightenment regarding the structure of being and value under which one stands with others. Once again the image recurs that a person is surrounded by being and values richer than he can ever comprehend by himself, and yet sociologism insists he can never grow in appreciation of such wealth because all one is able to find is what one's own paltry socio-cultural background has already taught one to see.[39]

# 6

# Rationality and Dialogic Ethics

Husserl's interests, as well as Scheler's, extended from the life-world—the lived layer of experience out of which all theorizing arises—to transcendental phenomenology's highest-level reflections on rationality. In order to bring out the strengths and weaknesses of Scheler's handling of the rationality problematic, his thought should be compared and contrasted with that of Jürgen Habermas. While Scheler seems to have anticipated several of Habermas's valid criticisms of Weberian and Kantian rationality, he failed to appreciate the positive role of rationality in ethics—principally due, perhaps, to his struggle against rationalism and the mechanistic worldview. Scheler, however, shows himself masterful in exploring the intuitive experiences of intersubjectivity that precede theoretical ethics and all other theory. His findings foreshadow the dialogic ethics of Habermas and Emmanuel Levinas. Nevertheless, a confrontation with Levinas's dialogic ethics will highlight revisions necessary for Scheler's ethical theory if it is to escape the mechanistic framework. With these improvements in Scheler's theory of rationality and ethics, his phenomenology could better protect intercultural dialogue.

## Scheler and Habermas on Rationality

Habermas and Scheler both criticize Max Weber's account of rationality, which is symptomatic of Western modernity's predicament. For Scheler the modern Western *Weltanschauung* tends to evacuate this world of all objective values with the result that moral values become nothing more than subjective appearances in human consciousness. Weber, an articulate supporter of that *Weltanschauung*, affirmed the dichotomy between objective science and subjective values in spite of the regrettable modern disenchantment that resulted. In the value domain, with the demise of Christianity, old and new gods have arisen and entered into a competitive struggle, whose final outcome science cannot adjudicate.

Jürgen Habermas, however, dissents from Weber's opinion that a polytheism of gods and demons makes any rational redemption of objective, ethical claims impossible. For Habermas, Weber's own diagnosis of the times is symptomatic of a culture whose institutional embodiment of available cognitive potentials is unbalanced. The cognitive-instrumental rationality of science and technology has assumed dominance in the West, thereby largely overriding moral-practical rationality and aesthetic-practical rationality. To rectify this situation, Habermas rehabilitates these alternative modes of rationality. Similarly, Scheler's essential ranking of values and his theory of the tripartite structure of knowledge (science, metaphysics, religion) precede, situate, and limit the mechanistic exaltation of science. Striking similarities exist, however much Scheler and Habermas may otherwise disagree.[1]

Scheler's critique of Weberian ethics, instead of developing a strong notion of moral-practical rationality as does Habermas's, relies on his a priori value ranking. In Scheler's opinion, Weber represents a form of ethical nominalism wherein science provides valuefree objects to which one arbitrarily assigns values depending on the gods one serves. But science's insistence on the priority of valuefree objects ignores how scientific attitudes abstract from an already value-laden world. One does not begin with valuefree objects onto which he might project values at his subjective whim. Rather, a pregiven value order affectively engages one before he ever artifically withdraws from such "lived valuing" in order to grapple with that artificial "late arrival" on the human scene: the valuefree object.[2]

Scheler's own critique of Weber is concise:

> The essential point where we sharply separate ourself from Max Weber and Schumpeter is the following: Even science rests on a *metaphysics:* on the precritical metaphysics of the "natural attitude." Max Weber hands over those questions which exceed his scientific conception of the "technically important" to a fully, a-rational, individual option of will—and therefore to a mere struggle between parties and groups. It is his radical error that the material values have only subjective significance and that *there cannot be* any path of *binding knowledge of objective things and values,* of goods and systems of goods, beyond the positive sciences. In addition, there can be no "conviction" and spiritual fructification between representatives of different value-systems.[3]

As this text suggests, like every ethical nominalism, Weber's is antidialogic. Scheler rightly perceives how the subjectivization of values leads to merely strategic struggles between self-interested groups and parties, as Nietzsche and Hobbes believed. This reduction of the search for ethical consensus to turf battles between conflicting powers destroys the possibility of mutual cross-fertilization between dialogue partners bound to each other in solidarity. For Habermas too, an orientation to success, wherein cognitive-instrumental rationality usurps the place of communicative rationality, undermines an orientation toward reaching understanding. If Scheler has accurately diagnosed this deterioration of dialogue as a symptom of the mechanistic worldview and its self-encapsulating impetus for control, then only a willingness to relinquish control and to surrender in love can achieve the missing "decentration," also valued by Habermas and Piaget. Hence whether one is talking about carrying on a dialogue in solidarity, ethical acting, achieving a "national" culture, finding pleasure, or performing heroically—the best is done when one gives up all self-conscious efforts to manage outcomes and entrusts oneself in love to the activities, values, and dialogue partners at hand.[4]

Kant stands out as one of the few modern philosophers who recognized this need for decentration. His ethics attempted to prove that the Cartesian turn to the subject need not issue in subjectivism. On the contrary, for Kant, rational agency discovers itself bound by universal ethical norms emerging from its own very nature. These norms, formulated in the categorical imperative, demanded that agents think beyond their private desires and constrain their practical, instrumental behavior, governed as it is by hypothetical imperatives. Scheler repeatedly affirms such universal norms. Only after a person has satisfied these requirements binding all people, can she begin to comply with the individual ethical "demand of the hour." Scheler differs from Kant in that every ought—including universal ones—is founded in the a priori ranking of values he has uncovered.[5]

Scheler, however, thanks to Nietzsche's influence, understood how universal ethics can do the bidding of a covert will to power. In Scheler's view, Kant reduces the objective worth of the good to the mere generalizability of a maxim. Kant thereby neglects that those personal, individual demands, which apply at one moment in time to one individual and to no one else, are not merely "subjective," but are objective. According to Scheler, the tendency to seek social confirmation in one's actions is so prevalent that such Kantian universalism can be used to foster a certain conformism. Such conformism, although contrary to Kant's own emphasis on autonomy, tends to exempt individuals from responsibilities uniquely their own and to prevent the emergence of creative value contributions in human history. Scheler's a priori ranking of values calls for historically variable moral and cultural systems to appreciate and realize fully those values. Rationalistic ethics, by stressing ethical universalism, would more likely find such diversity relativistic and enemical to ethical objectivity. Scheler's value theory, prompting both his acceptance of ethical universals and his suspicion of their potential for tyrannic use, provides a corrective to any forced uniformity that would seem to bear the stamp of the mechanistic zeal to control. Habermas, too, recognizes these hazards and hence prefers a dialogic process of reaching universal norms to Kant's monological method.[6]

While Scheler defends a richer and more comprehensive theory of values than either Weber or Kant, he treats rationality more narrowly than Kant and Habermas, who consider both moral-practical and aesthetic-practical rationality in detail. In Scheler's opinion, ethics is the judgmental formulation of what is given in the sphere of moral cognition. This entire sphere of moral cognition, completely independent from the sphere of propositions and judgments, depends upon functions such as preferring or loving. Such functions differ *toto caelo* from thinking and supply the *only* access to values. When it comes to apprehending the ranking of values, no logical deduction can ever replace intuitive preference evidence. Scheler thus associates his ethics with G. E. Moore's emotional intuitionism.[7]

Scheler emphases on affective over rational sources of ethical judgments both defends affectivity against the mechanistic worldview's onslaught and counters rationalistic tendencies toward conformism and the suppression of individuals. But if mechanistic rationalism may be responsible for these errors, one need not impugn reason in general. Both Kant and Habermas, for instance, develop the distinctive domain of practical rationality, which can restrain and direct forms of scientific instrumental rationality. Scheler, in his *Formalism*, never seems to consider the distinctiveness of such practical rationality. Without hesitation, for instance, he immediately applies Husserl's eidetic method, originally a tool of speculative rationality, to the practical domain. In addition, Scheler grounds his ethical theory in affectivity largely in reaction against the mechanistic rationalism that reigned supreme among modern Western thinkers. Scheler's move here resembles that of the earlier Frankfurt school in Habermas's view. Horkheimer and Adorno did not look to reason to ground ethics because the only model of rationality available at that time was that of cognitive instrumental rationality. One can and should maintain the importance of refined moral intuitions prior to reasoning, as even Kant and Habermas do. One can utilize them as a source for grounding ethics and challenging mistaken theory, as Scheler does. But is it necessary *also* to deny that one can present rational justifications for behaviors also demanded by the intuitively grasped spiritual values of "justice" and "right"? Can one not justify the superiority of these values over others *also* through testing one's maxims for consistency against one's own rational self or against the norm of an ideal speech situation? Scheler's emphasis on the intuitions preceding theory resembles phenomenological investigations of the life-world that attempt to get at what preexists all theorizing. But Scheler neglects other Husserlian concerns, including the task of disclosing the foundations of theory in the sedimentations of everyday life. Because Scheler failed to appreciate a more complementary and less antithetical relationship between feeling and reason, intuition and theory, the mechanistic viewpoint still seems to hold him in its spell in spite of his resistance to it.[8]

## Intersubjective Ethics

If the nominalist ethics of the mechanistic worldview encourage self-encapsulation, the way to liberation lies as much in dialogue, particularly with Eastern culture, as in a system of a priori essences and value rankings. As noted earlier, Scheler's defense of the otherness of the Other in fellow feeling proceeds in tandem with his attempt to maintain objective values and an objectively structured world, which stand over against every selective culture pattern and illuminate its one-sidedness. Interpersonal and intercultural dialogue, with different persons and cultures embodying and bearing different values or the same values in different ways, decenters as much as the objective value schemes themselves do.

Scheler's propaganda attack on England during the First World War presents a counterexample to the type of dialogue he later urged between West and East in *Some Problems of a Sociology of Knowledge.* In that attack, Scheler deploys reason as a weapon, as literally an instrument of war, distorting the other party and sowing seeds of distrust so that the Other's defenses and self-justifications will be read as a covert strategy for domination. Scheler's deployment of his own value ranking as an armament, when he construes Germany as upholding life values against the British who represent lesser use values, does not per se disprove the value scheme. Rather, it suggests that the mere existence of objective values does not secure their implementation, as Scheler would have been the first to acknowledge. Such an implementation seems to require an open and unconstrained dialogue to uncover value distortions and mediate their application. But dialogue of itself cannot suffice since, even in dialogue, reason can degenerate into a mere instrument of power, as Nietzsche thought was always the case. Scheler's war writing masterfully wields Nietzschean method to interpret Britain, and, at the same time, Scheler's very arguments seem to substantiate the basic Nietzsche principle that all argumentation really serves power even as it pretends not to do so.

That one can recognize how distorted Scheler's understanding of Britain was shows that a standard of mutual understanding, which even the neurosis of war cannot abolish and which approaches Habermas's "ideal speech situation" exists. Scheler himself certainly hoped for undistorted communication between West and East. Indeed, the phenomenological method had convinced him that "Nothing is more certain that this, that we can think the thoughts of the Other as well as our own and feel her feelings as well as our own." The situation of communication is not such that one is confined within her interpretation of the Other and even her interpretations of the Other's interpretations of her. The Other need not always submit to categories one imposes, nor vice versa. However much war and violence may disfigure communication, phenomenology suggests that Nietzsche does not have the final word.

In fact, as this book has argued, Scheler's critique of the modern Western *Weltanschauung* constitutes an effort to defend the possibility of dialogue. For Scheler rejects the view that people are isolated within subjective worldviews—a view based on far-reaching epistemological and metaphysical premises. He further denies the thesis that agreements amount to no more than artificially constructed contracts wherein each party manages to protect his own interests against attacks from without. At a political level, it need not be simply the case that the common will means only that a majority secures its interests at the expense of a minority from whom they are otherwise cut off. Fully opposed to this mode of thinking, which is more a victim of *Gesellschaft*-type relationships than it cares to recognize, Scheler provides an epistemological, metaphysical, and ethical defense of an objective, shared order of being and value that comes to light piecemeal in the selective stances of individuals and cultures. This discovery of being and value, though, necessitates a common search in solidarity with others in the hope that the narrowness of viewpoints can be broken down. In Scheler's view, solidarity replaces isolation to such an extent that even criminals do not commit crime on their own, apart from the rest of society, with no responsibility on others' parts for them because there is no contractual bond. Rather their crime breaches one's self-enclosure since all are responsible for their crime insofar as the community never gave them the love that might have evoked their counterlove.[9]

Given that fellow feeling, as Scheler conceives it, overleaps egocentrism and reaches the Other, one could conceive of a trajectory of liberation from self—growing in proportion as the distinctiveness of the Other and the Other's independence from one is recognized and honored. Emmanuel Levinas envisions freedom in precisely this fashion:

> Conscience welcomes the Other. It is the revelation of a resistance to my powers that does not counter them as a greater force, but calls in question the naive right of my powers, my glorious spontaneity as a living being. Morality begins when freedom, instead of being justified by itself, feels itself to be arbitrary and violent. The search for the intelligible and the manifestation of the *critical* essence of knowing, the movement of a being back to what precedes its condition, begin together.
>
> Existence is not in reality condemned to freedom, but is *invested* as freedom. Freedom is not bare. To philosophize is to trace freedom back to what lies before it, to disclose the investiture that liberates freedom from the arbitrary. . . . The essence of reason consists not in securing for man a foundation and powers, but in calling him in question and in inviting him to justice.[10]

Scheler and Levinas converge in their opposition to the Nietzschean-mechanistic belief that freedom essentially involves maximal control.[11]

Scheler at his best—and in a reversal of his subsumption of England under hostile, warlike categorizations—maintains a focus on the Other as one not to be subjugated to theoretical, interpretive, or action frameworks that are not the Other's own. Scheler, for instance, opposes monistic metaphysics in favor of reciprocity between act centers, which are given first and foremost as phenomenally different. Furthermore, love for the Other as if the Other were "I" is not authentic love of an *Other*. After all, love basically consists in an understanding going toward the Other as distinctive from one and affirming the Other in the Other's otherness. Scheler's critique of Wundt's assertion that other times have considered murder praiseworthy for reasons moderns would find objectionable provides another illustration of his concentration on the Other as irreducible to present frameworks. Scheler, in the name of the moral solidarity of humanity throughout history, reconsiders the meaning of "murder." He ends up interpreting the practice of human sacrifice, to which Wundt seems to be referring, not as murder, but as an affirmation of the worth of sacrificed individuals and a compliance with the a priori value scheme, which places the values of the holy over those of life. Thus human solidarity enjoins the abolition of ethnocentric judgments and painstaking efforts to illuminate the otherness of the Other (and paradoxically here the Other's moral likeness to others). Other examples of Scheler's suggest how the otherness of the Other is crucial if the Other is to teach and reshape one in the practical domain. The Buddha, raised in pomp and pleasure, is moved to complete conversion upon meeting the Other who is sick and poor. Tolstoy's hard-hearted master, when face to face with his freezing servant, learns fellow feeling for the first time and sees the world anew. Even though the rapprochement between East and West involves reciprocal learning, Scheler focuses more on what the East has to teach the West. Finally, Francis of Assisi manifested most clearly this reverent welcoming of the Other, of which Levinas speaks. For Francis, in defiance of medieval aristocratic-hierarchic metaphysical views, forsook all condenscension to look upon the sun and moon and wind as brothers and sisters, apart from whatever significance they may have possessed for humanity (e.g., as materials for parables or fables).[12]

When Scheler discusses the reciprocity of all moral comportment, which characterizes solidarity, he not only maintains the independence of the Other, but places a priority on one's responsibility to the Other. When addressing the meaning of love, for example, he emphasizes not the love that the Other owes, but rather the love of the Other, which confronts one and makes its demand whether one responds to it or not.

> The possible understanding of a love, for example, a good act done to me, implies at least the co-experience of the demand for a return love, which belongs to the essence of that act. This demand realizes itself in my psyche (insofar as I actually reciprocate love or feel a

tendency to reciprocate love, even if other motives prevent me, or even if I only feelingly represent an act of reciprocal love). I say: the mere *understanding* of the act implies this. Whoever does not see this, does not really grasp the *experience*. To be sure, it is always possible for me to refuse respect to the one who respects me and whose respect I understand. It is always possible to refuse love to someone who loves me or to refrain from obeying a command that I understand. I can also refuse to accept a promise offered. Still, in all these cases, I must in someway [deliberately] refuse and deny something to the Other. But I cannot understand the meaning of his intention and comport myself as if nothing at all in general had happened.[13]

Even though Scheler generally favors a reciprocity between agents, perhaps because he detected the pervasiveness of the will to control, he often speaks of a subservience to the Other, a passivity before the Other, as a central ingredient in dialogue. Reciprocity and efforts to teach the Other about the being and values held in common can often disguise hidden power motives. This is why, perhaps, the notion of an objective order of being and value appear less power-laden if one envisions such an order as a basis for *being educated* by the Other.

Others not only make demands, their very presence constitutes a demand. In their presence, one experiences an absolute value, given in emotive immediacy.

In the very experience of an authentic, pure act of love for a person— there is no need for proof of that person's place in the changing fortunes of happiness and suffering and the inner and outer fate of life. The *value* of the person possesses a detachment from all simultaneously existing, feeling-given value layers of our personal value-world, especially those layers which are still bound to our senses and our life feelings. But this takes place in such a way that *immediately* in this kind of value givenness a *guarantee* appears (not as a kind of "conclusion") that here an absolute value lies before us. It is not the factual continuity in experience or the generalizability of the judgment "This is an absolute value for *all* life moments of our lives" which gives us that *evidence* of absolute value. Rather it is the *felt absoluteness* of this value which leads us to feel that the thought of giving up this value or waiving it for some other value itself involves a "*possible* guilt" or a "fall" from the height of our value existence which we have just reached.

Often we discover the "relativity" of the values to unities of goods (and also therewith to our psychophysical constitution) first through a process of judgment and conclusion—through comparison and induction. *This relativity* and *absoluteness*, however, are even *given immediately in feeling*.[14]

Of course, one could point out that unethically behaving persons seemingly lack any such "valueception" of this absoluteness. Others could argue that this absoluteness really only comes into existence if a correlative agent freely chooses to recognize this absoluteness, by, for instance, contracting to respect the Other. But, at this point, Scheler would no doubt suggest that the modern *Weltanschauung* looms behind these objections: the world is value-barren until one perceives values or until contractual arrangements give birth to them.

If a person is to recognize this absolute value of the Other at all, let alone embark upon a self-liberating dialogue with the Other, then many of the attitudes necessary for philosophizing will be indispensable. Love plays a crucial role insofar as it abandons all striving, rests in its object, does not seek that the object be otherwise than it is, and allows the Other to be and unfold on the Other's own terms. Receptiveness to the unearned "grace" of the Other and refusal to seek mastery, key components of authentic philosophizing and dialoguing, actually constitute a law of life, as Scheler comments.

Thus that is a law of our life, that the things, the higher they stand in the order of their rank, are that much the less capable of being immediately produced through a rationally defined will. Faith, love in the spirit, the beauty of woods and sea, the holiness, harmony, and cheerfulness of existence, a prayer which rises up to God and palpably reaches God's ear, the genius and the work surging from the genius, the blessing of children—everything wherein we feel that our being reaches its end and wins its final meaning—even the joyful power of our own rational will itself—these all require a system of protections that our will can achieve and that hold at bay whatever might hinder or disturb the coming into being of all these things. But these things themselves come without being called forth, "as if to the children of God," as Goethe says. The magician who prefers to summon them forth blocks their way to us all the more. Only the lower world of the mechanizable is completely capable of that kind of will-directed mastery and artificial "organization." Thus [one can will] the drill, but not the education which three-fourths of exemplary educators live. Thus [one can will] the advance according to a method in the sciences, but not the discovery of the method itself and its spirit. Thus [one can will] the establishment of constitutions in the state, but not the free disposition thirsting for responsibility or the [alternate] disposition anxiously and reprehensibly avoiding that responsibility, even as it yet makes use of those constitutions.[15]

Moreover, Scheler's realism could buttress the givenness of the Other, who defies all attempts at subsumption under what Levinas calls one's "totalities." If the resistance of the world precedes consciousness and is not derivative from it, as Scheler holds, then he could agree with Levinas's depiction of the infinity of the Other, stronger than murder, who resists one in the face, whose first word is "You shall not commit murder," and who thus offers "ethical resistance." Levinas remarks, in his essay "Meaning and Sense," that "the putting into question of consciousness [by the Other] is not initially a consciousness of the putting into question. The first is the condition of the second."[16] If, as Scheler believes, one does not deduce reality from reasoning processes, and if reality precedes the reason that is aroused when ecstatic consciousness encounters obstacles, then Scheler might concur with Levinas regarding that most powerful source of resistance evoking and preceding language and reason—the irreducible Other:

> If, on the contrary, reason lives in language, if the first rationality gleams forth in the opposition of the face to face, if the first intelligible, the first signification, is the infinity of the intelligence that presents itself (that is speaks to me) in the face, if reason is defined by signification rather than signification being defined by the impersonal structures of reason, if society precedes the apparition of these impersonal structures, if universality reigns as the presence of humanity in the eyes that look at me, if, finally, we recall that this look appeals to my responsibility and consecrates my freedom as responsibility and gift of self—then the pluralism of society could not disappear in the elevation to reason, but would be its condition.[17]

In addition, Scheler reverts to Pascal's "the heart has its reasons"—reasons that differ from those of thinking, that precede every theoretical ethics, and that every theoretical ethics worthy of the name must attentively consult. His stance implies the prerational founding experience of ethics for Levinas. The totality-shattering face of the Other makes its demand before one ever reasons. Similarly, Levinas finds theoretical ontology suspect since it is repeatedly guilty of reducing the Other to the categories of sameness. Hence, ethics, articulated through a suitable "metaphysics," must take precedence over any theoretical ontology.

> Its [metaphysis's] critical intention then leads it beyond theory and ontology: critique does not reduce the other to the same as does ontology, but calls into question the exercise of the same. A calling into question of the same—which cannot occur within the egoist

spontaneity of the same—is brought about by the other. We name this calling into question of my spontaneity by the presence of the Other ethics. The strangeness of the Other, his irreducibility to the I, to my thought and my possessions, is precisely accomplished as a calling into question of my spontaneity, as ethics. Metaphysics, transcendence, the welcoming of the other by the same, of the Other by me, is concretely produced as the calling into question of the same by the other, that is, as the ethics that accomplishes the critical essence of knowledge. And as critique precedes dogmatism, metaphysics precedes ontology.[18]

Indeed, Scheler's a priori ranking of values and the demands they issue precede not just theoretical ethics, but also every kind of knowing. They correspond to the founding order of acts since, in Scheler's view, the human being is first an *ens amans*—before an *ens volens* or *ens cogitans*. Concurring with Augustine's view (which Scheler interprets as one of the primacy of love and not primacy of will), Scheler argues that the act of love has a primacy over acts of cognition and striving and willing. According to Scheler, even interest-taking acts, the lower impulses of love, precede all perceiving, representing, remembering, and thinking acts, which mediate meaning contents. As such, then the a priori ranking of values, which well-ordered acts of preference apprehend and which perdures despite the changing fortunes of intellectual systems, makes its demand before reasoning commences as does Levinas's Other.[19]

In setting this intuitive apprehension of ethical demands at the foundation of rationality, one may seem to undermine the earlier criticism that Scheler was too intuitive and not sufficiently rational. This possible antirational slant of both Scheler's and Levinas's thought further manifests itself in that the priority they place on the Other might seem to jeopardize the reciprocity and equality between dialogic partners upon which a properly rational ethics might insist. A bridge, though, is possible between these intuitive and rational levels through Levinas's conception of the "Third." The existence of the third person forces one to modify the ethical asymmetry between the Other and him and to adopt rational procedures. When one considers the third person, he realizes that the Other whom he serves also serves the third, and he recognizes his equality with the Other in the service of that third. By extending this discovery, a person discovers her equality with all of humanity, and all persons experience each other commanding them to command Others. That is, one is commanded to uphold her *own* rights in the name of the entirety of humanity represented in every individual, including herself. Notice, though, that one ought to maintain an Other focus even in the defense of one's own rights, according to Levinas, since one defends one's rights not for one's own sake, not in one's own self-interest, but because each person represents all humanity and, in his own self-defense, he really defends them.[20]

### Value Theory

Although the overlapping between the intuitive ethics of Scheler and Levinas has been explored, the last quotation from Levinas raises a critical question for Scheler's view: Does the a priori value ranking ultimately subject the Other to the absolutes of Scheler's categorical system? Scheler's separation of the personal value-bearers from the material values makes it possible that those who serve merely as bearers of values could be sacrificed for the values they bear.

His earlier example of human sacrifice should be considered. The sacrifice of virgins and the most beautiful youth actually fulfills Scheler's value ranking since life values, by no means absolute, are inferior to the values of the spiritual and holy. Other than two references to the superstitious underpinnings of this belief in human sacrifice—a form of religious, but not ethical, criticism—Scheler pronounces *no ethical judgment against such human sacrifice!* In addition to the rather strange dualism, criticized by others, that one can take someone's life and yet be elevating and affirming their Person, Scheler seems to contradict himself in the following way. Scheler develops a painstaking interpretation of Other, past cultures out of a sense of moral solidarity with them, to offset Wundt's uncomprehending charge that they have felt murder to be praiseworthy. But if Scheler shows such sensitivity to another culture to prevent it from falling prey to demeaning modern categorizations, how can he allow the taking of a human lives, even for the best of motives, without a word of ethical protest? Scheler overlooks this inconsistency because his focus on the material ranking of values distracts his attention from what is happening to the bearers of those values. There is a danger that as long as one observes the material value ranking, one can incur no ethical blame, no matter what happens to the bearers of those values, whether they be persons or things.[21]

Kaspar Hurlimann, in a lengthy essay "Person und Werte," presents a possible Schelerian response to these charges. Hurlimann contends that Scheler proposed his ethical personalism in the second part of his *Formalism* to concretize and complement the abstract a priori material value-ethic advanced in the first part. Even in that first part, Scheler's dual value system of values and value-bearers becomes evident in the fact that certain value-bearers cannot bear certain values. Hence, while moral values pertain especially to persons, persons cannot bear the values of the useful or the pleasant that belong only to things. Furthermore, the higher material values encompass attributes that only a person can bear, but lower values reside in things or in the lower aspects of the human person. A hierarchy of values extends from the useful to the holy in the material value system, while in the value-bearer system, persons outrank things. Hurlimann believes that Scheler envisioned no contradiction between these two orders, but rather a mutual complementarity.[22]

Hurlimann, however, does not find Scheler's solution satisfactory, because as long as these dual value systems exist, the value of the person is never definitively anchored in the being of the person. The person only possesses superior value to things indirectly, insofar as the person can bear higher values than a thing. Because these two value systems exist side by side, the human personality, always capable of being subjected to the material value ranking, can never constitute an ultimate normative principle. These dangerous implications are not merely peripheral since, according to Hurlimann, Scheler's thought attempted to establish that "humanity is not the measure of value, but rather humanity is itself to be measured against values."[23]

Hurlimann's final comment strikes at the heart of the issue. As this study has shown, in contrast to the mechanistic worldview that stripped the world of its own values to make room for the subjective values imposed by diverse groups, Scheler relied on Husserlian eidetic method to establish an objective scheme of values that human beings do not create and that survives the contingencies and varieties of cultures. If Scheler had allowed humanity to be the measure of values, he would have fallen into the very ethical nominalism he criticized. By measuring humanity against the values, he prescribes boundaries for the mechanistic will to control and opens up the possibility of an intercultural dialogue under the firmament of common values. But, paradoxically, in this praiseworthy effort to escape the mechanistic worldview, which in general subordinates persons to use values, Scheler ends up devising a ranking of values to which persons could be no less subordinated.

Scheler would have done better to separate his ethics from his value theory and to anchor this (intuitive) ethics in the person, as Hurlimann suggests, in a manner comparable to Levinas who posits the face of the Other as the source of ethical demand. This ethical framework based on the Other's demand would prescribe the behavioral limits within which one might respond to the pervasive allurements and demands of other values. In other words, Scheler's theory of affectivity and values would form the background for his ethics. After all, the *Formalism* involves precisely an effort to provide a long-needed theory of human affect and human valuing in order to correct the errors of the Western *Weltanschauung* and Kant, in particular. It is suggested that one read the *Formalism* as a contribution to philosophical anthropology along the line of most of the work of Scheler's later period, which he himself claims grew out of the *Formalism*. Better sources for Scheler's ethics, although not fully developed by Scheler, lie in his *Wesen und Formen der Sympathie*, in the repeated forays he makes into the realm of intersubjective *Verstehen*, and in his doctrine of solidarity.[24]

Where, though, do these suggested revisions leave Scheler's whole phenomenological project, namely that of offering an inexhaustible structure of being and value, to which one attends selectively because of socio-historical, real factors and whose comprehension, therefore, requires the solidary cooperation of all humanity? The face of the Other, whose imperious demand pries open one's world-shrinking totalities, can help fulfill this purpose as much as the values and being that also impinge upon one. Indeed, with great frequency, Scheler envisions value structures, for instance, becoming discoverable through dialogue with the Other who is totally different. Nature speaks to Francis of Assisi, the poor and sick to the Buddha, the freezing servant to Tolstoy's master, and Asia reveals to the West the importance of passive resistance and metaphysics. Of course, if one embarks upon an intersubjective dialogue only with those he feels have something to teach him and neglects those who he suspects cannot instruct him, then he is simply inflating his own totality by dismissing those who do not fit. Levinas's ethics, wherein the Other commands one's obedience simply as Other, ensures maximal decentration, promises the discovery of unforeseen insights, and thus fulfills several of the central purposes of Scheler's phenomenology. Indeed, the disclosure of values, their a priori rank relationships, and their creative realization would be sustained and even enhanced—if, first and foremost, one refrains from subordinating the Other to one's own category systems and allows oneself to be taught by the Other. It can be argued that each such submission before the Other coheres perfectly with the main lines of Scheler's thought, particularly his often neglected treatments of intersubjectivity and solidarity.

Phenomenology would be needed still. The process of reduction as Scheler describes it, or variants of it, for instance, would involve a loving refusal to control, abandonment of social and historical prejudices, and freedom from linguistic presuppositions—all those impediments which deny access to the "things themselves," in this case, the Other and the Other's individual essence. In addition, phenomenology could clarify meanings in order to reveal the Other on the Other's terms and not one's own, as Scheler did so artfully with the concept of "murder" in relation to earlier practitioners of infant sacrifice. Finally, phenomenology can correct mistaken cultural suppositions, such as those of the mechanistic worldview and its sociology of knowledge, which reduce all ideal factors to causal products. If such a view were valid, then no universal ethics could ever be propounded, relativism would rule, the height from which the Other addresses one would be levelled, and one's hope in solidarity that the Other might teach about the firmanent of truths and values, under which all stand together, would dissipate. Phenomenology should continue to be, as it always was for Max Scheler, the guardian of dialogue.

# Afterword: Scheler's Rigorous Philosophy: Beyond Naturalism and Historicism

From as early as "Philosophy as Rigorous Science" (1911) to as late as *The Crisis of European Sciences and Transcendental Philosophy* (1937), Edmund Husserl battled against two philosophical enemies. On the one hand, he struggled with naturalistic philosophy, which imitated the natural sciences in their concentration on physical-material nature and refused to provide any meaning for life. On the other hand, he opposed the historicist, relativist, or sceptical currents that reacted against scientific-oriented philosophy usually on the basis of their studies of processes in human consciousness. Dilthey's *Weltanschauungen* philosophy, for instance, furnished the historicist-relativist target of Husserl's critique in "Philosophy as Rigorous Science," and, in the *Crisis*, Hume's scepticism climaxed the philosophical/psychological reaction to the meteoric rise of Galilean science. This polarization between scientific naturalism and psychological scepticism has its origins in Descartes's separation of the body—available for study by mechanistic science—from the soul, the theme of philosophical/psychological analysis. Indeed this conflict continues to haunt contemporary philosophy, sliding as it has from retreating positivism toward forms of postmodernist scepticism. In this afterword, Max Scheler's potential contribution to contemporary philosophical, scientific, and social scientific discussions that crystallize around the poles of this naturalist/historicist debate will be considered. The complex, diverse positions constituting the contemporary spectrum render these comments no more than suggestive.[1]

## Scheler and Recent Naturalism

Scheler's critique of mechanistic science as unreflectively overstepping its boundaries in the areas of epistemology, theories of intersubjectivity, and ethics converges with recent efforts in the

166

same direction. The project of logical positivists, such as Carnap, who attempted to establish a sense-datum language against which theoretical statements could be tested, has foundered. Ever since Quine's "The Two Dogmas of Empiricism," the interplay between theoretical frameworks and observation statements, correlative to and not independent of those frameworks, has formed the centerpiece of the philosophy of science developed by philosophers such as Kuhn, Popper, and Lakatos. Indeed, this revolution in the philosophy of the natural sciences, has impacted epistemologists such as Hilary Putnam, who has articulated an internal realism wherein objects are always given correlatively to subjective-linguistic activities:

> What is wrong with the notion of objects existing "independently" of conceptual schemes is that there are not standards for the use of even the logical notions apart from conceptual choices. What the cookie-cutter metaphor [i.e., that the things independent of concepts are like dough awaiting our conceptual cookie cutters] tries to preserve is the naive idea that at least one Category—the ancient category of Object or Substance—has an absolute interpretation. The alternative to this idea is not the view that it's all *just* language. We can and should insist that some facts are there to be discovered and not legislated by us. But this is something to be said when one has adopted a way of speaking, a language, a "conceptual scheme."[2]

On the one hand, Scheler, would argue that the objects and essential features accessible to *phenomenological reflection* on the natural attitude (e.g., Husserl's description of the material thing in *Ideas II*) take precedence over other conceptual-linguistic systems and their correlative objects, and phenomenology assigns these systems their regions. After all, it is from some often implicit viewpoint that one demarcates the place of other conceptual-linguistic systems and their objects. Phenomenology's quest has always been to supply a self-consciousness of that often implicit viewpoint, without reverting to naive notions of "substance." On the other hand, Scheler would laud these epistemological developments precisely for becoming self-consciously reflective of the diverse subjective processes whereby objects present themselves without forfeiting their autonomy and irreducibility.[3]

As Scheler himself has contended, when one becomes self-aware of the mechanistic optics toward the world, one becomes simultaneously aware that other modes of attending to the world are possible (e.g., redemptive or self-formative modes of knowing). Correlatively, the world thus given to accesses other than one bent upon domination reveals itself to be rich in qualities, colors, tones, aromas, and structures that the mechanistic perspective never apprehends. Although Scheler gives free reign to the mechanistic worldview in the natural sciences as long as it recognizes its merely instrumental usefulness, his view that nature discloses itself differently to the one surrendering to it, instead of seeking to dominate it, anticipates later feminist critiques of science. Such critiques tend to favor an attitude similar to that of plant geneticist Barbara McClintock's affectionate "listening to the material" of nature as if it were a friend over Francis Bacon's virile desire to bind nature "to your service and make her your slave." Such feminist critics, however, go further than Scheler since they are not merely pointing to other attitudes paralleling natural science's mechanistic approach. They indicate how these alternative attitudes toward nature could (and should) affect the actual conduct of science itself.[4]

According to Scheler, the phenomenological principle that objects appear differently to different cognitional attitudes can have its impact on the social sciences and their endeavor to understand (*Verstehen*) persons. For Scheler, social scientists intent on grasping the meaning of others rely upon interpretive understanding and only resort to causal explanation when behavior appears aberrant and resists efforts to make sense of it. Behaviorist and causal/mechanistic social sciences thus explain normal processes by paradigms appropriate only for abnormal cases. Scheler thus offers a philosophical foundation for the social sciences consistent with his predecessor, Max Weber, and compatible with the later correctives to positivistic accounts of the social sciences, namely those of phenomenology (Schutz, Berger, and Luckmann) and ordinary language philosophy (Wittgenstein and Winch). Scheler's work here also antedates Habermas's important distinction between cognitive-instrumental action and communicative action oriented to achieving understanding. Glifford Geertz's preference for an interpretive sociology and anthropology instead of causal and reductionistic accounts explaining individuals and cultures behind their backs could easily have been Scheler's own:

> The culture of a people is an ensemble of texts, themselves ensembles, which the anthropologist strains to read over the shoulders of those to whom they properly belong. There are enormous difficulties in such an enterprise, methodological pitfalls to make a Freudian quake, and some moral perplexities as well. Nor is it the only way that symbolic forms can be sociologically handled. Functionalism lives

and so does psychologism. But to regard such forms as "saying something of something," and saying it to somebody, is at least to open up the possibility of an analysis which attends to their substance rather than to reductive formulas professing to account for them.[5]

The behavioristic/mechanistic foundation for the social sciences that positivism had espoused in the past has been generally replaced by game theoretic accounts of intersubjectivity. The "Prisoner's Dilemma," wherein self-interested agents decide whether to cooperate with or defect from their partners, depending on their differing degrees of knowledge and the differing rewards for courses of action, has provided a central model of intersubjectivity. Instead of preoccupying itself with questions of causal determinism dominating earlier mechanistic descriptions of action, this model prides itself on its compatibility with economic science.

Nevertheless, the narrowing and constrictive traits typical of the mechanistic worldview criticized by Scheler appear in game theoretic accounts of intersubjectivity. For instance, Russell Hardin prescinds from talking about moral, altruistic, familial motivations since these "extrarational" motivations admit of only the crudest measurement. The meaning of rationality is reduced to being "efficient in securing one's self-interest." Such constraints might be permissible insofar as these game theoretic accounts are methodologically helpful in describing how someone would act if motivated economically only. One gets the impression, however, that this truncated version of intersubjectivity has come to substitute for a richer notion of intersubjectivity, such as Scheler's, from which it is abstracted in the first place. Hardin, for instance, chides the "team-spirited boosterism" and "childhood Kantianism" of those who do not recognize how statistically insignificant their own contributions are to large organizations. He insists that contractarians would do as they would have others do so long as there are enough others who do likewise to produce net benefits for the contractarians. In all cases, one would adamantly not contribute to benefit others less responsible than oneself. In order to secure cooperation with another, one punishes the Other by tit for tat retribution for the Other's defections. Hardin's position can be summed up in the words of Mackie Messer ("Mack the Knife") whom Hardin quotes favorably: "Erst kommt das Fressen, dann kommt die Moral."[6]

The self-interested players in the "Prisoner's Dilemma" display all the characteristics of Scheler's type of *der Bourgeois*: self-concerned, desperate for "security" and "guaranty" in all things, calculating, competitive, quantitatively directed, and mistrustful of the Other. Here higher values in the Schelerian scheme are by-passed, even deleted from the conversation, in favor of economic ones. The one-sided self-responsibility of *Gesellschaft* replaces the coresponsibility of *Gemeinschaft*, and a precariously maintained balance of power takes the place of mutual solidarity. The objective forms of human loyalty, such as promises given, marriages conjoined, or communities formed, are subjectivized and left to arbitrary choice. The drive to self-preservation occludes from sight Scheler's (and Levinas's) assertion of a primordial ethical demand that precedes theorizing itself.[7]

The ethics growing out of game theoretic explanations of inter-subjectivity also evidence their *gesellschaftlicher* origin. Gilbert Harman, for instance, argues that moral obligations arise from contracts. Harman argues that the self-interested wealthy person would never enter into an contract with the poor according to which the poor ought to be helped. Both rich and poor, however, could together agree to a system wherein no one ought to hurt another or be hurt since both of their interests are at stake. As a result, only the latter prohibition against hurting another could be established as a moral obligation. Similarly, David Gauthier begins his *Morals by Agreement* by positing a premoral context wherein self-interested actors can be persuaded to overrule their narrow self-interest only for the sake of greater, long-run self-interests. In such an ethical system, one would never consent to redistribution of goods unless benefits were ensured for oneself and the reciprocity of the Other guaranteed. Gauthier admits that no reason can be given as to why a more powerful party ought not to benefit from coercing a less powerful one. In order to provide such a reason, Gauthier asserts that one would have to appeal to a strong, controversial conception of reason that would incorporate prior moral suppositions.[8]

These arguments suggest that Harman and Gauthier reduce all motivation to self-interest and acknowledge only one's responsibility for oneself, as is typical of solidarity-barren *Gesellschaft*. They ignore the pretheoretical nature of ethical demands, which would render any "pre-moral" context impossible. Furthermore, Harman and Gauthier are proponents of ethical nominalism, the belief that neither values nor ethical requirements exist unless an agent decides that they exist or a group contracts to recognize them. Their theory thus presents self-enclosed agents and groups, bent on satisfying themselves, and immune to the criticism and will formation potentially emergent from a dialogue with an irreducible Other under a firmament of values and standards not of their own making. Finally, in response to Gauthier's question about a stronger, more controversial type of rationality, Scheler would argue that his notion of solidarity is grounded in the essential nexus of basic types of social interactions such as love, esteem, promising, or giving orders that require as ideal correlates responses of love, esteem, accepting, or obeying. One grasps this essential nexus not on the basis of induction, but through intuitive apprehension. No doubt further discussion would be required about the essence of rationality, which, according to phenomenology, can only be grasped when such an essence in all its fullness, without any one-sidedness, presents itself to the intuition of an autonomous investigator. Certainly one cannot accept a definition of rationality simply because it is the prevailing definition in a particular science, such as economics, or because it is defined so minimally as to be unobjectionable to most.[9]

## Scheler and Recent Forms of Historicism

Scheler reacted to positivism by taking account of subjective activity through which objects presented themselves, thereby opening up alternative ways of viewing the world and alternative ways wherein the world could be given. It has been suggested that he would have found contemporary game theoretic approaches to intersubjective relationships and ethics an impoverished abstraction from the richer real thing. Richard Rorty, too, criticizes positivism for preserving a god in notion of Science, "a portion of culture where we touched something not ourselves, where we found Truth naked, relative to no description."[10] But while Rorty's inclusion of the subjective elements in the pragmatic tradition leads to relativism, Scheler's would not.

Rorty proposes that one be an ironist who doubts the final vocabulary he uses because he has been impressed by other vocabularies, who realizes that these doubts cannot be dispelled in his present vocabulary, and who does not think that his vocabulary is closer to truth than others, that is, in touch with a power not oneself. Rorty's reserve about any claims to have an ultimate vocabulary converges with Nietzsche's suspicions about the will to truth wherein the will to power disguises itself as "humble submission" to what on the surface has nothing to do with power: truth. Instead of sending the will to power underground by seeking to make contact with something larger and more enduring than oneself, it is better to manifest one's power openly in creative activity, "recreating all 'it was' into a 'thus I willed it.'" In the end, the Nietzschean-Heideggerian insight into one's rootedness in the world underlies Rorty's—and for that matter most postmodernism's—rejection of any pretense to attain transtemporal or transcultural vocabularies.[11] "The fundamental premise of the book is that a belief can still regulate action, can still be thought worth dying for, among people who are quite aware that this belief is caused by nothing deeper than contingent historical circumstance."[12]

Rorty's ethics is quite consistent with his epistemology. He believes that if one is ironic enough about her final values and curious enough about everyone else's, there will be no need to worry about whether she is in direct contact with moral reality, whether she is blinded by ideology, or whether she is being mildly relativistic. For Rorty, one only believes that philosophy must give reasoned answers to a question like "Why not be cruel?" only because of one's metaphysical upbringing. Instead of philosophical demonstrations of a common human nature, novels and ethnographies have the responsibility for sensitizing one to the pain of those who do not speak his language. Solidarity is to be built up out of little pieces rather than found waiting in the form of a ur-language eliciting the acceptance of all who hear it.[13]

Given Scheler's keen awareness of the usefulness of Nietzsche for analyzing value inversions and the concealment of power motives, as is evident in his war writings and in his account of phenomenological reduction, he might well endorse many of Rorty's and postmodernism's suspicions. But for Scheler, as for Levinas and Habermas, Nietzschean scepticism provides a valuable tool for unmasking distortions, but by no means can account for the origin of ethical demands. The discovery of covert power motives in the search for truth or value or rightness opens up the possibility of greater authenticity, but need not discredit the entire enterprise of seeking it. As happens so frequently with postmodernist thought, disillusionment with philosophy's past cancels any hope for its future and leads one to relinquish philosophy's responsibilities to literature and ethnography.[14]

In a similar way, Rorty seems to assume that any commitment to an ethical absolute—such as an a priori ranking of values, the face of the Other, or an ideal speech situation implicitly and mutually presupposed in every conversation—inevitably leads to the suppression of diversity. Scheler precisely attempts to show that a commitment to such an absolute exacts a continual vigilance as to how the Other might illuminate the very values under which all stand together. In Scheler's case, commitment to absolute values properly understood attunes one all the more to the distinctiveness of the Other.[15]

Rorty, like most postmodernists, displays a laudible concern that one be curious about others' final values, sensitized to their pain, and impressed by their vocabularies. These are indeed the ingredients of human solidarity. But he assumes that the best way to achieve such solidarity is by exercising one's own creativity rather than by reaching out to a power not of oneself or something larger and more enduring. There is, however, certainly a question whether Rorty's route will arrive at solidarity better than Scheler's. If the problem of egocentrism and ethnocentrism is *one's own* self-enclosure, is it consistent to recommend as medicine one's own creativity or self-generated Nietzschean mistrust of one's projects? Could it not rather be the case that creative exertions undertaken in response to values one does not produce, to the face of the Other preceding and evoking all one's initiatives, or to a nonmanipulable structure of communication might better crumble the barriers of egoism, dissipate ethnocentrism, and produce solidarity? Further, Rorty does not seem to consider the perils that relativism poses for authentic solidarity. Relativists, surveying other cultures from a comfortable distance, can regard their differences as curious, interesting, or quaint. But nonrelativists, who believe in values shared with these others and perhaps better embodied among them, experience a critical impetus to scrutinize their own possible failures to grasp or to live such values. Relativism all too easily lapses into the *gesellschaftlichen* pattern wherein the Other has significance for and makes a claim on one only on one's terms, according to one's interests, or at one's leisure. The linkages drawn between Scheler's independent value scheme, querying everyone, and Levinas's insistence that Others enjoin all to become their apprentices indicate that commitment to ethical absolutes set one on a surer path toward solidarity than the denial of such absolutes. In the end, postmodern ethics comes to resemble game theoretic ethics since in each case ethical demands arise from the decision to recognize them instead of calling that decision forth.[16]

Finally, Rorty and other postmodernists seem to accept uncritically that beliefs are caused by contingent historical circumstances. Scheler presents a plausible alternative sociology of knowledge with his subtle distinction that historico-cultural factors do not produce the objective orders of being and value or conjure up the Other, but lead one to appreciate selectively these orders and the Other. As the confrontation with Mannheim's thought has shown, this approach follows on Scheler's phenomenological starting point that seeks to establish a prior context within which causal factors can be inserted. The one-sided selectivity, induced by such cultural factors, invites a cooperative endeavor to overcome such limitations in dialogue. Once again, Scheler, through his sociology of knowledge, would seem to foster solidarity more than those who deny anything beyond what each socio-cultural milieu produces within its own historically conditioned setting and from its own limited resources.[17]

# Notes

## Introduction: Scheler's Sociology of Knowledge

1. Peter Gay, *Weimar Culture: The Outsider as Insider* (New York and Evanston: Harper & Row, 1968), 9–14, 105; Dagmar Barnouw, *Weimar Intellectuals and the Threat of Modernity* (Bloomington and Indianapolis: Indiana University Press, 1988), 12–14, 44–45; Irving Fetscher, "Max Scheler's Auffassung von Krieg und Frieden," *Max Scheler im Gegenwartsgeschehen der Philosophie, Max Scheler im Gegenwartsgeschehen der Philosophie*, ed. Paul Good (Bern and Munich: Francke Verlag, 1975), 247–48; Hannah Arendt, *The Origins of Totalitarianism* (San Diego, New York, London: Harcourt Brace Jovanovich, 1973), 3–120. For a treatment of Scheler's own life and particularly how his life history intersects with his different philosophical periods, cf. John H. Nota, S.J., *Max Scheler, the Man and His Work*, trans. by Theodore Plantinga and John H. Nota, S.J. (Chicago: Franciscan Herald Press, 1983).

2. Gay, *Weimar Culture*, 96.

3. Ibid., 12–13, 77–80; Barnouw, *Weimar Intellectuals and the Threat of Modernity*, 37–38, 44–46; Gordon Craig, *The Germans* (New York and Scarborough, Ontario: New American Library, 1982), 208, 329.

4. Max Scheler, "Die deutsche Philosophie der Gegenwart," with his *Wesen und Formen der Sympathie*, ed. Manfred S. Frings, vol. 7 of *Gesammelte Werke* (Bern and Munich: Francke Verlag); Jürgen Habermas, *The Philosophical Discourse of Modernity*, trans. Frederick Lawrence (Cambridge: MIT Press, 1987), 150–51, 157.

5. Max Scheler, "Probleme einer Soziologie des Wissens," in his *Die Wissensformen und die Gesellschaft*, 2d ed., ed. Manfred S. Frings, vol. 8 of *Gesammelte Werke* (Bern and Munich: Francke Verlag, 1960); idem, *Problems of a Sociology of Knowledge*, trans. Manfred S. Frings, ed. Kenneth W. Stikkers (London: Routledge & Kegan Paul, 1980). German pages are followed by English translation pages, separated by a slash. The following pages mark out these parts: (1) 17–23/33–39, (2) 24–39/39–53, (3) 39–41/53–55, (4) 41–50/55–62, and (5) 50–51/62–63.

6. Ibid., 58–59/72–73.

7. Max Scheler, "Der Genius des Krieges und der Deutsche Krieg," in his *Politisch-pädagogische Schriften*, ed Manfred S. Frings, vol. 4 of *Gesammelte Werke* (Bern and Munich: Francke Verlag, 1982), 36; idem, "Von kommenden Dingen," in his *Politisch-pädagogische Schriften*, ed. Manfred S. Frings, vol. 4 of *Gesammelte Werke* (Bern and Munich: Francke Verlag, 1982), 547–48.

8. Max Scheler, "Weltanschauungslehre, Soziologie und Weltanschauungssetzung," in his *Schriften zur Soziologie und Weltanschauungslehre*, ed. Maria Scheler, vol. 6 of *Gesammelte Werke* (Bern and Munich: Francke Verlag, 1963), 25–26.

9. Max Scheler, "Probleme einer Soziologie des Wissens," 93, 107/101, 113–14.

10. Ibid., 125–26, 128–29, 155/129–30, 132–33, 154–55.

11. Ibid., 86–87, 91, 154, 162, 178–79, 182–83/95–96, 99, 154–55, 160–61, 175–77, 178–80; Charles Taylor, "Rationality," in *Rationality and Relativism*, ed. Martin Hollis and Steven Lukes (Cambridge: MIT Press, 1982), 102–5; Robin Horton, "Tradition and Modernity Revisited," in *Rationality and Relativism*, ed. Martin Hollis and Steven Lukes (Cambridge: MIT Press, 1982), 201–60.

12. Kenneth Stikkers, "Introduction," to Scheler, *Problems of a Sociology of Knowledge*, 23.

13. I concur with Heinz Leonardy that Scheler's thought divides into three phases: the first under Eucken's influence until 1902–4, the second, a phenomenological period running to around 1922, and a final metaphysical phase. In Leonardy's view, these phases involve differences, but no abrupt breaks. Heinz Leonardy, *Liebe und Person: Max Schelers Versuch eines "phänomenologischen" Personalismus* (The Hague: Martinus Nijhoff, 1976), 9.

14. Edward Vacek, S.J., "Scheler's Evolving Methodologies," in *Morality within the Life and Social World*, ed. A. T. Tymieniecka, vol. 22 of *Analecta Husserliana* (Dordrecht: D. Reidel, 1987), 165–83.

## Chapter 1. The Modern Western *Weltanschauung*

From Max Scheler, *Ressentiment*, edited with an Introduction by Lewis A. Coser and translated by William W. Holdheim. Translation, Copyright © 1961 by The Free Press, a Division of Macmillan, Inc. Reprinted with the permission of the publisher.

1. Max Scheler, "Erkenntnis und Arbeit," in *Die Wissensformen und die Gesellschaft*, 2d ed., ed. Maria Scheler, vol. 8 of *Gesammelte Werke* (Bern and Munich: Francke Verlag, 1960), 257.

2. Ibid.

3. Max Scheler, "Manuskripte zu den Metaszienzien," in his *Schriften aus dem Nachlass*, Vol. 2: *Erkenntnislehre und Metaphysik*, ed. Manfred S. Frings, vol. 11 of *Gesammelte Werke* (Bern and Munich: Francke Verlag, 1979), 166–67.

4. Max Scheler, *Wesen und Formen der Sympathie*, ed. Manfred S. Frings, vol. 7 of *Gesammelte Werke* (Bern and Munich: Francke Verlag, 1973); idem, *The Nature of Sympathy*, trans. Peter Heath (New Haven: Yale University Press, 1954). Routledge and Kegan Paul holds translation rights to this book. Henceforth English translation pages will follow German edition pages separated by a slash. Idem, "Erkenntnis und Arbeit," 328.

5. Max Scheler, "Vorbilder und Führer," in his *Schriften aus dem Naclass*, Vol. 1: *Zur Ethik und Erkenntnislehre*, ed. Maria Scheler, vol. 10 of *Gesammelte Werke* (Bern: Francke Verlag, 1957), 310. An English translation, "Exemplars of Persons and Leaders," appears in *Person and Self-Value: Three Essays*, ed., trans. (partially) by Manfred Frings (The Hague: Martinus Nijhoff, 1987), 188.

6. Max Scheler, "Versuche einer Philosophie des Lebens," in his *Vom Umsturz der Werte*, vol. 3 of *Gesammelte Werke* (Bern and Munich: Francke Verlag, 1955), 321; idem, "Erkenntnis und Arbeit," 253, 262.

7. Scheler, *Wesen und Formen der Sympathie*, 181/182.

8. Max Scheler, "Die transzendentale und die psychologische Methode," in his *Frühe Schriften*, ed. Maria Scheler, vol. 1 of *Gesammelte Werke* (Bern and Mu-

nich: Francke Verlag, 1971), 207–8, 270; idem, "Das Ressentiment im Aufbau der Moralen," in his *Vom Umsturz der Werte,* 5th ed., vol. 3 of *Gesammelte Werke* (Bern and Munich: Francke Verlag, 1982), 135; idem, *Ressentiment,* ed. Lewis Coser, trans. William W. Holdheim (New York: The Free Press of Glencoe, 1961), 160–61. Henceforth German pages of "Das Ressentiment" will precede the English translation. Idem, "Zu den Metazienzien," in his *Schriften aus dem Nachlass,* Vol. 2: *Erkenntnislehre und Metaphysik,* ed. Manfred S. Frings, vol. 11 of *Gesammelte Werke* (Bern and Munich: Francke Verlag, 1979), 165, 180. Idem, *Der Formalismus in der Ethik und die materiale Wertethik,* 5th ed., ed. Maria Scheler, vol. 2 of *Gesammelte Werke* (Bern: Francke Verlag, 1966), 168; idem, *Formalism in Ethics and Nonformal Ethics of Values: A New Attempt toward the Foundation of an Ethical Personalism,* trans. Manfred S. Frings and Roger L. Funk (Evanston, Ill.: Northwestern University Press, 1973), 154–55. Henceforth German text pages will precede English translation. Idem, "Die Idole der Selbsterkenntnis," in his *Selected Philosophical Essays,* trans. David R. Lachterman (Evanston, Ill.: Northwestern University Press, 1973), 77–78. Henceforth the German pagination will precede English translation pages.

9. Max Scheler, "Manuskripte zur Wesenslehre und Typologie der metaphysischen Systeme und Weltanschauungen (Weltanschauungslehre)," in his *Schriften aus dem Nachlass,* Vol. 2: *Erkenntnislehre und Metaphysik,* ed. Manfred S. Frings, vol. 11 of *Gesammelte Werke* (Bern and Munich: Francke Verlag, 1979), 57; idem, "Zu den Metaszienzien," 157; idem, "Das Ressentiment im Aufbau der Moralen," 145/172; Scheler, "Versuche einer Philosophie des Lebens," 332–33; idem, "Die Stellung des Menschen im Kosmos," in his *Späte Schriften,* ed. Manfred S. Frings, vol. 9 of *Gesammelte Werke* (Bern and Munich: Francke Verlag, 1976), 63; idem, *Man's Place in Nature,* trans. Hans Meyerhoff (Boston: Beacon Press, 1961), 82. Henceforth German pages will precede those of English translation.

10. Evelyn Fox Keller, *Reflections on Gender and Science* (New Haven and London: Yale University Press, 1985), 20, 31, 36, 44, 51–52, 70, 138, 162; Elizabeth Fee, "Critiques of Modern Science: The Relationship of Feminism to Other Radical Epistemologies," in *Feminist Approaches to Science,* ed. Ruth Bleier (New York: Pergamon Press, 1986), 48, 50; Arlene Kaplan Daniels, "Feminist Perspectives in Sociological Research," in *Another Voice: Feminist Perspectives on Social Life and Social Science,* ed. Marcia Millman and Rosabeth Moss Kanter (New York: Octagon Books, 1976), 347–58; Nancy Chodorow, *The Reproduction of Mothering: Psychoanalysis and the Sociology of Gender* (Berkeley, Los Angeles, London: University of California Press, 1978), 173–90.

11. Scheler, "Manuskripte zu Wesenslehre und Typologie," 58; idem, "Versuche einer Philosophie des Lebens," 333; idem, "Von kommenden Dingen," 549–50; infra, 103–4.

12. Scheler, "Die Idole der Selbsterkenntnis," 272/72–73. Evelyn Fox Keller refers extensively to the work of developmental psychologist Ernest Schachtel who distinguishes between an instrumentalist perspective ("secondary autocentricity") that views objects only in terms of their need for the perceiver, with regard to their suitability for manipulation and control and an "allocentricity" that grasps the object in "its own right"; her *Reflections on Gender and Science,* 118–20, 165–66; cf. Ernest G. Schachtel, *Metamorphosis: On the Development of Affect, Perception, Attention, and Memory* (New York: Basic Books, 1959), 167–72, 182, 185, 189, 220–27.

13. Scheler, *Der Formalismus in der Ethik,* 170–71/157–58.

14. Scheler, "Erkenntnis und Arbeit," 291.

15. Ibid., 316–18, 323.
16. Ibid., 344, 352.
17. Scheler, "Zur Wesenslehre und Typologie," 44.
18. Supra, 28–29.
19. Max Scheler, "Kant und die moderne Kultur," in his *Frühe Schriften*, ed. Maria Scheler and Manfred S. Frings, Vol. 1 of *Gesammelte Werke* (Bern and Munich: Francke Verlag, 1971), 360–61.
20. David Hume, *A Treatise of Human Nature*, ed. L. A. Selby-Biggs (Oxford: Clarendon Press, 1967), 218; Scheler "Der Genius des Krieges und der deutsche Krieg," 227.
21. Scheler, "Erkenntnis und Arbeit," 221–22.
22. Ibid., 220–22.
23. Max Scheler, "Probleme der Religion," *Vom Ewigen in Menschen*, ed. Maria Scheler, vol. 5 of *Gesammelte Werke* (Bern and Munich: Francke Verlag, 1954), 251; idem, *On the Eternal in Man*, trans. Bernard Noble (New York: Harper & Brothers, 1960), 256–57. Henceforth German page numbers will be followed by those of English translation. Idem, "Erkenntnis und Arbeit," 328.
24. Scheler, *Der Formalismus in der Ethik*, 85/68.
25. "Erkenntnis und Arbeit," 376–77.
26. "Von kulturellen Wiederaufbau Europas," in his *Vom Ewigen in Menschen*, 5th ed., ed. Maria Scheler, vol. 5 of *Gesammelte Werke* (Bern and Munich: Francke Verlag, 1968), 447/447.
27. Max Scheler, "Absolutsphäre und Realsetzung der Gottesidee," in his *Schriften aus dem Nachlass*, Vol. 1; *Zur Ethik und Erikenntnislehre*, 2d ed., ed. Maria Scheler, vol. 10 of *Gesammelte Werke* (Bern: Francke Verlag, 1957), 209–10; idem, "Tod und Fortleben," in his *Schriften aus dem Nachlass*, Vol. 1; *Zur Ethik und Erkenntnislehre*, 2d ed., ed. Maria Scheler, vol. 10 of *Gesammelte Werke* (Bern: Francke Verlag, 1957), 34, 46.
28. Max Scheler, "Die Idole der Selbsterkenntnis," 273–74/74–5.
29. Max Scheler, "Zusätze aus den nachgelassenen Schriften," in his *Späte Schriften*, ed. Manfred S. Frings, vol. 9 of his *Gesammelte Werke* (Bern and Munich: Francke Verlag, 1976), 268; idem, "Der Bourgeois und die religiosen Mächte," in his *Vom Umsturz der Werte*, 5th ed., vol. 3 of *Gesammelte Werke* (Bern and Munich: Francke Verlag, 1972), 357–58, 371. A reduced translation can be found entitled, "The Thomistic Ethic and the Spirit of Capitalism," trans. Gertrude Neuwith, *Sociological Analysis* (1968): 4–19.
30. Scheler, "Der Bourgeois und die religiosen Mächte," 373/13; Max Weber, *The Protestant Ethic and the Spirit of Capitalism*, trans. Talcott Parsons (New York: Charles Scribner's Sons, 1958), 106, 155–83.
31. Scheler, "Der Bourgeois und die religiosen Mächte," 375, 376–77/12–15.
32. Scheler, "Das Ressentiment im Aufbau der Moralen," 115, 117/138, 140; idem, "Zur Idee des Menschen," in his *Vom Umsturz der Werte*, 5th ed., vol. 3 of *Gesammelte Werke* (Bern and Munich: Francke Verlag, 1972), 188; idem, "Arbeit und Ethik," in his *Frühe Schriften*, ed. Marid Scheler and Manfred S. Frings, vol. 1 of *Gesammelte Werke* (Bern and Munuch: Francke Verlag, 1971), 188–90; idem, "Der Bourgeois und die religiosen Mächte," 365/7–8; idem, "Die Ursachen des Deutschenhasses," in his *Politisch-pädagogische Schriften*, ed. Manfred S. Frings, vol. 4 of *Gesammelte Werke* (Bern and Munich: Francke Verlag, 1982), 322–25; idem, "Das Ressentiment im Aufbau der Moralen," 133/156–57.
33. Max Scheler, "Christlicher Sozialismus als Antikapitalismus," in his *Politi-*

*sch-pädagogische Schriften*, ed. Manfred S. Frings, vol. 4 of *Gesammelte Werke* (Bern and Munich: Francke Verlag, 1982), 616, 619–21; idem, "Der Bourgeois," 347.

34. Scheler, "Der Bourgeois," 356–57.

35. Ibid.; Scheler, "Das Ressentiment im Aufbau der Moralen," 117/139; idem, "Die Ursachen des Deutschenshasses," 297; Scheler, "Der Genius des Krieges und der Deutsche Krieg," 30, 229.

36. Max Scheler, "Die Zukunft des Kapitalismus," in his *Vom Umsturz der Werte*, 5th ed., vol. 3 of *Gesammelte Werke* (Bern and Munich: Francke Verlag, 1972), 383–84.

37. Ibid., 384.

38. Scheler, "Christlicher Sozialismus als Antikapitalismus," 673–74; idem, "Die Zukunft des Kapitalismus," 393.

39. Scheler, "Zur Wesenslehre und Typologie," 66–67.

40. Scheler, "Versuche einer Philosophie des Lebens," 317; idem, *Der Formalismus in der Ethik und die materiale Wertethik*, 282, 294–95/277, 290–91.

41. Scheler, "Das Ressentiment im Aufbau der Moralen," 123–24/145–46.

42. Ibid., 101–1/116–18.

43. Scheler, *Der Formalismus in der Ethik*, 529/541; idem, "Zusätze aus den nachgelassenen Manuskripten," 437–38.

44. Scheler, *Der Formalismus in der Ethik*, 517–18, 530/528–29, 542; idem, "Zusätze aus den nachgelassenen Manuskripten," 436–37.

45. Scheler, *Der Formalismus in der Ethik*, 517–18, 544/528–29, 556–57; idem, "Der Genius des Krieges und der Deutsche Krieg," 192; idem, "Soziologische Neuorientierung und die Aufgabe der deutschen Katholiken nach dem Krieg," in his *Politisch-pädagogische Schriften*, ed. Manfred S. Frings, vol. 4 of *Gesammelte Werke* (Bern and Munich: Francke Verlag, 1982), 406, 440; idem, "Recht, Staat und Gesellschaft," in his *Politisch-pädagogische Schriften*, ed. Manfred S. Frings, vol. 4 of *Gesammelte Werke* (Bern and Munich: Francke Verlag, 1982), 574; idem, "Christliche Demokratie," in his *Politisch-pädagogische Schriften*, ed. Manfred S. Frings, vol. 4 of *Gesammelte Werke* (Bern and Munich: Francke Verlag, 1982), 684.

46, Scheler, "Christliche Demokratie," 683–84.

47. Scheler, *Der Formalismus in der Ethik*, 518–19/528–29.

48. Scheler, "Soziologische Neuorientierung und die Aufgabe der deutschen Katholiken nach dem Krieg," 441.

49. Scheler, *Wesen und Formen der Sympathie*, 57–58/46–47.

50. Ibid., 232, 238, 252–58/238, 244, 259–64; R. M. MacIver, *Social Causation* (Boston: Ginn and Company, 1942), 378–93; Jürgen Habermas, *On the Logic of the Social Sciences*, trans. Shierry Weber Nicholsen and Jerry A. Stark (Cambridge: Polity Press, 1988), 178–86.

51. Scheler, *Wesen und Formen der Sympathie*, 257/263.

52. Scheler, *Der Formalismus in der Ethik*, 482–84/490–92; idem, "Der Genius des Krieges und der Deutsche Krieg," 239.

# Chapter 2. Phenomenology and the Objective Order of Being

1. Scheler, "Die deutsche Philosophie der Gegenwart," 307–11.

2. Johannes Daubert was instrumental in this process. Daubert had bicycled to Göttingen in 1903, conversed with Husserl twelve hours, and returned to Munich a convinced phenomenologist.

3. Edmund Husserl, *Ideen zu einer reinen Phänomenologie und phänomenologischen Philosophie*, Book 1: *Allgemeine Einführung in die reine Phänomenologie*, ed. Walter Biemel, vol. 3 of *Husserliana* (The Hague: Martinus Nijhoff, 1950), 42; idem, *Ideas: General Introduction to Pure Phenomenology*, trans. W. R. Boyce Gibson (New York: Collier Books; London: Collier Macmillan Publishers, 1962), 76–77. Henceforth English translation pages follow German pages.

4. Ibid., 54–55/86–87; Edmund Husserl, *Die Krisis der Europäischen Wissenschaften und die transzendentale Phänomenologie*, ed. Walter Biemel, vol. 6 of *Husserliana* (The Hague: Martinus Nijhoff, 1954), 1–3; idem, *The Crisis of European Sciences and Transcendental Phenomenology*, trans. David Carr (Evanston, Ill.: Northwestern University Press, 1970), 3–5. Henceforth English translation pages follow German pages.

5. Edmund Husserl, *Ideen zu einer reinen Phänomenologie und phänomenologischen Philosophie*, 43/74–75; Scheler, "Probleme der Religion," 250/255–56.

6. Husserl, *Ideen zu einer reinen Phänomenologie und phänomenologischen Philosophie*, 1: 43–44/74–76.

7. Edmund Husserl, *Logische Untersuchungen*, vol. 2, 2d part: *Untersuchungen zur Phänomenologie und Theorie der Erkenntnis*, ed. Ursula Panzer (The Hague, Boston, Lancaster: Martinus Nijhoff, 1984), 667–85, 711–14; idem, *Logical Investigations*, vol. 2, trans. J. N. Findlay from the second German Edition (New York: Humanities Press, 1970), 782–95, 817–19; Scheler, "Die deutsche Philosophie der Gegenwart," 308; Robert Sokolowski, *Husserlian Meditations: How Words Present Things* (Evanston, Ill.: Northwestern University Press, 1974), 31.

8. Husserl, *Ideen zu einer reinen Phänomenologie und phänomenologischen Philosophie*, 1: 46, 52/77–78, 83–84; the italics on the word "stunted" are mine.

9. Husserl, "Die Krisis des Europäischen Menschentums und die Philosophie," in his *Die Krisis der Europäischen Wissenschaften und die transzendentale Phänomenologie*, 333–34, 347–48/286–87, 299.

10. Husserl, *Ideen zu einer reinen Phänomenologie und phänomenologischen Philosophie*, 1: 44/75–76; Herbert Spiegelberg, *Doing Phenomenology* (The Hague: Martinus Nijhoff, 1975), 80–109; Manfred S. Frings, "Insight—Logos—Love (Lonergan—Heidegger—Scheler)," *Philosophy Today* 14 (1970):108, 113.

11. Max Scheler, "Zur Erkenntnis- und Methodenlehre," in his *Schriften aus dem Nachlass*, Vol. 2: *Erkenntnislehre und Metaphysik*, ed. Manfred S. Frings, vol. 11 of *Gesammelte Werke* (Bern and Munich: Francke Verlag, 1979), 115–17.

12. Husserl, *Ideen zu einer reinen Phänomenologie und phänomenologischen Philosophie*, 1: 14–15, 46–47, 48–49, 52/48–49, 77–78, 78–79, 83–84.

13. Ibid., 100–101/124–25.

14. Ibid., 70–73, 76–78, 84–85, 112, 119, 147–49, 170, 173–74, 235–37, 247–49, 264, 340–41, 355/101–3, 105–7, 111–12, 134–35, 139–40, 165–67, 190–91, 192–93, 253–55, 265–67, 281–82, 356–57, 370–71; Husserl, *Die Krisis der Europäischen Wissenschaften und die transzendentale Phänomenologie*, 235–36, 252–53/233–35, 249–50.

15. Husserl, *Ideen zu einer reinen Phänomenologie und phänomenologischen Philosophie*, 162/182–83.

16. Ibid., 163/183–84.

17. Ibid., 127–29/146–49.

18. Michel Foucault, "The Discourse on Language" in his *The Archeology of Knowledge*, trans. A. M. Sheridan Smith (New York: Pantheon Books, 1972), 226–228; Jacques Derrida, *Speech and Phenomena*, trans. David B. Allison (Evanston, Ill.: Northwestern University Press, 1973), 50–51; Jean-François Lyotard and

Jean-Loup Thebaud, *Just Gaming*, trans. Wlad Godzich (Minneapolis: University of Minnesota Press, 1985), 10, 23, 60, 94.

19. Supra, 28; Scheler's essay "Arbeit und Ethik," referred to in chapter 1, 28, was published in 1899 before his exposure to phenomenology; finally, his critique of Kant is from his *Frühe Schriften*, but published in 1904, after his encounter with Husserl. Scheler, "Die deutsche Philosophie der Gegenwart," 308; Edmund Husserl, *Logische Untersuchungen*, 2: 667–85, 711–14; idem, *Logical Investigations*, 2: 782–95, 817–19.

20. Scheler, "Vorwort zur ersten Auflage," in his *Die Wissensformen und die Gesellschaft*, 2d ed., ed. Maria Scheler, vol. 8 of *Gesammelte Werke* (Bern and Munich: Francke Verlag, 1960), 11–12. Scheler's subsequent metaphysical works can be found in his *Schriften aus dem Nachlass*, Vol. 2: *Erkenntnislehre und Metaphysik*, ed. Manfred S. Frings, vol. 11 of *Gesammelte Werke* (Bern and Munich: Francke Verlag, 1979).

21. Scheler, "Vorwort zur ersten Auflage," 9.

22. Infra, 140–41.

23. Supra, 30–36.

24. Scheler, "Erkenntnis und Arbeit," 203–4.

25. Ibid., 226–28.

26. Ibid., 203–4.

27. Max Scheler, "Über die positivistische Geschichtsphilosophie des Wissens," in his *Schriften zur Soziologie und Weltanschauungslehre*, 2d ed., ed. Maria Scheler, vol. 6 of *Gesammelte Werke* (Bern and Munich: Francke Verlag, 1963), 30; the italics here are Scheler's. There is an English translation: "On the Positivistic Philosophy of the History of Knowledge and Its Laws of Three Stages," trans. Ranier Koehne, in *The Sociology of Knowledge: A Reader*, ed. James E. Curtis and John W. Petras (New York: Praeger Publishers; London: Duckworth, 1970), 164.

28. Scheler, "Erkenntnis und Arbeit," 205–6.

29. Ibid., 206, 208, 211; Scheler, "Die transzendentale und die psychologische Methode," 289–94; idem, "Lehre von den drei Tatsachen," *Schriften aus dem Nachlass*, Vol. 1, *Zur Ethik und Erkenntnislehre*, 2d ed., ed. Maria Scheler, vol. 10 of *Gesammelte Werke* (Bern: Francke Verlag, 1957), 501–2; idem, "The Theory of the Three Facts," *Selected Philosophical Essays*, 285–87.

30. Scheler, "Erkenntnis und Arbeit," 217–18.

31. Ibid., 230–31, 237–38.

32. Ibid., 241.

33. Ibid., 244.

34. Ibid., 245–60.

35. Ibid., 260–61, 266–67, 273; Peter Winch, "Understanding a Primitive Society" in *Rationality*, ed. Bryan R. Wilson (Oxford: Basil Blackwell, 1970), 78–94.

36. Scheler, "Erkenntnis und Arbeit," 270–71.

37. Ibid., 273–75.

38. Ibid., 275.

39. Ibid., 275–76.

40. Ibid., 276–78; Simone de Beauvoir, *The Second Sex*, trans. and ed. H. M. Parshley (New York: Vintage Books, 1974), 157–223.

41. Scheler, "Erkenntnis und Arbeit," 283.

42. Ibid., 289–90.

43. Ibid., 313.

44. Ibid., 298, 311; Ernest Gellner, "Relativism and Universals" in *Rationality*

*and Relativism,* ed. Martin Hollis and Steven Lukes (Cambridge: The MIT Press, 1982), 197–200.

45. Scheler, "Erkenntnis und Arbeit," 284.

46. Ibid., 289–90, 292, 324.

47. Ibid., 316–22.

48. Ibid., 323.

49. Ibid., 324.

50. Ibid., 293, 317–18.

51. Ibid., 314–15, 326, 347.

52. Ibid., 326–28.

53. Ibid., 332, 339–43; Barry Barnes, "On the Conventional Character of Knowledge and Cognition," *Philosophy of the Social Sciences* 11 (1981):318.

54. This question of reality will be discussed in chapter 6, focusing on Scheler's late essay "Idealismus-Realismus," in his *Späte Schriften,* ed. Manfred S. Frings, vol. 9 of *Gesammelte Werke* (Bern and Munich: Francke Verlag, 1976).

55. Manfred S. Frings, *Zur Phänomenologie der Lebensgemeinschaft: Ein Versuch mit Max Scheler* (Meisenheim am Glan: Verlag Anton Hain, 1971), 68.

## Chapter 3. Common Values and Self-Critical Dialogue

1. Scheler, *Der Formalismus in der Ethik und die materiale Wertethik/Formalism in Ethics and Non-formal Ethics of Values,* 9–10, 234/xvii–xviii, 227.

2. Ibid., 32/9–10.

3. Ibid., 37, 47, 65–66, 215, 226/14, 25, 45–46, 207–8, 219); Immanuel Kant, *Grundlegung zur Metaphysik der Sitten* in his *Schriften zur Ethik und Religionsphiloso-phie,* Erster Teil (Darmstadt: Wissenschaftliche Buchgesellschaft, 1968), 33–40; idem, *Grounding for the Metaphysics of Morals,* trans. James W. Ellington (Indian-apolis and Cambridge, Eng.: Hackett, 1981), 19–23.

4. Scheler, *Der Formalismus in der Ethik,* 138/123.

5. Ibid., 38, 46, 51, 127, 138/15–16, 24–25, 30, 112, 123.

6. Immanuel Kant, *Kritik der praktischen Vernunft* in *Schriften zur Ethik und Religionsphilosphie,* 180; idem, *Critique of Practical Reason,* trans. Lewis White Beck (Indianapolis: Bobbs-Merrill, 1956), 65; Scheler, *Der Formalismus in der Ethik und die materiale Wertethik,* 46, 51/24–25, 30.

7. Scheler, *Der Formalismus in der Ethik,* 138–43, 267/123–28, 262.

8. Ibid., 43–43, 148–52/20–21, 133–37.

9. Ibid., 145–48, 152/130–33, 138.

10. Ibid., 148, 151/133, 137.

11. Ibid., 152/137–38.

12. Ibid., 172/159.

13. Ibid., 67–72/48–53; supra, 55–56.

14. Ibid., 72–73/53–54.

15. Ibid., 72–82/54–64; Friedrich Nietzsche, *On the Genealogy of Morals,* trans. Walter Kaufmann and R. J. Hollingdale, with his *Ecce Homo* (New York: Vintage Books, 1967), p. 26; supra, 53–54.

16. Scheler, *Der Formalismus in der Ethik und die materiale Werthethik,* 83–84/63–65.

17. Ibid., 85/67; Alfred Schutz, *Studies in Phenomenological Philosophy,* vol. 3 of *Collected Papers,* ed. I. Schutz (The Hague: Martinus Nijhoff, 1975), 155–63.

18. Scheler, *Der Formalismus in der Ethik, Werthethik*Ibid, 89–92/71–74.

19. Ibid., 92–96, 501/74–78, 510.

20. Ibid., 20, 96–99, 491/xxviii–xxix, 78–81, 500.

21. Ibid., 45–51, 99–126/23–30, 81–110.

22. Ibid., 177–80/167–71.

23. Ibid., 177–203/167–94.

24. Ibid., 203/194.

25. Ibid., 185–86/176–77.

26. Ibid., 205–6/197–98; Max Weber, *The Methodology of the Social Sciences*, trans. and ed. Edward A. Shils and Henry A. Finch (New York: The Free Press, 1949), 74.

27. Scheler, *Der Formalismus in der Ethik*, 207–8, 264–65/198–200, 259–60.

28. Ibid., 13–14, 88, 106–7, 116, 260–61/xxi–xxiii, 69, 88–90, 99, 254–55.

29. Ibid., 123/105–6.

30. Ibid., 91, 166, 249, 272, 375, 379/72, 153, 242–43, 267, 376, 379.

31. Ibid., 98, 183, 197–98, 567/79, 173, 189, 582.

32. Ibid., 338–40, 508/336–38, 517–18.

33. Ibid., 353–54/352–53.

34. Ibid., 338–50/336–49.

35. Supra, 86; Scheler, *Der Formalismus in der Ethik*, 48–49, 192, 496, 405, 541, 555/27, 182–83, 499, 508, 553, 569.

36. Scheler, *Der Formalismus in der Ethik*, 132–33, 298, 379, 389, 415–69, 478, 496–97, 556, 569/117, 294, 379, 390, 417–76, 486, 506, 557, 571.

37. Ibid., 219, 233/212, 226–27.

38. Ibid., 233/226–27.

39. Ibid., 161–63/147–50.

40. Ibid., 358, 410–12/357, 412–14.

41. Ibid., 250, 330/243–44, 327.

42. Ibid., 193–94, 322, 328, 484–85/184–85, 319, 325, 492–93.

43. Ibid., 124, 233, 282, 284–88, 350, 420, 508, 567/107, 226, 277, 279–83, 349, 423, 518–19, 582; Peter L. Berger and Thomas Luckmann, *The Social Construction of Reality: A Treatise in the Sociology of Knowledge* (Garden City, N.Y.: Doubleday and Company, 1966), 1–17.

44. Scheler, *Der Formalismus in der Ethik*, 250–51/244.

45. Ibid., 330, 363–365, 449/327, 363–65, 454; Manfred S. Frings, "Social Temporality in George Herbert Mead and Max Scheler," *Philosophy Today* 29 (1983): 282–83.

46. Scheler, *Der Formalismus in der Ethik*, 170/157.

47. Ibid., 97–99, 169–70, 292–4, 492/78–80, 156–57, 288–90, 501.

48. Ibid., 246–48, 403–6, 428–29/239–41, 405–8, 432–33.

49. Ibid., 275/270.

50. Ibid., 266, 480, 524–25/261, 488, 535–36.

51. Ibid., 308/304.

52. Ibid., 313–17/309–13.

53. Ibid., 319/316; supra, 95; Alfred Schutz, *The Phenomenology of the Social World*, trans. George Walsh and Frederick Lehnert (Evanston, Ill.: Northwestern Univeristy Press, 1967).

54. Scheler, *Der Formalismus in der Ethik*, 296–99/292–95.

55. Ibid., 307–8/303–4.

56. Ibid., 485/494.

## Chapter 4. The Fundaments of Dialogue: Scheler's Theory of Intersubjectivity

1. Scheler, *Wesen und Formen der Sympathie*, 34/23.
2. Ibid., 26, 28–29/15, 17–18.
3. Ibid., 37–39/26–28; supra, 88–93.
4. *Wesen und Formen der Sympathie*, 50–52, 57–58/39–42, 46–47.
5. Ibid., 57/46.
6. Ibid., 58–61/47–49.
7. Ibid., 58–59/47–48.
8. Ibid., 61/50.
9. Ibid., 69–70, 77, 80–81, 87, 221, 226/58–59, 66, 70–71, 76, 225, 231.
10. Ibid., 87–90/77–80.
11. Ibid., 42, 94–96/31, 83–85.
12. Ibid., 97–103/87–93.
13. Ibid., 117–109.
14. Supra, 68–70.
15. *Wesen und Formen der Sympathie*, 113/105.
16. Ibid., 44/32.
17. Ibid., 113/105.
18. Ibid., 19–20, 24–25, 105–11/8–9, 13–14, 96–102.
19. Ibid., 112, 114–15,/103–4, 106–7.
20. Ibid., 118, 123, 133–34, 204–5/110, 115, 124–25, 204–5; Bruno Rutishauser, *Max Schelers Phänomenologie des Fühlens: Eine kritische Untersuchung seiner Analyse von Scham und Schamgefühl* (Bern and Munich: Francke Verlag, 1969), 142.
21. Scheler, *Wesen und Formen der Sympathie*, 17–18, 145–46, 147–48/5, 140–41, 142–43.
22. Ibid., 150–56/147–53.
23. Ibid., 155–57, 160, 162–63/152–54, 157, 160.
24. Ibid., 161–64/158–60.
25. Ibid., 162/160.
26. Ibid., 164–67/162–65.
27. Ibid., 175–79/175–79.
28. Ibid., 180–81/181–82.
29. Ibid., 186, 199–200, 202/187, 200–201, 202–3.
30. Ibid., 11/xlvi.
31. Ibid., 218–219/222–24.
32. Ibid., 220/225; Alfred Schutz, *The Problem of Social Reality*, vol. 1 of *Collected Papers*, ed. Maurice Natanson (The Hague, Boston, London: Martinus Nijhoff, 1962), 55–59; Max Weber, *Economy and Society: An Outline of Interpretive Sociology*, ed. Guenther Roth and Claus Wittich (Berkeley, Los Angeles, London: University of California Press, 1978), 1: 4–22; Peter Winch, *The Idea of a Social Science and Its Relation to Philosophy* (London, Melbourne, Henley: Routledge & Kegan Paul; Atlantic Highlands, N.J.: Humanities Press, 1958), 111–20.
33. Scheler, *Wesen und Formen der Sympathie*, 219–20/224–25.
34. Ibid., 228–32/234–37; Michael Theunissen, *The Other: Studies in the Social Ontology of Husserl, Heidegger, Sartre, and Buber*, trans. Christopher Macann (Cambridge, Mass. and London: MIT Press, 1984), 171.
35. Scheler, *Wesen und Formen der Sympathie*, 232, 234–36, 238/238, 240–42, 244.
36. Ibid., 238, 239, 241/244, 245, 247.

37. Ibid., 244–47/251–54.
38. Ibid., 254/260.
39. Ibid., 247, 254–255/253, 260–61.
40. Ibid., 255–257/261–63.
41. Ibid., 257/263.
42. Ibid., 227/231.
43. Ibid., 226–27/230–31; A. R. Luther, *Persons in Love: A Study of Max Scheler's Wesen und Formen der Sympathie* (The Hague: Martinus Nijhoff, 1972), 150.
44. Scheler, *Wesen und Formen der Sympathie*, 227–228/232–33; idem, *Der Formalismus in der Ethik*, 522–31/533–43.
45. Scheler, "Der Bourgeois," 349–50; idem, "Das Ressentiment im Aufbau der Moralen," 121/143; idem, *Wesen und Formen der Sympathie*, 228/234–35; idem, *Der Formalismus in der Ethik*, 522–31/533–43.
46. Supra, 23–24; Scheler, *Der Formalismus in der Ethik*, 515, 527/525, 538–39. Erhard Denninger, *Rechtsperson und Solidarität; Ein Beitrag zur Phänomenologie des Rechtsstaates unter besonderer Berücksichtigung der Sozialtheorie Max Schelers* (Frankfurt and Berlin: Alfred Metzner Verlag, 1967), 302–6. Denninger's comments on solidarity portray Scheler as aiming at a type of communication which anticipates Habermas's "ideal speech situation" where force has no place.

# Chapter 5. The Way beyond Sociologism

1. Supra, 95–96; Friedrich Nietzsche, *Beyond Good and Evil,* trans. R. J. Hollingdale (Harmondsworth: Penguin Books, 1972), 151–72.
2. Scheler, "Der Genius des Krieges und der Deutsche Krieg," 53–54, 70–71; Denninger, *Rechtsperson und Solidarität,* 153; Fetscher, "Max Schelers Auffassung von Krieg und Frieden," 246–47.
3. Scheler, "Der Genius des Krieges und der Deutsche Krieg" 27–32, 53–54, 70–71, 192.
4. Ibid., 35.
5. Ibid., 34–35, 41; idem, "Die Ursachen des Deutschenhasses," 347, 352.
6. Scheler, "Der Genius des Krieges und der Deutsche Krieg," 49, 54–55.
7. Ibid., 56, 86, 147.
8. Ibid., 29, 36, 136–37, 193, 220–21, 227–44.
9. Ibid., idem, "Die Ursachen des Deutschenhasses," 344–45.
10. Supra, 90–92. Peter H. Spader, "The Primacy of the Heart: Scheler's Challenge to Phenomenology," *Philosophy Today* 29, no. 3/4 (Fall 1985): 226; Alfred Schutz, *Studies in Social Theory,* vol. 2 of *Collected Papers,* ed. Arvid Brodersen (The Hague: Martinus Nijhoff, 1976), 258–62; Michael Barber, "Alma Gonzalez: Otherness as Attending to the Other," in *The Question of the Other: Essays in Contemporary Continental Philosophy,* ed. Arleen B. Dallery and Charles E. Scott (Albany: State University of New York Press, 1989), 119–26; Friedrich Nietzsche, *Joyful Wisdom,* trans. Thomas Common (New York: Frederick Ungar, 1960), 300–301; Howard Schwartz and Jerry Jacobs, *Qualitative Sociology* (New York: The Free Press; London: Collier Macmillan, 1979), 247–65; Clifford Geertz, *The Interpretation of Cultures* (New York: Basic Books, 1973), 412–53.
11. Karl Mannheim, "Das Problem einer Soziologie des Wissens," in his *Wissenssoziologie: Auswahl aus dem Werk,* ed. Kurt H. Wolff (Berlin and Neuwied: Luchterhand, 1964), 328–29; idem, "The Problem of a Sociology of Knowledge," *From Karl Mannheim,* ed. Kurt H. Wolff (New York: Oxford University Press,

1971), 75. Henceforth German text references will be followed by a slash and the pages in the English translation.

12. Ibid., 340, 346/83, 88; supra, 18, 132.

13. Ibid., 344, 348–49/86, 90–91; Karl Mannheim, *Ideology and Utopia*, trans. Louis Wirth and Edward Shils (New York and London: Harcourt, Brace, Jovanovich, 1936), 266–86; David Bloor, *Knowledge and Social Imagery* (London, Henley, Boston: Routledge & Kegan Paul, 1976), 1–10; Gilbert Harman, "Is There a Single True Morality?" in *Relativism: Interpretation and Confrontation*, ed. Michael Krausz (South Bend, Ind.: University of Notre Dame Press, 1989), 363–86.

14. Mannheim, "Das Problem einer Soziologie des Wissens," 352/93.

15. Ibid., 352–53/93–94. How much Scheler's essences reflect his own existential background also appear in recurrent comments that nowadays would be considered blatantly sexist, e.g., to the effect that housework and not labor in the marketplace pertains to women (e.g., Scheler, "Von kommenden Dingen," 558; idem, "Zur Sinn der Frauenbewegung," *Vom Umsturz der Werte*, 5th ed., vol. 3 of *Gesammelte Werke* (Bern and Munich: Francke Verlag, 1972), "Concerning the Meaning of the Feminist Movement, trans. Manfred S. Frings, *Philosophical Forum* 9 (1978): 45–46, that "virile" characteristics should not be found in women (Scheler, "Zur Sinn der Frauenbewegung," 201–2); that a young virgin's defenses before sexual intercourse are often accompanied by the hidden wish to be conquered by the male [Max Scheler, "Über Scham und Schamgefühl," in his *Schriften aus dem Nachlass*, Vol. 1; *Zur Ethik und Erkenntnislehre*, 2d ed., ed. Maria Scheler, vol. 10 of *Gesammelte Werke* (Bern: Francke Verlag, 1957), 121/59]; that women live less expansive, more childlike, less problematic existences since the female is the genius of life whereas the male is the genius of the spirit (Scheler, "Über Scham und Schamgefühl," 1: 146–47/83–85). Scheler betrays anti-Semitism when, for instance, he attributes the subjection of sexuality to reproduction not to German or Christian sources but to the goal orientedness which belongs to the essence of the Jewish spirit (Scheler, "Über Scham und Schamgefühl," 1: 136/73). This comment evokes Bruno Rutishauser's wonder and criticism also in his *Max Schelers Phänomenologie des Fühlens*, 146. There is even an enigmatic racist-sounding comment at the end of Schelen's *Wesen und Formen der Sympathie* that Americans do not hate Negroes because they are black, but that they scent the Negro under the blackness of his skin (Scheler, *Wesen und Formen der Sympathie*, 257–258, footnote/263). Such comments involve the kind of reading of one's existential background into supposed "essences" against which Mannheim complains. The problem, however, may not be with essences, but with the force of Scheler's prejudices, which hinder him from truly utilizing phenomenological method.

16. Mannheim, "Das Problem einer Soziologie des Wissens," 356–60, 361/96–99, 100.

17. Ibid., 370–71/103.

18. Scheler, "Probleme einer Soziologie des Wissens," 19, 22/35, 38.

19. Ibid., 28–29/43–44.

20. Ibid., 75, 107/86, 114; idem, "Über die positivistische Geschichtsphilosophie des Wissens (Dreistadiengesetz)," 30–31/164–165.

21. Scheler, "Probleme einer Soziologie des Wissens," 24, 26, 28, 29, 39, 40/40, 41–42, 43, 44, 53–54; Robert K. Merton, "Paradigm for the Sociology of Knowledge," in *The Sociology of Knowledge*: A Reader, ed. James E. Curtis and John W. Petras (New York and Washington: Praeger Publishers), 342–44.

22. Scheler, "Probleme einer Soziologie des Wissens," 153–54/154; idem, *Der*

*Formalismus in der Ethik*, 484–85/492–93; supra, 88–89; Reinhold J. Huskamp, *Spekulativer und phänomenologischer Personalismus* (Munich: Verlag Karl Alber, 1966), 151–55, 174; Peter H. Spader, "The Non-Formal Ethics of Value of Max Scheler and the Shift in His Thought," *Philosophy Today* 18, no. 3/4 (Fall 1974): 220.

23. Karl Mannheim, *Wissenssoziologie: Auswahl aus dem Werk*, ed. Kurt H. Wolff (Berlin and Neuwid: Luchterhand, 1964), 357; idem, *From Karl Mannheim*, ed. Kurt H. Wolf (New York: Oxford University Press, 1971) 96–97.

24. Max Scheler, "Vom Wesen der Philosophie und der moralischen Bedingung des philosophischen Erkennens," in his *Vom Ewigen im Menschen*, 5th ed., ed. Maria Scholer, vol. 5 of *Gesammelte Werke* (Bern and Munich: Francke Verlag, 1968), 67/73.

25. Ibid., 65–68, 79/72–74, 85: idem, "Zusätze aus den nachgelassenen Manuskripten," 250.

26. Scheler, "Vom Wesen der Philosophie und der moralischen Bedingung des philosophischen Erkennens," 84/89–90.

27. Ibid., 83; idem, "Liebe und Erkenntnis," in his *Schriften zur Soziologie und Weltanschauungslehre*, 2d ed., ed. by Maria Scheler, vol. 6 of *Gesammelte Werke* (Bern and Munich: Francke Verlag, 1963), 82, 84, 95–96, 97.

28. Scheler, "Vom Wesen der Philosophie," 88, 89–90, 91–92/94, 95, 96–98; idem, "Zur Wesenslehre und Typologie," *Schriften aus dem Nachlass*, Vol. 2: *Erkenntnislehre und Metaphysik*, ed. Manfred S. Frings, vol. 11 of *Gesammelte Werke* (Bern and Munich: Francke Verlag, 1979), 64–65.

29. Scheler, "Idealismus-Realismus," 190, 194–99/295, 300–8; idem, "Zusätze aus den nachgelassenen Schriften," 262; idem, "Manuskripte zur Erkenntnis- und Methodenlehre der Metaphysik als positive Erkenntnis (Auseinandersetzung mit Gegnern)," in his *Schriften aus dem Nachlass*, Vol. 2: *Erkenntnislehre und Metaphysik*, ed. Manfred S. Frings, vol. 11 of *Gesammelte Werke* (Bern and Munich: Francke Verlag, 1979), 107, 110; supra, 107–8, 125–26. Idem, "Zur Erkenntnis- und Methodenlehre," 2: 103–17; idem, "Die Idole der Selbsterkenntnis," 239–40; idem, "The Idols of Self-Knowledge," 33–35.

30. Scheler, "Idealismus-Realismus," 208, 214/317–25; idem, "Die Stellung des Menschen im Kosmos," 15/11–12; idem, "Die Idole der Selbsterkenntnis," 257/55. Maurice Merleau-Ponty, *Phénoménologie de la Perception* (Paris: Librairie Gallimard, 1945), viii.

31. Scheler, "Idealismus-Realismus," 193, 207/299, 315; idem, "Zur Erkenntnis- und Methodenlehre," 2: 95–96.

32. Scheler, "Zur Erkenntnis- und Methodenlehre," 2; 72–81, 93, 95, 99–100, 102, 103; idem, "Die Idole der Selbsterkenntnis," 273–74, 283/75–76, 86; Kenneth W. Stikkers, "Phenomenology as Psychic Technique of Non-Resistance," in *Phenomenology in Practice and Theory*, ed. William S. Hamrick (Dordrecht, Boston, Lancaster: Martinus Nijhoff Publishers, 1985); Michael Barber, "Finitude Rediscovered," *Philosophy and Theology* 5 (1990): 73–80.

33. Scheler, "Zur Erkenntnis- und Methodenlehre, 2: 113–17; idem, "Idealismus-Realismus," 185–87, 200–4/288–91, 308–12; idem, "Manuskripte zur Metaphysik der Erkenntnis," 2: 117;

34. Max Scheler, "Das Nationale im Denken Frankreichs," in his *Schriften zur Soziologie und Weltanschauungslehre*, 2d ed., ed. Maria Scheler, vol. 6 of *Gesammelte Werke* (Bern and Munich: Francke Verlag, 1963), 132–33.

35. Schutz, *The Phenomenology of the Social World*, 159–63; Michael D. Barber, *Social Typifications and the Elusive Other: The Place of Sociology of Knowledge in Alfred Schutz's Phenomenology* (Lewisburg, Pa.: Bucknell University Press, 1988), 85–87;

Ernst Grünwald, *Das Problem der Soziologie des Wissens: Versuch einer kritischen Darstellung der wissenssoziologischen Theorien* (Wien and Leipzig: Wilhelm Braumuller, 1934), 232–33.

36. Scheler, "Die Idole der Selbsterkenntnis," 257–59/55–57.

37. Ibid., 259/57.

38. Supra, 85, 94.

39. Supra, 100–106; Jürgen Habermas, *Communication and the Evolution of Society*, trans. Thomas McCarthy (Boston: Beacon Press, 1979), 95–129; Thomas McCarthy, *The Critical Theory of Jürgen Habermas* (Cambridge and London: MIT Press, 1978), 246, 253–58.

## Chapter 6. Rationality and Dialogic Ethics

1. Supra, 67–70; Max Weber, "Science as a Vocation," in *From Max Weber: Essays in Sociology*, ed. H. H. Gerth and C. Wright Mills (New York: Oxford University Press, 1946), 147–49; Jürgen Habermas, *Reason and the Rationalization of Society*, vol. 1 of his *The Theory of Communicative Action*, trans. Thomas McCarthy (Boston: Beacon Press, 1984), chapter 2.

2. Supra, 90–91.

3. Max Scheler, "Zusätze aus den nachgelassenen Manuskripten," 430–31.

4. Habermas, *Reason and the Rationalization of Society*, 273–95; supra, 88, 93–94.

5. Scheler, *Der Formalismus in der Ethik*, 211–18/203–10; supra, 97.

6. Scheler, *Der Formalismus in der Ethik*, 322, 327–28, 483–85/319, 324–25, 491–93.

7. Ibid., xxi–xxii, 87–88, 107/13–14, 68–69, 89–90; supra, 90–91.

8. Kant appeals to such moral intuitions into the nature of the good will and moral experience before one embarks upon theoretical considerations in practical philosophy and the metaphysics of morals in his first section of *Grounding for the Metaphysics of Morals*. Cf. Jürgen Habermas, *Moral Consciousness and Communicative Action*, trans. Christian Lenhardt and Shierry Weber Nicholsen (Oxford: Polity Press, 1990), 199–203; idem, *Reason and the Rationalization of Society*, chapter 4; Manfred S. Frings, *Zur Phänomenologie der Lebensgemeinschaft*, 33.

9. Supra, 119–20, 127–29.

10. Emmanuel Levinas, *Totality and Infinity: An Essay on Exteriority*, trans. Alphonso Lingis (The Hague: Martinus Nijhoff, 1979), 84–85, 88.

11. Supra, 111–12.

12. Scheler, *Wesen und Formen der Sympathie*, 75, 80–81/64–65, 69–70; supra, 90–91, 110, 111–12.

13. Scheler, *Der Formalismus in der Ethik*, 524–25/536.

14. Ibid., 116/99; Emmanuel Levinas, *Otherwise than Being or Beyond Essence*, trans. Alphonso Lingis (The Hague, Boston, London: Martinus Nijhoff, 1981), 61–97.

15. Scheler, "Soziologische Neuorientierung und die Aufgabe der deutschen Katholiken nach dem Krieg," 446; supra, 143–44, Enrique Dussel, *Philosophy of Liberation*, trans. Aquilina Martinez and Christine Morkovsky (Maryknoll, N.Y.: Orbis Books, 1985), 59, 64–66; Sandra Lee Bartky, *Femininity and Domination: Studies in the Phenomenology of Oppression* (New York and London: Routledge, 1990), 39–40, 63–82.

16. Levinas, *Totality and Infinity*, 199; idem, *Collected Philosophical Papers*, trans. Alphonso Lingis (Dordrecht: Martinus Nijhoff, 1987), 99.

17. Levinas, *Totality and Infinity*, 208.

18. Ibid., 43; supra, 90–96.

19. Max Scheler, "Ordo Amoris," in his *Schriften aus dem Nachlass*, Vol. 1; *Zur Ethik und Erkenntnislehre*, 2d ed., ed. Maria Scheler, vol. 10 of *Gesammelte Werke* (Bern: Francke Verlag, 1957), 356; idem, "Ordo Amoris," in his *Selected Philosophical Essays*, trans. David R. Lachtermann (Evanston, Ill.: Northwestern University Press, 1973), 110–11; idem, "Liebe und Erkenntnis," 95–96; Heinz Leonardy, *Liebe und Person*, 101.

20. Levinas, *Totality and Infinity*, 213; Judith Butler, *Gender Trouble: Feminism and the Subversion of Identity* (London and New York: Routledge, 1990) 28–34, 140–49.

21. Scheler, *Der Formalismus in der Ethik*, 315–17/311–13; Felix Hammer, *Theonome Anthropologie* (The Hague: Martinus Nijhoff, 1972), 83, 91–93, 102, 152, 161, 187–88, 201.

22. Scheler, *Der Formalismus in der Ethik*, 117, 103–4/85–86, 100; Kaspar Hurlimann, "Person und Werte: Eine Untersuchung über den Sinn von Max Schelers Doppeldevise 'Materiale Wertethik' und 'Ethischer Personalismus,'" *Divus Thomas* 30 (1952): 278, 288, 295.

23. Hurlimann, "Person und Werte," 296–98.

24. Scheler, *Der Formalismus in der Ethik*, 17/xxvi.

# Afterword: Scheler's Rigorous Philosophy: Beyond Naturalism and Historicism

1. Edmund Husserl, "Philosophie als strenge Wissenschaft" in his *Aufsätze und Vorträge (1911–1921)*, ed. Thomas Nenon and Hans Rainer Sepp, vol. 25 of *Husserliana* (Dordrecht, Boston, Lancaster: Martinus Nijhoff, 1987), 7–8, 8–41, 41–62; idem, "Philosophy as Rigorous Science" in his *Phenomenology and the Crisis of Philosophy*, trans. Quentin Lauer (New York: Harper and Row, 1965), 78–79, 79–122, 122–47; idem, *Die Krisis der Europäischen Wissenschaften und die transzendentale Phänomenologie* 3–5, 62–71, 91–100, 194–276/5–7, 61–70, 88–97, 191–265.

2. Hilary Putnam, *Representation and Reality* (Cambridge and London: MIT Press, 1988), 114.

3. W. V. Quine, "The Two Dogmas of Empiricism," in *Analyticity*, ed. James F. Harris, Jr., and Richard H. Severens (Chicago: Quadrangle Books, 1970), 43–53; Thomas S. Kuhn, *The Structure of Scientific Revolutions*, 2d edition, (Chicago and London: The University of Chicago Press, 1970), 4, 9, 16, 18, 37, 46, 103, 113–16, 120–23, 125–27, 150, 201; Imre Lakatos, *The Methodology of Scientific Research Programmes*, vol. 1 of his *Philosophical Papers*, ed. John Worrall and Gregory Currie (Cambridge: Cambridge University Press, 1978), 44; Karl Popper, *Objective Knowledge: An Evolutionary Approach* (Oxford: Clarendon Press, 1972), 30–31; idem, *Conjectures and Refutations: The Growth of Scientific Knowledge* (New York and Evanston, Ill.: Harper & Row, 1965), 22–23; Husserl, *Ideen zu einer reinen Phänomenologie und phänomenologischen Philosophie*, 2: 27–55.

4. Supra, 62–69; Keller, *Reflections on Gender and Science*, 33–42, 162–65; Ruth Bleier, ed., *Feminist Approaches to Science*, (New York: Pergamon Press, 1986), 6; Sarah Blaffer Hrdy, "Empathy, Polyandry, and the Myth of the Coy Female," in *Feminist Approaches to Science*, ed. Ruth Bleier (New York: Pergamon Press, 1986), 119–41.

5. Geertz, *The Interpretation of Cultures*, 452–53; Weber, *Economy and Society*, 1: 13; Winch, *The Idea of a Social Science and its Relation to Philosophy*, 40–65, 111–20; Schutz, *The Problem of Social Reality*, 48–66; Richard Bernstein, *The Restructuring of Social and Political Theory* (Philadelphia: University of Pennsylvania Press, 1978), xv–xxiv.

6. Russell Hardin, *Collective Action* (Baltimore and London: The Johns Hopkins University Press, 1982), 10, 14, 116–24, 149–54.

7. Supra, 39–47/100.

8. Gilbert Harman, "Moral Relativism Defended" in *Relativism, Cognitive and Moral*, ed. Jack W. Meiland and Michael Krausz (South Bend, Ind. and London: University of Notre Dame Press, 1982), 196–97; David Gauthier, *Morals by Agreement* (Oxford: Clarendon Press, 1986), 9–17, 47–58.

9. Supra, 49–50, 53–54, 83–84, 85–86, 88–89, 90–93, 100, 120; Scheler, *Der Formalismus in der Ethik*, 523–25/535–36.

10. Richard Rorty, "Pragmatism and Philosophy," in *After Philosophy: End or Transformation?*, ed. Kenneth Baynes, James Bohman, and Thomas McCarthy (Cambridge and London: MIT Press, 1987), 61.

11. Richard Rorty, *Contingency, Irony, and Solidarity* (Cambridge: Cambridge University Press, 1989), 29, 73.

12. Ibid., 189.

13. Ibid., 94, 176–77

14. Supra, 88–96, 137–38,143–44, 152; Habermas, *The Philosophical Discourse of Modernity*, 56, 86 101–3, 248, 265, 270, 274; Levinas, *Otherwise than Being or Beyond Essence*, 59.

15. Supra, 100–106, especially 104–5.

16. Supra, 100–106, 157–62.

17. Supra, 9–13, 141–42.

# Select Bibliography

## Scheler's Works

### German

**GESAMMELTE WERKE**

Scheler, Max. *Frühe Schriften*. Edited by Maria Scheler and Manfred S. Frings. Vol. 1 of *Gesammelte Werke*. Bern and Munich: Francke Verlag, 1971.

———. *Der Formalismus in der Ethik und die materiale Wertethik: Neuer Versuch der Grundlegung eines ethischen Personalismus*. 5th ed. Edited by Maria Scheler. Vol. 2 of *Gesammelte Werke*. Bern and Munich: Francke Verlag, 1966.

———. *Vom Umsturz der Werte*. 5th ed. Vol. 3 of *Gesammelte Werke*. Bern and Munich: Francke Verlag, 1972.

———. *Politisch-pädagogische Schriften*. Edited by Manfred S. Frings. Vol. 4 of *Gesammelte Werke*. Bern and Munich: Francke Verlag, 1982.

———. *Vom Ewigen im Menschen*. 5th ed. Edited by Maria Scheler. Vol. 5 of *Gesammelte Werke*. Bern and Munich: Francke Verlag, 1968.

———. *Schriften zur Soziologie und Weltanschauungslehre*. 2d ed. Edited by Maria Scheler. Vol. 6 of *Gesammelte Werke*. Bern and Munich: Francke Verlag, 1963.

———. *Wesen und Formen der Sympathie: Die deutsche Philosophie der Gegenwart*. Edited by Manfred S. Frings. Vol. 7 of *Gesammelte Werke*. Bern and Munich: Francke Verlag, 1973.

———. *Die Wissenformen und die Gesellschaft*. 2d ed. Edited by Maria Scheler. Vol. 8 of *Gesammelte Werke*. Bern and Munich: Francke Verlag, 1960.

———. *Späte Schriften*. Edited by Manfred S. Frings. Vol. 9 of *Gesammelte Werke*. Bern and Munich: Francke Verlag, 1976.

———. *Schriften aus dem Nachlass*. Vol. 1, *Zur Ethik und Erkenntnislehre*. 2d ed. Edited by Maria Scheler. Vol. 10 of *Gesammelte Werke*. Bern: Francke Verlag, 1957.

———. *Schriften aus dem Nachlass*. Vol. 2, *Erkenntnislehre und Metaphysik*. Edited by Manfred S. Frings. Vol. 11 of *Gesammelte Werke*. Bern and Munich: Francke Verlag, 1979.

———. *Schriften aus dem Naclass*. Vol. 3, *Philosophische Anthropologie*. Edited by Manfred S. Frings. Vol. 12 of *Gesammelte Werke*. Bonn: Bouvier Verlag Herbert Grundmann, 1987.

OTHER

————. *Logik*. Amsterdam: Editions Rodopi, 1975.

## English Translations

————. "Concerning the Meaning of the Feminist Movement." Translated by Manfred S. Frings. *Philosophical Forum* 9 (1978): 42–54.

————. *Formalism in Ethics and Non-Formal Ethics of Values: A New Attempt toward the Foundation of an Ethical Personalism*. Translated by Manfred S. Frings and Roger L. Funk. Evanston, Ill.: Northwestern University Press, 1973.

————. *Man's Place in Nature*. Transplanted by Hans Meyerhoff. Boston: Beacon Press, 1961.

————. *The Nature of Sympathy*. Translated by Peter Heath. New Haven: Yale University Press, 1954.

————. *On the Eternal in Man*. Translated by Bernard Noble. New York: Harper & Brothers, 1960.

————. "On the Positivistic Philosophy of the History of Knowledge and Its Laws of Three Stages." Translated by Ranier Koehne. In *The Sociology of Knowledge: A Reader*. Edited by James E. Curtis and John W. Petras, 161–69. New York: Praeger Publishers; London: Duckworth, 1970.

————. *Person and Self-Value*. Edited and partially translated by Manfred S. Frings. Dordrecht, Boston, Lancaster: Martinus Nijhoff, 1987.

————. *Philosophical Perspectives*. Translated by Oscar A. Haac. Boston: Beacon Press, 1958.

————. *Problems of a Sociology of Knowledge*. Translated by Manfred S. Frings. Edited by Kenneth W. Stikkers. London, Boston, Henley: Routledge & Kegan Paul, 1980.

————. *Ressentiment*. Translated by Wiliam W. Holdheim. Edited by Lewis A. Coser. New York: The Free Press of Glencoe, 1961.

————. *Selected Philosophical Essays*. Translated by David R. Lachtermann. Evanston, Ill.: Northwestern University Press, 1973.

————. "The Thomistic Ethic and the Spirit of Capitalism." Translated by Gertrude Neuwith. *Sociological Analysis* 25 (1964): 4–19.

# Books and Articles on Scheler

Becker, Howard, and Helmut Otto Dahlke. "Max Scheler's Sociology of Knowledge." *Philosophy and Phenomenological Research* 2, no. 3 (1942):310–22.

Deeken, Alfons. *Process and Permanence in Ethics: Max Scheler's Moral Philosophy*. New York: Paulist Press, 1974.

Denninger, Erhard. *Rechtsperson und Solidarität: Ein Beitrag zur Phänomenologie des Rechstaates unter besonderer Berücksichtigung der Sozialtheorie Max Schelers*. Frankfurt and Berlin: Alfred Metzner Verlag, 1967.

Fetscher, Irving. "Max Schelers Auffassung von Krieg und Frieden." In *Max Scheler im Gegenswartsgeschenen der Philosophie*. Edited by Paul Good, 241–56. Bern and Munich: Francke Verlag, 1975.

Frings, Manfred S. "Insight—Logos—Love (Lonergan—Heidegger—Scheler)." *Philosophy Today* 14, no. 3/4 (1970):106–15.

―――. "Max Scheler Centennial 1874–1974." *Philosophy Today* 18, no. 3/4 (1974):211–16.

―――. *Person und Dasein: Zur Frage der Ontologie der Wertseins.* The Hague: Martinus Nijhoff, 1969.

―――. "Social Temporality in George Herbert Mead and Max Scheler." *Philosophy Today* 27 (1983):281–89.

―――. *Zur Phänomenologie der Lebensgemeinschaft: Ein Versuch mit Max Scheler.* Meisenheim am Glan: Verlag Anton Hain, 1971.

―――, ed. *Max Scheler (1874–1928): Centennial Essays.* The Hague: Martinus Nijhoff, 1974.

Good, Paul, ed. *Max Scheler im Gegenwartsgeschenen der Philosophie.* Bern and Munich: Francke Verlag, 1975.

Hafkesbrink, Hanna. "The Meaning of Objectivism and Realism in Max Scheler's Philosophy of Religion: A Contribution to the Understanding of Max Scheler's Catholic Period." *Philosophy and Phenomenological Research* 2, no. 3 (1942):292–309.

Hammner, Felix. *Theonome Anthropologie: Max Schelers Menschenbild und Seine Grenzen.* The Hague: Martinus Nijhoff, 1972.

Hartmann, Wilfried, ed. *Max Scheler, Bibliographie.* Stuttgart, Bad Cannstaat: Friedrich Frommann Verlag (Günther Holzboog), 1963.

Hurlimann, Kaspar. "Person und Werte: Eine Untersuchungen über den Sinn von Max Schelers Doppeldevise 'Materiale Wertethik' und 'Ethischer Personalismus.'" *Divus Thomas* 30 (1952):273–98, 385–416.

Huskamp, Reinhold J. *Spekulativer und phänomenologischer Personalismus.* Munich: Verlag Karl Albert, 1966.

Kelly, Eugene. "Ordo Amoris: The Moral Vision of Max Scheler." *Listening* 21, no. 3 (1986):226–42.

Lenk, Kurt. *Von der Ohnmacht des Geistes: Kritische Darstellung der Spätphilosophie Max Schelers.* Tübingen: Hopfer Verlag, 1959.

Leonardy, Heinz. *Liebe und Person: Max Schelers Versuch eines "phänomenologischen" Personalismus.* The Hague: Martinus Nijhoff, 1976.

Lorscheid, Bernhard. *Das Leibphänomen: Schelers Wesensontologie des Leiblichen.* Bonn: H. Bouvier und Co. Verlag, 1962.

Luther, A. R. *Persons in Love: A Study of Max Scheler's Wesen und Formen der Sympathie.* The Hague: Martinus Nijhoff, 1972.

―――. "Scheler's Interpretation of Being as Loving." *Philosophy Today* 14, no. 3/4 (1970):217–28.

―――. "Scheler's Order of Evidence and Metaphysical Experiencing." *Philosophy Today* 23, no. 3/4 (1979):249–59.

―――. "Scheler's Person and Nishida's Active Self as Centers of Creativity." *Philosophy Today* 21, no. 2/4 (1977):126–42.

Mader, Wilhelm. *Max Scheler.* Reinbeck bei Hamburg: Rowohlt Taschenbuch Verlag, 1980.

Mannheim, Karl. *Ideology and Utopia: An Introduction to the Sociology of Knowledge.* Translated by Louis Wirth and Edward Shils. New York and London: Harcourt Brace Jovanovich, 1936.

————. "Das Problem einer Soziologie des Wissens." In his *Wissenssoziologie: Auswahl aus dem Werk*. Edited by Kurt H. Wolff. Berlin and Neuwied: Luchterhand, 1964.

————. "The Problem of a Sociology of Knowledge." In his *From Karl Mannheim*. Edited by Kurt H. Wolff. New York: Oxford University Press, 1971.

McGill, V. J. "Scheler's Theory of Sympathy and Love." *Philosophy and Phenomenological Research* 2 (1942):273–91.

Miller, George David. "Ordo Amoris: The Heart of Scheler's Ethics." *Listening* 21, no. 3 (1986):210–25.

Nota, John H., S.J. *Max Scheler, The Man and His Work*. Translated by Theodore Plantinga and John H. Nota, S.J. Chicago: Franciscan Herald Press, 1983.

Ranly, Ernest W. *Scheler's Phenomenology of Community*. The Hague: Martinus Nijhoff, 1966.

Rothacker, Erich. *Schelers Durchbruch zur Wirklichkeit*. Bonn: H. Bouvier und Co., 1946.

Rutischauser, Bruno. *Max Schelers Phänomenologie des Fühlens: Eine kritische Untersuchung seiner Analyse von Scham und Schamgefühl*. Bern and Munich: Francke Verlag, 1969.

Schutz, Alfred. "Max Scheler's Epistemology and Ethics." In his *Studies in Phenomenological Philosophy*. Vol. 3 of *Collected Papers*. Edited by I. Schutz. The Hague: Martinus Nijhoff, 1975.

————. "Max Scheler's Philosophy." In his *Studies in Phenomenological Philosophy*. Vol. 3 of *Collected Papers*. Edited by I. Schutz. The Hague: Martinus Nijhoff, 1975.

————. "Scheler's Theory of Intersubjectivity and the General Thesis of the Alter Ego." In his *The Problem of Social Reality*. Vol. 1 of *Collected Papers*. Edited by Maurice Natanson. The Hague, Boston, London: Martinus Nijhoff, 1962.

Spader, Peter H. "A Change of Heart: Scheler's Ordo Amoris, Repentance and Rebirth." *Listening* 21, no. 3 (1986):188–96.

————. "The Facts of Max Scheler." *Philosophy Today* 23, no. 3/4 (1979):260–66.

————. "The Non-Formal Ethics of Value of Max Scheler and the Shift in His Thought." *Philosophy Today* 18, no. 3/4 (1978):217–33.

————. "The Primacy of the Heart: Scheler's Challenge to Phenomenology." *Philosophy Today* 23, no. 3/4 (1983):223–30.

Strikkers, Kenneth. "'Ethos,' Its Relationship to Real and Ideal Sociological Factors in Scheler's Philosophy of Culture." *Listening* 21, no. 3 (1986):243–52.

————. "Phenomenology as Psychic Technique of Non-Resistance." In *Phenomenology in Practice and Theory*. Edited by William S. Hamrick, 129–51. Dordrecht, Boston, Lancaster: Martinus Nijhoff, 1985.

Theunissen, Michael. "Wettersturm und Stille: Über die Weltdeutung Schelers und ihr Verhältnis zum Seinsdenken." In *Max Scheler im Gegenwartsgeschenen der Philosophie*. Edited by Paul Good, 91–109. Bern and Munich: Francke Verlag, 1975.

Vacek, Edward, S.J. "Personal Development and the Ordo Amoris." *Listening* 21, no. 3 (1986):197–209.

————. "Scheler's Evolving Methodologies." In *Morality within the Life and Social World*. Edited by Anna-Teresa Tymieniecka, 165–83. Vol. 22 of *Analecta Husserliana*. Dordrecht: D. Reidel, 1987.

Williams, Richard Hays. "Scheler's Contributions to the Sociology of Affective Action with Special Attention to the Problem of Shame." *Philosophy and Phenomenological Research* 2, no. 3 (1942):348–58.

Wojtyla, Karol (Johannes Paul II). *Primat des Geistes: Philosophische Schriften.* Edited by Juliusz Stroynowski. Stuttgart, Degerloch: Seewald Verlag, 1980.

# Related Works

Arendt, Hannah. *The Origins of Totalitarianism.* San Diego, New York, London: Harcourt Brace Jovanovich, 1973.

Barber, Michael D. "Alma Gonzalez: Otherness as Attending to the Other." In *The Question of the Other: Essays in Contemporary Continental Philosophy.* Edited by Arleen B. Dallery and Charles Scott. Albany: State University of New York Press, 1989. 119–26.

———. "Finitude Rediscovered." *Philosophy and Theology,* no. 1 (1990):73–80.

———. *Social Typifications and the Elusive Other: The Place of Sociology of Knowledge in Alfred Schutz's Phenomenology.* Lewisburg, Pa.: Bucknell University Press, 1988.

Barnes, Barry. "On the Conventional Character of Knowledge and Cognition." *Philosophy of the Social Sciences* 11 (1981):303–33.

Barnouw, Dagmar. *Weimar Intellectuals and the Threat of Modernity.* Bloomington and Indianapolis: University of Indiana Press, 1968.

Bartky, Sandra Lee. *Femininity and Domination: Studies in the Phenomenology of Oppression.* New York and London: Routledge, Chapman & Hall 1990.

Baynes, Kenneth, James Bohman, and Thomas McCarthy, eds. *After Philosophy: End or Transformation?* Cambridge and London: MIT Press, 1987.

Beauvoir, Simone de. *The Second Sex.* Translated by E. M. Parshley. New York: Vintage, 1973.

Berger, Peter L. and Thomas Luckmann. *The Social Construction of Reality: A Treatise in the Sociology of Knowledge.* Garden City, N.Y.: Doubleday, 1966.

Bernstein, Richard. *The Restructuring of Social and Political Theory.* Philadelphia: University of Pennsylvania Press, 1978.

Bleier, Ruth, ed. *Feminist Approaches to Science.* New York: Pergamon Press, 1986.

Bloor, David. *Knowledge and Social Imagery.* London and Boston: Routledge & Kegan Paul, 1976.

Butler, Judith. *Gender Trouble: Feminism and the Subversion of Identity.* New York and London: Routledge, Chapman & Hall, 1990.

Chodorow, Nancy. *The Reproduction of Mothering: Psychoanalysis and the Sociology of Gender.* Berkeley, Los Angeles, London: University of California Press, 1978.

Craig, Gordon. *The Germans.* New York and Scarborough, Ontario: New American Library, 1982.

Curtis, James E., and John W. Petras, eds. *The Sociology of Knowledge: A Reader.* New York: Praeger, 1970.

Dallery, Arleen B., and Charles E. Scott, eds. *The Question of the Other: Essays in Contemporary Continental Philosophy.* Albany: State University of New York Press, 1989.

Daniels, Arlene Kaplan. "Feminist Perspectives in Sociological Research." In *Another Voice: Feminist Perspectives on Social Life and Social Science.* Edited by Marcia Millman and Rosabeth Moss Kanter, 347–58. New York: Octagon Books, 1976.

Derrida, Jacques. *Speech and Phenomena.* Translated by David B. Allison. Evanston, Ill.: Northwestern University Press, 1973.

Dussel, Enrique. *Philosophy of Liberation.* Translated by Aquilina Martinez and Christine Morkovsky. Maryknoll, N.Y.: Orbis Books, 1985.

Fee, Elizabeth. "Critiques of Modern Science: The Relationship of Feminism to Other Radical Epistemologies." In *Feminist Approaches to Science.* Edited by Ruth Bleier, 42–56. New York: Pergamon Press, 1986.

Foucault, Michel. "The Discourse on Language." In his *The Archeology of Knowledge.* Translated by A. M. Sheridan Smith. New York: Pantheon Books, 1972.

Gauthier, David. *Morals by Agreement.* Oxford: Clarendon Press, 1986.

Gay, Peter. *Weimar Culture: The Outsider as Insider.* New York and Evanston, Ill.: Harper & Row, 1968.

Geertz, Clifford. *The Interpretation of Cultures: Selected Essays.* New York: Basic Books, 1973.

Gellner, Ernest. "Relativism and Universals." In *Rationality and Relvativism.* Edited by Martin Hollis and Steven Lukes, 181–200. Cambridge: MIT Press, 1982.

Grünwald, Ernst. *Das Problem der Soziologie des Wissens: Versuch einer kritischen Darstellung der wissenssoziologischen Theorien.* Wien and Leipzig: Wilhelm Braumuller, 1934.

Habermas, Jürgen. *Communication and the Evolution of Society.* Translated by Thomas McCarthy. London: Heinemann, 1976.

———. *Moral Consciousness and Communicative Action.* Translated by Christian Lenhardt and Shierry Weber Nicholsen. Oxford: Polity Press, 1990.

———. *On the Logic of the Social Sciences.* Translated by Shierry Weber Nicholsen and Jerry A. Stark. Cambridge: Polity Press, 1988.

———. *The Philosophical Discourse of Modernity.* Translated by Frederick Lawrence. Cambridge: MIT Press, 1987.

———. *Reason and the Rationalization of Society.* Vol. 1 of his *Theory of Communicative Action.* Translated by Thomas McCarthy. Boston: Beacon Press, 1984.

Hardin, Russell. *Collective Action.* Baltimore and London: The Johns Hopkins University Press, 1982.

Harman, Gilbert. "Is There a Single True Morality?" In *Relativism: Interpretation and Confrontation.* Edited by Michael Krausz, 363–86. South Bend, Ind.: University of Notre Dame Press, 1989.

———. "Moral Relativism Defended." In *Relativism, Cognitive and Moral.* Edited by Jack W. Meiland and Michael Krausz, 189–204. South Bend, Ind., and London: University of Notre Dame Press, 1986.

Harris, James F., Jr., and Richard H. Severens. *Analyticity.* Chicago: Quadrangle Books, 1970.

Hollis, Martin, and Steven Lukes, eds. *Rationality and Relativism.* Cambridge: MIT Press, 1982.

Horton, Robin. "Tradition and Modernity Revisited." In *Rationality and Relativism.* Edited by Martin Hollis and Steven Lukes, 201–60. Cambridge: MIT Press, 1982.

Hrdy, Sarah Blaffer. "Empathy, Polyandry, and the Myth of the Coy Female." In *Feminist Approaches to Science*. Edited by Ruth Bleier, 119–41. New York: Pergamon Press, 1986.

Hume, David. *A Treatise of Human Nature*. Edited by L. A. Selby-Biggs. Oxford: Clarendon Press, 1967.

Husserl, Edmund. *The Crisis of European Sciences and Transcendental Phenomenology*. Translated by David Carr. Evanston, Ill.: Northwestern University Press, 1970.

———. *Ideas: General Introduction to Pure Phenomenology*. Translated by W. R. Boyce Gibson. New York: Collier Books; London: Collier Macmillan, 1962.

———. *Ideen zu einer reinen Phänomenologie und phänomenologischen Philosophie*. Book 1: *Allgemeine Einführung in die reine Phänomenologie*. Edited by Walter Biemel. Vol. 3 of *Husserliana*. The Hague: Martinus Nijhoff, 1950.

———. *Ideen zu einer reinen Phänomenologie und phänomenologischen Philosophie*. Book 2: *Phänomenologischen Untersuchungen zur Konstitution*. Edited by Marly Biemel. Vol. 4 of Husserliana. The Hague: Martinus Nijhoff, 1952.

———. *Die Krisis der Europäischen Wissenschaften und die transzendentale Phänomenologie*. Edited by Walter Biemel. Vol. 6 of *Husserliana*. The Hague: Martinus Nijhoff, 1954.

———. *Logical Investigations*. Vol. 2. Translated by J. N. Findlay from the Second German Edition. New York: Humanities Press, 1970.

———. *Logische Untersuchungen*. Vol. 2, 2d Part: *Untersuchungen zur Phanomenologie und Theories der Erkenntnis*. Edited by Ursula Panzer. The Hague, Boston, Lancaster: Martinus Nijhoff, 1984.

———. "Philosophie als strenge Wissenschaft." In *Grundsätze und Vorträge (1911–1921)*. Edited by Thomas Nenon and Hans Rainer Sepp, 3–62. Vol. 25 of *Husserliana*. Dordrecht, Boston, Lancaster: Martinus Nijhoff, 1987.

———. "Philosophy as Rigorous Science." In his *Phenomenology and the Crisis of Philosophy*. Translated by Quentin Lauer, 71–147. New York: Harper and Row, 1965.

Kant, Immanuel. *Critique of Practical Reason*. Translated by Lewis White Beck. Indianapolis: Bobbs-Merrill, 1956.

———. *Grounding for the Metaphysics of Morals*. Translated by James W. Ellington. Indianapolis and Cambridge, Eng.: Hackett, 1981.

———. *Grundlegung zur Metaphysik der Sitten*. In his *Schriften zur Ethik und Religionsphilosophie*, Part 1. Darmstadt: Wissenschaftliche Buchgesellschaft, 1968.

———. *Kritik der praktischen Vernunft*. In his *Schriften zur Ethik und Religionsphilosophie*, Part 1. Darmstadt: Wissenschaftliche Buchgesellschaft, 1968.

Keller, Evelyn Fox. *Reflections on Science and Gender*. New Haven: Yale University Press, 1985.

Krausz, Michael, ed. *Relativism: Interpretation and Confrontation*. South Bend, Ind.: University of Notre Dame Press, 1989.

Kuhn, Thomas S. *The Structure of Scientific Revolutions*. 2d edition. Chicago and London: The University of Chicago Press, 1970.

Lakatos, Imre. *The Methodology of Science Research Programmes*. Vol. 1 of *Philosophical Papers*. Edited by John Worral and Gregory Currie. Cambridge: Cambridge University Press, 1978.

Levinas, Emmanuel. *Collected Philosophical Papers.* Translated by Alphonso Lingis. Dordrecht: Martinus Nijhoff, 1987.

——. *Otherwise than Being or Beyond Essence.* Translated by Alphonso Lingis. The Hague, Boston, London: Martinus Nijhoff, 1981.

——. *Totality and Infinity: An Essay on Exteriority.* Translated by Alphonso Lingis. The Hague: Martinus Nijhoff, 1979.

Lyotard, Jean-François, and Jean-Loup Thebaud. *Just Gaming.* Translated by Wlad Godzich. Minneapolis: University of Minnesota Press, 1985.

MacIver, R. M. *Social Causation.* Boston: Ginn and Company, 1942.

McCarthy, Thomas. *The Critical Theory of Jürgen Habermas.* Cambridge: MIT Press, 1978.

Meiland, Jack W., and Michael Krausz, eds. *Relativism, Cognitive and Moral.* South Bend, Ind., and London: University of Notre Dame, 1986.

Merleau-Ponty, Maurice. *Phénoménologie de la Perception.* Paris: Librairie Gallimard, 1945.

Merton, Robert. "Paradigm for the Sociology of Knowledge." In *The Sociology of Knowledge: A Reader.* Edited by James E. Curtis and John W. Petras, 342–72. New York and Washington, D.C.: Praeger, 1970.

Millman, Marcia, and Rosabeth Moss Kanter, eds. *Another Voice: Feminist Perspectives on Social Life and Social Science.* New York: Octagon Books, 1976.

Nietzsche, Friedrich. *Beyond Good and Evil.* Translated by R. J. Hollingdale. Harmondsworth: Penguin Books, 1972.

——. *Joyful Wisdom.* Translated by Thomas Common. New York: Frederick Ungar, 1960.

——. *On the Genealogy of Morals.* With his *Ecce Homo.* Translated by Walter Kaufmann and R. J. Hollingdale. New York: Vintage Books, 1967.

Popper, Karl. *Conjectures and Refutations: The Growth of Scientific Knowledge.* New York and Evanston, Ill.: Harper & Row, 1965.

——. *Objective Knowledge: An Evolutionary Approach.* Oxford: Clarendon Press, 1978.

Putnam, Hilary. *Representation and Reality.* Cambridge and London: MIT Press, 1988.

Quine, W. V. "The Two Dogmas of Empiricism." In *Analyticity.* Edited by James F. Harris, Jr., and Richard H. Severens, 23–53. Chicago: Quadrangle Books, 1970.

Rorty, Richard. *Contingency, Irony, and Solidarity.* Cambridge: Cambridge University Press, 1989.

——. "Pragmatism and Philosophy." In *After Philosophy: End or Transformation?* Edited by Kenneth Baynes, James Bohman, and Thomas McCarthy, 26–66. Cambridge and London: MIT Press, 1987.

Schachtel, Ernest G. *Metamorphosis: On the Development of Affect, Perception, Attention, and Memory.* New York: Basic Books, 1959.

Schwartz, Howard, and Jerry Jacobs. *Qualitative Sociology: A Method to the Madness.* New York: The Free Press; London: Collier Macmillan, 1979.

Schutz, Alfred. *The Phenomenology of the Social World.* Translated by George Walsh and Frederick Lehnert. Evanston, Ill.: Northwestern University Press, 1967.

———. *The Problem of Social Reality.* Vol. 1 of his *Collected Papers.* Edited by Maurice Natason. The Hague, Boston, London: Martinus Nijhoff, 1962.

———. *Studies in Phenomenological Philosophy.* Vol. 3 of his *Collected Papers.* Edited by I. Schutz. The Hague, Boston, London: Martinus Nijhoff, 1975.

———. *Studies in Social Theory.* Vol. 2 of his *Collected Papers.* Edited by Arvid Brodersen. The Hague, Boston, London: Martinus Nijhoff, 1976.

Sokolowski, Robert. *Husserlian Meditations: How Words Present Things.* Evanston, Ill.: Northwestern University Press, 1974.

Spiegelberg, Herbert. *Doing Phenomenology.* The Hague: Martinus Nijhoff, 1975.

———. *The Phenomenological Movement.* The Hague: Martinus Nijhoff, 1960.

Taylor, Charles. "Rationality." In *Rationality and Relativism.* Edited by Martin Hollis and Steven Lukes, 87–105. Cambridge: MIT Press, 1982.

Theunissen, Michael. *The Other: Studies in the Social Ontology of Husserl, Heiddeger, Sartre, and Buber.* Translated by Christopher Macann. Cambridge and London: MIT Press, 1984.

Weber, Max. *Economy and Society: An Outline of Interpretive Sociology.* Translated by Ephraim Fischoff et al. Edited by Guenther Roth and Claus Wittich. 2 vols. Berkeley: University of California Press, 1978.

———. *The Methodology of the Social Sciences.* Translated and edited by Edward A. Shils and Henry A. Finch. New York: The Free Press, 1949.

———. *The Protestant Ethic and the Spirit of Capitalism.* Translated by Talcott Parsons. New York: Charles Scribner's Sons, 1958.

———. "Science as a Vocation." In *From Max Weber: Essays in Sociology.* Edited by H. H. Gerth and C. Wright Mills, 129–156. New York: Oxford University Press, 1946.

Wilson, Bryan R., ed. *Rationality.* Oxford: Basil Blackwell, 1970.

Winch, Peter. *The Idea of a Social Science and its Relation to Philosophy.* London, Melbourne, and Henley: Routledge & Kegan Paul; Atlantic Highlands, N.J.: Humanities Press, 1958.

———. "Understanding a Primitive Society." In *Rationality.* Edited by Bryan Wilson, 78–111. Oxford: Basil Blackwell, 1970.

# Index